At the Very Least
She Pays the Rent _____

**Recent Titles in
Contributions in Women's Studies**

Political Equality in a Democratic Society: Women in the United States
Mary Lou Kendrigan

Fantasy and Reconciliation: Contemporary Formulas of Women's Romance
Fiction
Kay Mussell

Three Who Dared: Prudence Crandall, Margaret Douglass, Myrtilla Miner—
Champions of Antebellum Black Education
Philip S. Foner and Josephine F. Pacheco

Insatiable Appetites: Twentieth-Century American Women's Bestsellers
Madonne M. Miner

Representations of Women: Nineteenth-Century British Women's Poetry
Kathleen Hickok

Women, Nazis, and Universities: Female University Students in the Third Reich,
1933–1945
Jacques R. Pauwels

Cassandra's Daughters: The Women in Hemingway
Roger Whitlow

The World of Women's Trade Unionism: Comparative Historical Essays
Norbert C. Soldon, editor

Traditionalism, Nationalism, and Feminism: Women Writers of Quebec
Paula Gilbert Lewis, editor

Only Mothers Know: Patterns of Infant Feeding Practices in Traditional Cultures
Dana Raphael and Flora Davis

"Give to the Winds Thy Fears": The Women's Temperance Crusade, 1873–
1874
Jack S. Blocker, Jr.

Film Feminisms: Theory and Practice
Mary C. Gentile

At the Very Least
She Pays the
Rent

WOMEN AND GERMAN
INDUSTRIALIZATION,
1871–1914

Barbara Franzoi

CONTRIBUTIONS IN WOMEN'S STUDIES, NUMBER 57

Greenwood Press
WESTPORT, CONNECTICUT · LONDON, ENGLAND

331.4
F83 ω

Library of Congress Cataloging in Publication Data

Franzoi, Barbara.
  At the very least she pays the rent.

  (Contributions in women's studies, ISSN 0147-104X ;
no. 57)
    Bibliography: p.
    Includes index.
    1. Women—Employment—Germany—History. 2. Women—
Germany—Economic conditions. 3. Home labor—Germany—
History. 4. Sexual division of labor—Germany—History.
I. Title. II. Series.
HD6149.F718 1985   331.4'0943   84-22455
ISBN 0-313-24487-1 (lib. bdg.)

Library of Congress Catalog Card Number: 84-22455
ISBN: 0-313-24487-1
ISSN: 0147-104X

First published in 1985

Greenwood Press
A division of Congressional Information Service, Inc.
88 Post Road West
Westport, Connecticut 06881

Printed in the United States of America

10 9 8 7 6 5 4 3 2 1

Copyright Acknowledgment
Portions of the "Introduction," chapter 3 "Classification by Sex: Women as Protected
Workers," and chapter 6 "Women Home Workers," appeared in different form as Bar-
bara Franzoi's "Domestic Industry: Work Options and Women's Choices," in *German
Women in the Nineteenth Century,* ed. by John C. Fout © 1984 by Holmes & Meier
(New York and London: Holmes & Meier, 1984), pp. 256–269 and is reprinted by per-
mission of the publisher.

For my daughter and son,
Bari and Adolph

Contents

Illustrations

Acknowledgments

Seeing this manuscript in print is a personal victory that I gratefully share with friends and colleagues who helped me throughout its preparation. I want to recognize the History Department at Rutgers University, where I was nurtured into academic adulthood. I reserve special thanks for John Gillis for his encouragement and continued support. Daniel Horn has been a critical mentor whom I am honored to know as a friend. And Mary S. Hartman, who introduced me to women's studies, is an important inspirational presence in my life. Peter Stearns at Carnegie-Mellon University gave me confidence as a historian and was always available when I needed advice. Many thanks are offered to Dennis Showalter at The Colorado College, who was instrumental in making the manuscript visible to my publisher.

I also want to acknowledge the library staff at Alexander Library, Rutgers University, and Firestone Library, Princeton University, for their thorough and systematic responses to my requests. To Hedy Seitz, at Alexander Library, I extend my warm and deep appreciation for her untiring efforts and her quiet, good humor.

The administration, my colleagues, and the library staff at the College of Saint Elizabeth offered unconditional support for the project. My students deserve recognition for their understanding and caring and for the moments of shared laughter that helped keep things in perspective. I express my gratitude to Lydia Samatar at Seton Hall University, who typed the manuscript, fitting the project into an already busy schedule.

I save personal regards for Sister Grace Roberta McBreen, who stayed with me for every detail of the indexing process.

To my family, who sustained my absence with understanding and patience, I joyfully return.

At the Very Least
She Pays the Rent

Introduction

Chances for relief, departure, or escape from the multiple demands on women's lives were neither enhanced nor aggravated by the economic transformation of the nineteenth century. This book examines the impact of industrialization on working women in the critical period of Germany's economic growth, a time crucial to that nation's social as well as political formation. Its purpose is to identify what work choices there were for women in industrializing Germany, to determine how women used those work options, and to understand how this affected their lives. Women were the point of intersection between work and family. The ways women interacted with work and with the family involved constant tension, a conflict that demanded continual resolution. Women were virtually caught in the middle of a recurrent dilemma which required handling economic need and family responsibilities simultaneously. Women attempted to integrate the two by bringing paid labor as closely as possible into coincidence with their domestic role.

By looking at the interaction between work options and women's choices, a great deal can be clarified regarding the process of German industrialization and women's response to industrial work. Continuity prevailed over change in the lives of working women because women continued to select work options that were familiar to them. Their choices established a pattern of adjustment that preserved a uniquely female response to work, even during a time of rapid economic transformation. The picture that emerges reveals a significant time lag between external circumstances, such as changes in the mode of production, and changes in the lives of women. Strong evidence confirms that women's work was particularly resistant to change. Women's response to industrialization illuminates the complexity and flexibility that form the human dimension of personal adjustment to work.

Understanding the interaction requires a close look at the structure and organization of work in Germany in the late nineteenth and early twentieth centuries. Such an examination will suggest some answers to questions about the historical integration of women into the labor force. German industrialization intensified diversity instead of creating economic uniformity because factories were only one part of capitalist expansion. Mechanization increased, but so also did hand work and home work. The search for profit and cost minimization strengthened industry's use of non-factory methods. Women's work in industry dramatically illustrated Germany's complex economy. Female labor was essential to industrial expansion because women could be employed both in factories and at home to do the kinds of tasks that industry required. For this reason, the work women did cannot be looked upon as pre-industrial, nor can women be viewed as incidental to industrial expansion.

Mechanization of production and concentration of work in factories were only part of capitalist economic growth. That process was neither uniform nor linear.[1] Tasks in many industries were combinations of both mechanized factory work and handicraft production. Some work processes involved both factory labor and home work in a sequential or interrupted schedule of operation. And factory work in almost every industry experienced periods of irregular employment because a great deal of production was subject to the demands of a seasonal market. Labor-intensive production methods were not curious survivals of past time, but integral parts of the burgeoning capitalist economy. Owners and employers sought the cheapest production methods available, and the cheapest was not always factory work. In many instances the factory was a burden, an unacceptable cost, and, because it meant a concentration of workers, a threat to labor and social order.

There were big discrepancies in the growth potential among industries and time lags in certain industries in adoption of mechanization and factory concentration. Most apparent was the difference between capital goods and consumer goods industries. Heavy industry could more profitably adopt mechanized methods because of the nature of production, a ready and expanding market, and an available pool of skilled and semi-skilled labor. Expanding markets produced a capital reserve that could be ploughed back into production in the form of machines and factories. However, in many industries, various factors related to a fluctuating market, foreign competition, and an abundance of unskilled labor made utilization of non-factory work forms more profitable. Textiles, clothing, and tobacco products were especially responsive to these conditions.

There was no master plan in German capitalist development. Rather, it is useful to view the process as a probing—an experiment with various methods of organizing production that resulted in the combination of machine and hand labor and an assimilation of traditional work forms with the needs of industrial production. Instead of counting factories as a measure of economic growth, we must take a closer look into the kitchens, attics, and cellars in Berlin, in Saxony, and scattered throughout Germany, where essentially non-mechanized hand labor formed the base of the production process. Only by doing so can we understand the labor that thousands of women performed in the largely unmechanized and domestic area of production.

Women's interaction with work defined particular kinds of labor patterns. Most women's industrial work was labor intensive, low skilled, irregular, and low paid. They folded cartons, sorted parts, sewed dolls' clothes, plaited wicker, knotted fish nets, and rolled tobacco. The conventional image of the mill girl was true for only a small part of Germany's industrially employed women, even among young, single girls. Almost 50% of the industrial female labor force was employed in the clothing industry; another third worked in foods and tobacco. Both industries were heavily home work. When women worked in a factory setting, it was often seasonal and intermittent. Women moved in and out of the factory as both industrial demand and personal necessity dictated. Most women who did factory work were young and single; married women chose other ways to earn money. They changed jobs frequently; they combined various kinds of work in agriculture, in domestic service, in factories, and in domestic industry. Multiple earnings were required in many working-class families, not as cash reserve or savings for the future, but to compensate for immediate need. Women juggled their various roles as earners, daughters, wives, and mothers, supplementing the family income when necessary, sometimes supporting themselves and their families entirely.

Women's work was also affected by a consistent and coherent ideology of the family and of womanhood that influenced industry's use of women and women's response to work. Sexual division of labor illuminates some of the key problematic areas in women's involvement with work. The construct picks up and ties together such issues as wages, skills, turnover, and legal protection as they must be applied specifically to women's work and not to work in general. Seen in this context, gender differentiation in these areas moves our understanding beyond descriptive narrative into the social dimension of work. The economic role, the issue of earning a living, was central to the definition of masculine and feminine responsibilities.[2] Gender segregation brought selected components of the economic system into compliance with the basic elements of Germany's patriarchal society. The connection was complementary and mutually reinforcive. Industrial work extended segmentation into new areas and new modes of production. It cemented separation in place with economic and institutional barriers that precluded access and transit.

Sexual division of labor was the fundamental condition of women's work in Imperial Germany. To argue that industry deliberately structured work in this way imputes a notion of conspiracy and attributes a measure of control that was not always present. However, capitalist expansion intended to maximize production, keep costs low, and regulate the labor force. Replicating societal gender definitions was immensely serviceable to accomplishing these ends. Controlled assignment of work segmented jobs by industry and task. Recruiting men and women separately and differently filled both ideological prescriptions and industrial needs.

Division of labor was discrimination. Sexual division of work preserved the contours of traditional gender roles by removing women as far as possible from active competition with men. Women were concentrated in specific industries—clothing, textiles, tobacco. They were assigned special jobs in so-called men's industries that were ancillary, and women were locked into domestic production across all industry branches. Protective legislation divided men and women workers by gender and institutionalized women's subordinate position in society and in the labor force. The same theme was picked up and used by male-dominated labor unions in an effort to diminish a female presence in the labor market.

Segmented jobs made women less economically visible. If not exactly hidden, at least they were not conspicuously present. Industry absorbed women in such a way as to convince an anxious society that industrial work was acceptable and not glaringly inconsistent with basic values of home and family. Isolating women as a group cut them off from the mainstream of labor. They were less able to assert control over the work experience, and consequently they were more vulnerable to exploitation. Reducing public visibility conveyed the impression that women could move through industrial work with little harm to themselves or to society. Denying women full participation in the labor market effectively prevented them from using work for anything more than supplemental earnings, thereby explicating the social message of subordination.

If women are fitted into the picture of gender division in juxtaposition, some of the negative aspects of its discriminatory effects can be seen from a different perspective. The shift focuses the dilemma, the paradox of women's work. Women accepted the sexual division of labor with little overt resistance. Why this quiescence and acquiescence? A fundamental explanation hinges on the fact that women functioned within their consigned economic space. They did not confront the system, but rather negotiated its limited possibilities to suit their needs. In the balancing act between work and family, women continued to mold their employment around their domestic role.[3] Low wages, poor job skills, and high turnover did not have to be engaged directly or urgently if work was perceived as temporary and supplemental. Resistance was just not worth the loss of immediate earnings if there were few long-term expectations of persistence or permanence. And dual responsibilities prevented women at the most elemental level from functioning on the same basis as men. Tenuous ties to work and personal limitations to full involvement with paid labor outside the home made jobs segregated by sex useable and manageable. In part by choice and in part by constriction, women defined their lives coincidentally as their lives were defined for them.

It is vital to recognize that women's work cannot be merged with men's work analytically. Due to both economic and complex social factors, the two were quite different. Because factories were primarily employers of male labor, industrial history that focuses on factory work tends to either neglect women's work entirely or subsume it under a set of generalizations that do justice to neither sex. The uneven process of German industrialization affected women differently from men.

Any treatment of industrialization that ignores the question of gender is incomplete, providing a picture that distorts not only the role of women, but that of men as well.

Significant interpretive models are emerging in the growing body of literature concerning the impact of economic change on women. The key problematic area is the degree to which women were affected by industrialization. Assessment hinges on the nature of women's work experience and their family relationships. At present, there are two main lines of argument. One suggests that changes in women's lives were limited and to a large extent manageable because the family acted as the interactive variable in women's relationship to work. With varying degrees of centrality, regarding the family as primary in defining work roles and social roles is the basic conceptualization in much of the new history. The Tilly-Scott material for Britain and France and the Tentler work on the United States emphasize a conservative approach by viewing women's interaction with work through the family.[4] Tamara Hareven and Carl Degler focus on the family as the pivotal unit. Hareven contends that the family was the primary adaptive mechanism to industrial work.[5] While Degler identifies a conflict between women's desire for autonomy and their family role, his conclusions indicate that women resolved the dilemma by putting family first.[6]

The other side of the debate suggests multiple levels of change in women's lives that created new tensions and forced new behavioral patterns. Branca's study of European women and Dublin's material on mill workers in New England point up women's new role—changes that in the aggregate resulted in basic modifications in their lives and a significantly altered developmental process.[7] In the Marxist literature, as the family is addressed, it is not the ameliorative mechanism, but rather one that extends and reinforces structural changes in society. Marxist feminists follow up on this theme by focusing on capitalist exacerbation of gender division of labor and its consequent oppression of women. Heidi Hartmann, for example, has challenged the analytical validity of using the family as the locus for conceptualization of the women-and-work question.[8] As the literature expands, it is positing areas for interaction among divergent emphases and conflicting positions. While the conservative view seems to dominate the historiography at present, new interpretations will provide more opportunities for testing theses and stretching current parameters.

A brief review of selected literature will extend the discussion of

German women and also set this study into perspective. In *Women, Work and Family* by Louise Tilly and Joan Scott, 1978, the authors suggest a model of continuity for women's work within industrial transformation. The kinds of work women did before industrial development were similar to those performed after the advent of factories and mechanization. Women and families adjusted to changed circumstances by preserving basic elements of customary behavior.[9] The primary reason for this persistence, the authors argue, was the significance of women's place in the family in determining their work activity. Scott and Tilly intend an analysis of the relationship between the family and social change. The book provides an insightful explanation for the nexus of personal, economic, and demographic determinants of women's work over two centuries. Scott and Tilly's work, relying heavily on French and English sources, does not deal with Germany directly, although many of their findings are applicable.

Because much of women's work remained outside the factory setting, it is necessary to understand such areas as household work and domestic service. Theresa McBride, *The Domestic Revolution*, 1976, provides an introduction to the subject of domestic service but, like so much of the literature, excludes Germany from consideration.[10] The study also suffers from an exaggerated optimism about opportunities for women to achieve upward mobility through service positions. It ignores class segregation and over-generalizes from a small sample of servants who successfully married into a better social class.

Tamara Hareven refutes the contention that industrialization caused the breakdown of the traditional family. In Hareven's model, based on study of New England mill workers, women appear as components of familial relationships. Her thesis is best represented in *Family Time and Industrial Time*, 1982. She argues that in the transition from nonindustrial to industrial work, the family acted as the primary adaptive mechanism. Functioning as an economic unit and an emotional support system, the family was able to control its environment and to control the work experience of its members. The family was the resource base that permitted a modern response to new economic conditions.[11]

Patricia Branca, *Women in Europe since 1750*, 1978, describes a process of transformation that produced today's modern woman.[12] Modernization is the conceptual framework for analysis of the female experience. The author examines women's work role, family role, and public role using sources from various European countries. Although a comparative perspective is intended, examples are rather limited to England and France. Material on Germany is sketchy and, because of its general nature, somewhat unreliable. A major problem with Branca's work is her tendency to categorize women in the past as a group sharing similar experience. "Modernization" happens to them all over two centuries. An important theme of the book is the operation of conscious choice as women selected options that worked for them in changed circumstances. This argument suggests a refutation of the notion that women in the past were without any power of self-determination. The theme has broad implications for the history of women and needs to be examined more closely for women in various countries and classes.

Until recently, German historians themselves paid little attention to women's work or its implications for social history. A major reason for the omission has been the continued preoccupation with questions of political power. This focus has tended to retard the development of a genuine social history and subsequently limited opportunity to explore women's questions. Early investigations of women in nineteenth-century Germany fall mainly into two groups. There is a significant body of Marxist literature that addresses the issue of women and work. Foremost is Jürgen Kuczynski, *Die Geschichte der Lage der Arbeiter unter dem Kapitalismus*, 1963.[13] While rich with detail, the book is heavily polemical on the topic of the evils of capitalism and its exploitation of women. Werner Thönnessen discussed women's work in the context of Social Democracy in *The Emancipation of Women*, 1973.[14] Thönnessen's focus is women's struggle for emancipation, which stresses the organizational gains of women brought about by the socialist movement.

Another dimension of scholarship on women in Germany in the nineteenth century concerns women in their public role, specifically German feminism. Richard Evans looked at liberal bourgeois feminism, while Jean Quataert has done a biographical investigation of socialist feminists.[15] Evans' study has a narrow focus, the Federation of German Women's Associations, and admittedly excludes the whole socialist movement for female emancipation. Quataert makes up for that omission. Looking at socialist feminists, she analyzes the ideological and personal conflicts among the leaders of the movement and discusses the broader questions of social antagonism to the changing roles of women both politically and economically.

Within the last decade women's history for Germany has expanded greatly. Women and work and women and the family are major themes. Karin Hausen has taken important initiative in raising these issues for the nineteenth and early twentieth centuries. Hausen's *Frauen suchen ihre Geschichte*, 1983, brings together a collection of new material that extends women's history in several directions.[16] The four-part study explores issues of women's submergence in men's history, gender as a social role determinant, women's work in industry and domestic service, and women's movements and organizations. Although Hausen states it might be too banal to reiterate the theme that women have a past, nevertheless for Germany it has been a real problem. Her work has seminal influence in the field.

Seeking to explain present economic conditions of women in Germany in perspective, two studies provide a developmental framework for women's work. *Die Entwicklung der Frauenerwerbstätigkeit im Deutschen Reich*, 1980, by Angelika Willms is a "macro-sociological" analysis of the gender consequences of industrialization.[17] Walter Müller, Willms, and Johann Handl collaborated on the study *Strukturwandel der Frauenarbeit 1880–1980*, 1983, a research project based in the "Comparative Analysis of Social Structure with Mass Data" (*Vergleichende Analysen der Sozialstruktur mit Massendaten*, VASMA).[18] The authors argue that industrial work historically has been preferential to men, leaving women out of important integration and omitting them from scholarly attention. Noting the dilemma of work and family for women, the authors indicate that the structure of work and women's participation in paid labor has been influenced by consistent constraints over time.

Local studies are providing specific focus for women's work. Rosemarie Beier, *Frauenarbeit und Frauenalltag im Deutschen Kaiserreich*, 1982, references the existence and extent of domestic industry in pre-war Germany and refutes the notion that home work was an integrative form of industrial labor.[19] Despite women's selection of clothing home work as a way of reconciling need for earnings with family responsibilities, the author argues that domestic industry really solved neither problem well. Its effects were largely negative and discrepant with family demands and income requirements. The study is enriched by oral history, interviews with children of women who worked in the Berlin clothing industry before World War I. *Hinterhof, Keller und Mansarde*, 1982, combines historical monographs with illustrations; the book is a unique mosaic that transports the reader into the streets and apartments of Berlin's working classes.[20] The faces of the people in the photographs tell their own stories. A regional study of women's work in Bavaria by Elisabeth Plössl, *Weibliche Arbeit in Familie und Betrieb*, 1983, argues the thesis that women prioritized their double role by placing family first, attempting to bring economic activity into consistency with home and children.[21] Plössl incorporates a large number of quotations, many are autobiographical, that convey the feelings and circumstances of women's lives in a dramatic way.

The German dimension is beginning to take shape in the literature. Women's work permits an important way of identifying common patterns in the organization of work and common themes in the societal response to changes associated with industrial transition as these factors impacted on women. Certain questions are suggested for further exploration. One important area is the degree to which industrial capitalism penetrated the work experience of women, especially work done in the home. Another concerns the incidence and energy with which the state intervened in a regulatory or normative fashion in women's work. And there is the general and pervasive methodological problem of locating women workers hidden within national statistics and camouflaged by ideological assumptions that women did not work.

By looking at the structure and organization of work, overlaid with social and political attitudes toward industrial transformation, parallels and departures for Germany can be suggested. Chapter One demonstrates that numerical increase of working women was deceptive because census data did not account for uneven capitalist development. Data on women workers do not give a correct picture of women's work, leading contemporaries and historians alike into interpretive gray areas. Chapter Two shows the difference between men and women workers in terms of wages, skills, and job expectations. Women's work was distinct from men's work and industry took full advantage of that difference. Chapter Three examines the social and practical reasons for regulatory legislation for women in the labor force. Legal protection sought to reconcile industrial use of female labor with society's sense of women's proper role.

Chapters Four through Six center women at the intersection between work and family. How women interacted with paid labor asserted a certain measure of control in manipulating work choices to fit the circumstances of their lives. The discussion of economic need and family strategies demonstrates that working-class families coped with necessity by utilizing the labor of wives and children in an irregular pattern that included multiple earnings and careful distribution of resources. Women's work in domestic industry is given special attention because home work invariably was a part of the labor experience of most working women. The tenacity of home work focuses capitalism's pursuit of women as workers and the female dilemma of combining work and family. Chapters Seven and Eight examine women's response to labor organization and the reasons that labor unions sought to impose a regulatory presence on women's work lives. Results were a mixed package of benefits and liabilities as women were classified by gender into a special place in the labor force.

This study is an effort to make German working women visible within the context of their nation's economic and social history and, by doing so, to expand possibilities for comparative analysis of the impact of industrialization. It focuses women at the intersection of work and family. Although the most important determinants of women's economic lives were embedded in the industrial organization of work, women scrambled for ways to use the structure to create areas and moments of safety and compatibility. Both the limitations and resources contained in their connection to the family reinforced continuity. The causal links between family and work patterns are not always easy to disentangle, but women actively sought to assert some measure of manageability over both. Tracing their participation in the labor force indicates that women had more success in modifying their work options than in altering their family responsibilities.

It is important to recognize that this process of adjustment did not take place in a vacuum. There were strong cultural and political pressures impinging on women and on owners and employers alike to observe the implicit rules of patriarchy and paternalism. Gender division of labor permeated the organization of work and institutional measures to protect women from work, and influenced the ambivalence of labor unions toward women workers. Reinforced in familial gender segregation, the mutuality of the message was pervasive. It can be suggested that this ideology contributed to the persistence of traditional work forms for women in agriculture, domestic industry, and domestic service and extended with little modification into the factory system.

NOTES

1. Raphael Samuel, "Workshop of the World, Steam Power and Hand Technology in mid-Victorian Britain," *History Workshop* (Spring, 1977), p. 10.

14   Introduction

2. William H. Chafe, *The American Woman: Her Changing Social, Economic, and Political Roles, 1920–1970* (New York: Oxford University Press, 1972), p. ix.

3. Carl Degler, *At Odds: Women and the Family in America from the Revolution to the Present* (New York: Oxford University Press, 1980), p. 430.

4. Louise A. Tilly and Joan W. Scott, *Women, Work and Family* (New York: Holt, Rinehart, and Winston, 1978); Leslie Woodcock Tentler, *Wage-Earning Women: Industrial Work and Family Life in the United States, 1900–1930* (New York: Oxford University Press, 1979).

5. Tamara Hareven, *Family Time and Industrial Time: The Relationship between the Family and Work in a New England Industrial Community* (Cambridge, Mass.: Cambridge University Press, 1982), pp. 363–70.

6. Degler, *At Odds.*

7. Patricia Branca, *Women in Europe since 1750* (London: Croom Helm, 1978); Thomas Dublin, *Women at Work: The Transformation of Work and Community in Lowell, Mass. 1826–1860* (New York: Columbia University Press, 1979), p. 40.

8. Heidi I. Hartmann, "The Family as the Locus of Gender, Class, and Political Struggle: The Example of Housework," *Signs*, Vol. 6, No. 2 (Spring, 1981).

9. Tilly and Scott, *Women, Work and Family*, p. 8.

10. Theresa McBride, *The Domestic Revolution: The Modernization of Household Service in England and France 1820–1920* (London: Croom Helm, 1976).

11. Hareven, *Family Time and Industrial Time.*

12. Branca, *Women in Europe.*

13. Jürgen Kuczynski, *Die Geschichte der Lage der Arbeiter unter dem Kapitalismus. Studien zur Geschichte der Lage der Arbeiterin in Deutschland von 1700 bis zur Gegenwart*, Band 18 (Berlin: Akademie Verlag, 1963).

14. Werner Thönnessen, *The Emancipation of Women: The Rise and Decline of the Women's Movement in German Social Democracy 1863–1933* (London: Pluto Press, 1973).

15. Richard Evans, *The Feminist Movement in Germany 1894–1933* (London: Sage Publishers, 1976); Jean H. Quataert, *Reluctant Feminists in German Social Democracy 1885–1917* (Princeton, N.J.: Princeton University Press, 1979).

16. Karin Hausen, ed., *Frauen suchen ihre Geschichte: historische Studien zum 19. und 20. Jahrhundert* (München: Beck'sche schwarze Reihe, 1983).

17. Angelika Willms, *Die Entwicklung der Frauenerwerbstätigkeit im Deutschen Reich* (Nürnberg: Graphische Betriebe F. Willmy, 1980).

18. Walter Müller, Angelika Willms, and Johann Handl, *Strukturwandel der Frauenarbeit 1880–1980* (Frankfurt/Main: Campus Verlag, 1983).

19. Rosemarie Beier, *Frauenarbeit und Frauenalltag im Deutschen Kaiserreich. Heimarbeiterinnen in der Berliner Bekleidungsindustrie 1880–1914*, Band 348 (Frankfurt/Main: Campus Verlag, 1983).

20. *Hinterhof, Keller und Mansarde. Einblicke in Berliner Wohnungselend 1901–1920* (Hamburg: Rowohlt Taschenbuch Verlag, GmbH, 1982).

21. Elisabeth Plössl, *Weibliche Arbeit in Familie und Betrieb. Bayerische Arbeiterfrauen 1870–1914*, Heft 119 (München: Kommissionsverlag UNI-Druck, 1983).

1

Working Women: Who and Where They Were

"We must take to heart what the statistics . . . tell us"*

This chapter identifies the regional and industrial distribution of the German female labor force and proposes an analysis of statistical data that refutes contentions that industrialization caused profound change for women workers. Results of the occupational census of 1907 were taken as proof that women's role was changing—that more women worked in factories and that more women remained in factories. Contemporaries accepted without question an apparent increase of 35% in the number of women working and a 78% increase in the number of married women in industry between 1895 and 1907. But if the results are subjected to closer scrutiny, methods used in the collection of data operate against reading numerical increase as necessarily industrial work in factories. In addition, and equally important, 1907 was an extraordinary time because the German economy was experiencing depression. Whatever increase was apparent did not mean permanent transition into factory work. Rather, the increase confirmed the emergency nature of most women's work.

There were several peculiarities in the 1907 census that tended to make the data on women workers artificially inflated. These conditions

*Elizabeth Gnauck-Kühne, *Die Deutsche Frau um die Jahrhundertwende* (Berlin: Verlag von Otto Liebmann, 1907), p. 125.

must be examined in light of both the contemporary and historical importance attached to this census as a symbol of structural change for women's work.

We must take to heart what the statistics and experience tell us about women's work . . . it is a fervent wish that all young girls will fulfill their responsibilities as wife and mother and abandon employment which rightly belongs to the man. . . . The statistics have shown us that women cannot realize their maternal instincts. . . . Only children bring the woman identity, not work.[1]

Those who were quick to condemn industry as destructive of the family and society found fuel in the 1907 census. Ostensibly, it constituted irrevocable confirmation of abandoned homes and children. "Industrial work brings about new spiritual and moral circumstances for the woman. . . . In the confines of the home, the woman is influenced by tradition. Entrance into the labor force brings about drastic social change."[2] But a comparison of the data from the occupational censuses of 1882, 1895, and 1907, while not contradicting a steady increase in the number of industrially employed women, cannot justify conclusions of profound change.

For women industrial workers, these comparative data should not be taken at face value. Examination of what the 1907 census really counted mitigates against the intensity of the apparently dramatic results. The most obvious limitation lies in the interpretation of the term *industrial worker*. The immediate assumption was that "industry" meant "factory"; it did not. The occupational census counted persons who worked. There were four major categories of occupation, signified by letter and name designation: A—Agriculture, B—Industry, C—Trade and Commerce, and D—Service. Division B, Industry, included all persons who were in some way related to industrial production. What is most significant is that the figures in the cumulative data did not differentiate between factory and home work. Division B included domestic industry, and home work for women increased between 1882 and 1907.[3]

Exaggeration of the extent of women's work in the census also resulted from the way questions about occupation were asked. In 1907, forms included directions to count family members working in the industrial establishment of the head of the family.[4] This meant both part-time and full-time family help. The Imperial Statistics Office was confident that the material from such detailed inquiry would be more

definitive than previous countings. It was, but only with difficult results for the historian looking for a reliable, systematic way to evaluate
the three censuses. Nineteen hundred and seven picked up most of the
strays—those women workers who had eluded exposure before. The
inclusion of female part-time family help increased the cumulative figures, but not necessarily with women who worked in factories. Most
of the women who fell into this category worked in domestic industry.
Most worked in traditionally female industries: clothing, textiles, and
tobacco.[5] A great many of these women who had not previously shown
up in official statistics were married.[6]

The year in which the census was taken also seriously affected results. Because women's pattern of employment most closely followed
the prosperity level of family economy, the female labor force tended
to swell during bad times. Fluctuation could be seasonal. Men who
were partially employed could not provide sufficient income. However, emergency situations could be more acute than seasonal reduction. Not only did women supplement family income, their earnings
often had to substitute for men's wages during periods of soft employment. Low wages for women tended to keep them viable in the labor
market even when men were being laid off. The German economy experienced two periods of slack employment in the first decade of the
twentieth century. Depressed conditions in 1902 precipitated increased
female employment. Trade papers noted that employers were laying
off men workers and substituting women in their place. "If the effects
of the unemployment of the last year of crisis are not alleviated . . .
the economic result of male unemployment will be compensated by a
significant increase in female work."[7]

The year in which the census was taken was a time of even greater
economic hardship. There were more women working in 1907 because
it was the only way large numbers of families sustained the economic
depression. Men were laid off and replaced by women who worked for
less money.[8] As industry expelled the more expensive male labor,
pressure to make ends meet became critical. Women acted as a substitute source of earnings for families and a substitute supply of labor
for industry. As early as 1906, scattered impressions from mistresses
in homes for women indicated perceptibly worsening conditions. Not
only did the homes face increased demands for lodging and services
from single girls, but more married women and women from "better
families" sought assistance. "We have recorded in our register in the

last year, more and more female persons who have sought refuge in our hostel who do not belong to the class of factory women, who are also seeking employment."[9]

In addition to more women seeking factory employment, domestic industry also increased in crisis years. Industry, looking to minimize production costs, "sent out" everything it could. Women who for personal reasons chose to remain out of the factory took whatever work was available. While the 1907 census did register more women working in industry, it should not be assumed that the data represented the result of cumulative structural change, nor that the moment confirmed a permanently altered situation. Rather, for reasons relating to method and moment, results were extraordinary.

The first census in the twentieth century provides material for comparison among the occupational data for 1882, 1895, and 1907 for women's work. Even with the artificial inflation in 1907, there was very little change. If industrial work is placed within the context of all women's work, the percentage employed actually decreased between 1882 and 1907. The following table indicates the percentage distribution of working women among the various occupational groups.[10]

Occupational Division	1882	1895	1907
A. Agriculture	59.5	52.2	55.8
B. Industry and Mining	26.4	28.9	25.5
C. Trade and Commerce	6.9	11.0	11.3
D. Service	4.3	4.4	3.9
E. Free Professions	2.7	3.3	2.4
	99.8	99.8	99.9

The profile of female employment shows the sharpest increase in Division C—Trade and Commerce. These jobs can loosely be described as white-collar employment, mostly in offices and department stores. Totals in agriculture and service registered decline, but in the first decade of the twentieth century, more than half the number of women working remained in agriculture. However, as was the case with industry, 1907 figures were inflated, again over-simplifying the effects of including family workers in the counting. Census data indicated a

700,000 drop in the number of men working in agriculture between 1882 and 1907 accompanied by a disproportionate increase in the number of women.[11] Well over half the female agricultural population was married, a figure that remained fairly stable between 1895 and 1907.[12]

The most significant increase in percentage employment for women was registered in Division C—Trade and Commerce. Despite its relatively small share of the female labor force, between 1882 and 1907 there was an increase of approximately 600,000 workers, raising the 1907 figure to 931,373, or 11.3% of employed women.[13] A little more than half were single. Office jobs and sales positions were more "acceptable" than factory work and consequently attracted daughters and wives of lower-middle-class families. In a Karlsruhe survey of girls employed in retail trade in 1906, more than two-thirds were daughters of artisans, shopkeepers, and lower government officials. Only 7% came from families where fathers were employed in factories or as day laborers.[14] Positions in trade and commerce included such jobs as bookkeeping, advertising, and shopkeeping. Office work experienced increasing feminization as the "technology" of the typewriter became more widely used.[15]

Domestic service registered decline in both total employment and female employment.[16] Percentage figures for domestic service were deceptively small because the category was narrowly defined. Numerically, women and girls in service were distributed among the various occupational groups, which tended to diffuse the significance of the total.[17] Geographic mobility from rural areas to cities was the general pattern for girls who went into domestic service. Largely from peasant background, mostly living apart from their families, female servants frequently went into industry when, for various reasons relating to wages and conditions of work, they found service no longer suitable. A common transition was the shift from service into clothing, an industry especially available in large cities.[18]

In the twenty-five-year period between the occupational censuses of the years 1882, 1895, and 1907, the composition of the German industrial labor force remained remarkably consistent—more surprisingly stable than it should have been given the inflated statistics of 1907. In 1882, the total number of persons involved with industrial production was 6,396,465. Women employed represented 17.6% of that number. In 1895, the total was 8,281,220, of which 18.3% were women. For 1907, even with the increase derived from the peculiarities of the method and the time the census was taken, the total labor force was

11,256,254; 18.6% were women.[19] Eighty-two percent of all women employed in industry in 1907 were concentrated in three branches—textiles, foods and specialties, and clothing and cleaning. The rest of the female work force was fairly evenly distributed among the other industries.[20]

Between 1871 and 1914, it is more valid to discuss regional rather than national economic development for Germany.[21] The most significant change in this period was a shift in the prominence of two specific regions and industries. By the beginning of the twentieth century, metals and textiles had switched positions, and the Ruhr had overtaken Saxony as the center of German industry. Limitations in the consumer market tended to restrict growth potential in those industries compared with heavy industry.[22] Disparity resulting from an unequal sharing in economic growth retarded regions that were heavily dependent on agriculture and consumer goods production in relation to areas that enjoyed expanding markets. Since declining or stabilized industries faced greater constraints in terms of the need for cost minimization, women were the most suitable labor source. Consumer goods industries frequently expanded by utilizing non-mechanized, non-factory labor. Because consumer goods industries were labor intensive, women's work maintained an older, more traditional pattern longer. This lag intensified the feminization of certain industries, principally textiles, tobacco, and clothing, and the feminization of certain work forms, specifically domestic industry.

Regional specification of industry underlay patterns of concentration for women's work. Where consumer goods industries predominated, there were large numbers of women working. Areas of heavy industry registered low levels of female labor. Identifying geographic distribution of industry suggests where to look for women workers. Of the six industries that employed the largest percentage of Germany's working population, five were regionally specific. In order of percentage employed in the total working population in 1907, these industries were construction, clothing and cleaning, foods and specialties, textiles, and metals and machines.[23] Of these branches, two industries, textiles and clothing, were the most geographically concentrated.[24] Both were largely female industries. Textiles employed 3.5% of the working population in 1907, a drop from 4.2% in 1895.[25] Germany's textile industry was concentrated in two regions: Saxony in south central Germany and Rhine-Westphalia in the west. The highest degree of specialization in terms of the proportion of population employed was in Reuss ältere Linie, where 38% of the working population was employed in textile production. No other single industry employed as large a percentage of the working population in a specific geographic area. The next two highest concentrations were in Reuss jüngere Linie and Saxony, with 19.6% and 13.8% respectively of the population working in textiles.[26]

Another highly geographically specific industry was clothing, with large concentrations in urban centers. Clothing and cleaning was a large employer in pre-war Germany; 5.7% of the working population was in this branch.[27] Thirteen-and-a-half percent of the working population in Berlin was employed in clothing.[28] A third regionally specific industry, foods and specialties, also employed large numbers of women. The industry included such branches as brewing, baking, and tobacco products manufacture. Employment exceeded textiles, but fell far short of clothing and cleaning; 3.7% of the working population was included in 1907.[29] In this branch, tobacco products manufacture was generally rural. Many tobacco centers overlapped textile areas, a coincidence that benefited working women. Where there was shrinking opportunity in textiles, a transfer into tobacco was an easy transition, particularly as tobacco became increasingly domestic production.

Metals and machines employed 3.9% and 3% of the population respectively in 1907.[30] Both industries were heavily concentrated in western Germany. There was considerably wider geographic distribution in machines due to the inclusion in this group of instruments and small products manufacture, which did not depend so heavily on specialized production methods. The largest industrial employer in pre-war Germany was construction, with 6.3% of the nation's population working in this branch.[31] Construction was an industry that had considerable geographic distribution. Of the six industries that employed the largest numbers of Germany's working population, five were geographically specialized. Three of these industries—clothing and cleaning, textiles, and tobacco—employed the largest numbers of women workers.

Generally, the kind of industry in an area determined the numbers of women working.[32] Where there were concentrations of heavy industry, female employment was light. Certain areas in western Germany were excepted because there was a geographic overlap of textiles with steel and iron and mining. Regions that were devoted primarily to consumer goods production had heavy female employment. In Prussia, three locations registered significant women's work. Berlin, Silesia, and the Rhineland all showed more than 100,000 women working. Bavaria registered over 150,000 and Saxony showed the highest concentration of working women with over 250,000 employed in industry.

Within the pattern of regional specialization, there was a perceptible shift in the employment picture in certain industries from rural to urban areas between 1882 and 1907. The new labor concentration contributed to increasing geographic specialization. Least fluctuation occurred in small and medium-sized cities. Industrial urbanization reinforced regional diversity. The designation "large city," *Grossstadt*, in the German statistics referred to cities with over 100,000 population. In 1871, there were eight such centers; by 1910, that number had risen to forty-eight.[33] No industry showed increase in proportional employment in rural areas between 1882 and 1907. The reverse was true for urban centers. Following is a table showing the percentage of population employed by industry location.[34]

Industry Location	1907	1895	1882
Rural	26.4	32.5	40.1
Small and medium cities	50.5	49.8	50.1
Large cities	23.1	17.7	9.8

Between 1895 and 1907, three industries shifted from rural to urban locations. They were clothing manufacture, textiles, and leather goods. Numbers of persons in clothing also diminished in small and medium-sized cities. Since there was no reduction in total numbers employed in these three industries, it must be concluded that they became more urbanized. The least change occurred in textiles, which continued to be heavily concentrated in small and medium cities. At least half, and in some instances well over half, the working population in each industry remained in areas within a middle population range. While there was substantial industrial urbanization, most industry remained outside large cities. However, the reversal in the industrial employment pattern between rural and urban locations mirrored and amplified regional diversity.

Industries most frequently found in urban centers were construction, machines, metals, clothing, and textiles. Cities with concentrations of production goods industries were generally distinct from those where consumer goods production was high. Female labor was low in cities with heavy employment in capital goods production. The reverse was true in consumer goods cities.[35] The following cities had heavy concentrations of mining and smelting works. The percentage of women employed in industry was: Gelsenkirchen—3.7, Bochum—4.6, Duisburg—5.4, and Dortmund—7.5. In cities where metals and machines were heavily represented combined with consumer goods industries, there were higher levels of female labor: Chemnitz—28.2, Nürnberg—27.2, Leipzig—26.1, and Düsseldorf—12.5. The following group of cities were large clothing and textile centers: Plauen—42.2, Barmen—24, Crefeld—28.4, Elberfeld—25, Aachen—28.2, Berlin—28, and Erfurt—22.3. Female employment was heavy, exceeding one quarter of the industrial labor force. In Plauen, a textile city, almost 50% of the industrial population was female. As already noted, women made up 18.6% of the industrial labor force in 1907. If the industrially employed in large cities are separated from the total, women constituted 28% of the industrial population. This rather significant difference was due both to the concentration of old industries in certain cities, specifically textile centers, and to the tremendous urbanization of clothing and cleaning, industries that employed mostly women.

Industrial specialization and extent of female employment point up sharp differences in both geographic and personal prosperity. Low incidence of women working in industry was not merely indicative of meager opportunity for female employment. Availability of jobs was not the primary explanation for high percentages of women working. Among Germany's major industries, textiles and tobacco as well as other consumer goods branches paid the lowest average wages for both men and women workers. Construction, metals, and machines paid well. Women whose husbands or fathers brought home adequate wages did not go out to work. In regions and cities where industry paid its male skilled and semi-skilled workers 35 and 40 M. a week, there was no urgent need for women to work. Even laborers in heavy industry were paid better than skilled men in textiles and tobacco. The primary reason women went to work was need, not opportunity.

Industrial distribution of women workers revealed that industry's need for women was voracious. Increasing opportunity for women to find employment in industry was related primarily to changing technology and to the desire on the part of employers to keep down the cost of production. Historically, technological change usually has been interpreted as progress toward mechanization and greater concentration of the work force in factories. Yet in Germany, for those industries that sought the woman worker, technological change did not always point in the direction of factory production.

It was not technology alone that determined a place for women in industry, but the interplay between technology and cost. It was precisely for this reason that several industries decentralized in favor of production methods that reduced cost. Two such industries were tobacco products and clothing manufacture. Industry's embrace of the woman worker brought about by the interlocking of technological change and cost minimization caused perceptible alteration in the pattern of industrial employment. The two most significant aspects of that change were the feminization of certain industries in which women had previously been employed and the introduction of female labor in industries that were almost exclusively male employers. Clothing, tobacco, and textiles were traditional employers of women; metals and machines were new employers of female labor.

Clothing and cleaning employed the largest number of women industrial workers in pre-war Germany. It was a large industry, second only to construction in terms of total employment including both men and women workers. In 1907, 42.6% of the female industrial labor force worked in clothing.[36] In 1882, women made up 43.4% of all persons working in this industry; by 1907 the figure had risen to 53%. The percentage difference is significant. It was not caused by a reduction of men workers; male employment remained stable. Instead, the change was linked to the extensive proliferation of jobs for women in clothing, an expansion due to industrial decentralization and urbanization. A decentralized and urbanized clothing industry expanded principally into home work.

Clothing and cleaning included all types of garment sewing, even the manufacture of doll dresses, shoemaking, flower and feather products, hat-making, corsets, ties and collars, fur goods, and laundry and cleaning establishments. A major characteristic of most of the occupations in this division was seasonal fluctuation. The industry was intimately tied to the consumer market in terms of the dictates of both weather and fashion. There were significant differences between men's and women's clothing manufacture. Men's industry was more stable. Excepting tailoring and made-to-order clothes, men's garments were more readily factory produced. The industry was less geographically specialized than women's clothing. Cities were the centers for women's clothing: Berlin and Breslau in the north, and Munich in the south.[37] It was not unusual for men's clothing manufacturing to be located in or near textile districts, where there was ready access to fabrics. Better men's garments were produced in Berlin, Stuttgart, and Munich. Essen, München-Gladbach, and Rheydt in western Germany were centers for the production of work clothes. These locations were close to concentrations of heavy industry where such garments were in demand.[38]

Women's clothing always suffered more harshly than men's from seasonal fluctuation. The manufacture of women's garments usually reached full production for only six months in the year; two or three months were light production, and three or four months were slack time when there was no work at all. The following example shows the kind of fluctuation many workers in clothing experienced in their yearly schedule: Frau K was the wife of a construction worker in Berlin. When her husband had work, he could earn 18 to 21 M. a week, but construction was seasonal employment. The husband assisted his wife on a second sewing machine when he was at home. The woman did all types of ladies' clothes, dress shirts, and bed linens. During three months of the year, she had very little work. Slack time occurred during January, February, and October. In contrast, June, July, and August were the busy season. During these months, it was not unusual for her to work from 4:00 A.M. to 9 or 10 P.M. with only a short time free for the mid-day meal.[39]

Because the clothing industry was geared to a fluctuating market, the best work form was one that could match production demands with the least outlay in equipment and wages. For this reason, structural change in the clothing industry, as well as with many other occupations in this division, did not move in the direction of increased factory production. Also, in clothing, mechanization did not automatically mean more factory work. The nineteenth-century technological breakthrough in clothing was the sewing machine, which had a dual effect. There was increased factory production with the concentration of many machines, in some cases exceeding 500 units per shop. But the sewing machine was a versatile instrument; it could also duplicate factory-produced goods at home.

Decentralization in clothing caused expansion into domestic industry. In Berlin, it was rare to find a clothing firm that did not employ, in addition to factory labor, countless numbers of persons working at home. The following information gives some indication of the type of arrangement common to clothing. These figures are for 1906, but should be considered only as approximations because home work was consistently under-reported. In women's and children's clothes, 350 firms employed 52,000 home workers; 22,000 home workers were attached to 210 establishments making men's and boys' wear; 320 firms making undergarments employed 47,000 in home work; 150 hat-making and flower-making shops employed 6,000 home workers; and 170 shoe manufacturing establishments employed 2,000 persons working at home.[40]

Characteristic of the clothing industry was the middleman system (*Zwischenmeistersystem*). Most clothing-making in Berlin was handled in this way. Rarely did the employer have direct contact with his home workers. Exchange of goods and wages was done by the middleman who supervised the employment, training, and production of his people. Middlemen usually worked out of a shop where jobs that could not be done at home were carried out. These operations usually included cutting the goods, matching and assembling pieces, and doing the finishing work.[41] Because clothing manufacture required a flexible work form, home work was cheaper than factory production. Proliferation of jobs for women in clothing, to the extent that this industry employed almost half the number of women working, certainly showed up in the 1907 census, but, significantly, expansion was not into factory work.

Tobacco products manufacturing was another major German industry that experienced decentralization at the end of the nineteenth century, and, as with clothing, decentralization meant more jobs done at home. Division XIII, Foods and Specialties, in which tobacco was listed, also included baking and brewing, foods processing, and sugar production.[42] Foods and Specialties was the third largest employer in Germany in 1907; women made up 24.7% of those persons employed. It also placed third, after clothing and textiles, in terms of female employment. Between 1882 and 1907, female employment leaped from 74,000 to over 300,000. This represented a change in the gender composition of the work force from 10% to 25% female.[43] Tobacco was a large employer in Prussia, Silesia, Saxony, Westphalia, and the Rhineland; other states with large concentrations were Bavaria and Baden.[44] In south Germany, tobacco was one of the most rapidly expanding industries.[45] Tobacco products industries were generally non-urban; in some instances tobacco concentration overlapped with areas that were also heavily textile, thereby reinforcing the tendency for regional specification in women's work.

Several interrelated factors brought about structural change in tobacco. By the 1870's, the industry had already begun to feel the pressure of demands for increased production at lower cost. Competition from the United States was particularly bothersome.[46] The pinch became acute in the 1890's, when costs for factory production increased. Restrictive legislation regarding conditions of work for women and the prohibition of child labor limited the use of what had been traditionally cheap sources of labor. These restrictions were severely felt in tobacco because jobs were sex segregated, with whole families usually working together at different tasks.[47] The prohibition of child labor especially damaged the vitality of small shops. Many of them went out of business. Their place was taken by domestic industry, which lay beyond the restrictions of factory regulation and could still make use of family help.

In addition, techniques in tobacco manufacturing changed very little in the nineteenth century and did not require a factory setting. Making tobacco products remained largely a manual process.[48] Processing raw tobacco was usually done in the factory. Fermentation, curing, and preparation of the leaves required sun or intense heat for drying. Rolling and wrapping the tobacco for cigars was done by hand, usually a two-step process with women rolling and men wrapping the finished outer leaves. Luxury cigars continued to be made by one person, usually a man who completed the whole operation by hand. Since there was no advantage to factory production in terms of machines and concentration of the work process, what could be done in the factory could be done more cheaply at home. Employers sought to expand production by bringing work to the labor supply instead of the reverse. Many firms opened affiliates in rural areas adjacent to the city in which the parent factory was located to take advantage of an available female labor source. The culmination of these various changes in tobacco manufacturing was an expanding domestic industry that embraced more women workers.

The textile industry was the second largest employer of women in Germany. This position was maintained through the period from 1882 to 1907. Twenty-five percent of all women workers were employed in

the textile industry in 1907.[49] Reduction in the male labor force resulted in increasing feminization of the industry. The number of women
working in textiles increased from 350,522 to 578,544 between 1882
and 1907. For the same period, male employment dropped by about
30,000 workers.[50] Composition of the textile labor force changed from
37.5% female in 1882 to 51% women by 1907. This transition was
closely related to changing technology in the industry.

As textiles, particularly weaving, mechanized, more work was done
in factories. It was the mechanization of weaving more than any other
factor that accounted for the reduction of men in textile domestic industry. As machines took over the bulk of the production process, home
weaving became the work of women and girls. Men weavers either
entered factory production or sought employment in other industries
where wages were higher.[51] A male home weaver in Erfurt, trying to
support his family on 10 M. a week, perceived a bleak future for his
trade. " . . . hand weaving is without a future. It is done now the
whole year only by the old, weak, or sick. Most able men weavers
take on farming or construction work in the summer months to make
ends meet."[52] Despite an over-all reduction in home work in textiles,
the industry maintained a sizable portion of its labor force in domestic
production. Men were conspicuously absent, contributing in part to the
intense feminization of textiles by the first decade of the twentieth century. In addition to weaving and spinning, Division IX, Textiles, included knitting, embroidery, fabric dyeing, and net- and sail-mak-
ing.[53] There were two major geographic areas for textile production—
the old center of German industry in Saxony and a western textile region in Rhineland-Westphalia; 48% of all textile production in 1907
was located in western Germany.[54]

While much less subject to seasonal fluctuation than the clothing industry, textiles had its own problems with style changes that contributed to instability. A male textile worker observed that the textile
industry was always seeking something new—that owners and employers might try hundreds of new fabrics in the hope that one would
catch the buyers' fancy.[55] The worker went on to say that one year
hundreds of looms in Saxony turned out velours for women's jackets,
a popular fabric that season. The following year velours had disappeared and workers had to accept reduced production in goods from
wool shoddy. Over-production for a sometimes capricious consumer
market was characteristic of the textile industry. Employers sought to

minimize losses built into this kind of inconsistent demand by paying low wages. For men, textiles was one of Germany's lowest-paying industries. Women were a more appropriate labor source.

While clothing, tobacco, and textiles were examples of major industries that experienced feminization in the pre-war period, metals and machines were new employers of women. Because both branches were models of industries in which changing technology made way for women workers, it was easy to exaggerate their presence. Women workers became symbolic of the cheapening of work in terms of both skill and wages. "Mainly women work on the automatic machines, which, by combining tasks, eliminate pure work earlier done by men."[56] Metals and machines were industries with strong traditions of artisanal qualification and male exclusivity.

The whole opportunity for substituting female labor rests increasingly on division of labor and technical improvements in machines, and this can only have the effect of making work more mechanical, more uninteresting, and more uniform, and rendering any qualification more and more superfluous.[57]

The woman worker not only constituted a material threat, but her presence was perceived as symptomatic of a decline in the dignity of work.

Despite high visibility, the number of women employed in these two industries was hardly noteworthy compared with the hundreds of thousands working in clothing, textiles, and tobacco. In 1907, metals employed 77,251 women; machines 45,648. Women constituted 6.3% of the total labor force in metals and 4.8% in machines.[58] The 1907 figures indicate a four-fold increase for metals, while machines jumped to nine times the number of women employed in 1882. Despite the increase, only 3.3% of the total female labor force was employed in metals in 1907; 2% in machines.[59]

Simplified jobs could be performed by women and cheap wages assured them of a place in the industry. In Division VI, Machines and Instruments, women were employed mostly in the manufacture of instruments and apparatuses, especially in the electrical industry. A large electrical firm in Berlin hired its first women in 1896 and subsequently hired women almost exclusively for assembling instruments.[60] With the exception of building locomotives and other large pieces of equipment, women worked in most branches of the machine industry. It was not unusual for one or two women to be hired as a test, *zur Probe*, in an all-male establishment to initiate broader changes later on.[61] In metals as well as machines, women also performed large numbers of non-mechanical jobs such as washing, polishing, and finishing, sorting, and packing. "It was in all cases the cheapness of women's work which guided the employer toward substitution of women for men."[62] Most of the work in metals and machines was done in factories, yet it was the very issue of cheap wages that allowed for an expanding home industry along with factory production. Mostly all women were employed for home work jobs. Obviously not all operations could be done at home, but for those tasks that could, the jobs were "sent out." Watchmaking, certain branches in fine mechanics, gold-smithing, glass-etching, and wire-making were all jobs that were normally done by domestic industry. As with all other data for 1907, these jobs were not listed separately from factory work.

If the issue of women's work was a sensitive one in pre-war Germany, the question of married working women was even more difficult. Yet as was the case with the results of general statistics on working women, caution must be exercised with the interpretation of data concerning married women. In 1895, 68.9% of the female industrial labor force was single and 31.1% were married, widowed, or separated. In 1907, there was perceptible change, but hardly a remarkable one: 67.1% of working women were single and 32.9% were married or previously married.[63] Again, recognizing the inflated results of the 1907 census which picked up many married women previously excluded, what is extraordinary was the stability in the marital composition of the female industrial labor force. A profile of the marital status of working women in the four major occupational groups—agriculture, industry, trade and commerce, and service—further confirmed that industry was not the most attractive occupation for the married woman. A table indicating the percentage of women working by marital status in 1907 follows on page 33.[64] The largest percentage of single women worked in industry, the lowest in agriculture.

Locating married women by industry revealed that approximately 78% of all married women working in 1907 were employed in three branches: textiles, 30.2%; clothing and cleaning, 28.6%; and foods and specialties including tobacco, 19.5%.[65] Compared with figures for 1895 in the same industries, the total remained fairly stable, but there was significant change among the three branches: 82.8% of all married women

Occupational Division	Marital Status	Percentage
A. Agriculture	Single	45.4
	Married	43.7
	Widowed and separated	10.7
B. Industry	Single	67.1
	Married	21.3
	Widowed and separated	11.6
C. Trade and Commerce	Single	55.8
	Married	28.2
	Widowed and separated	15.8
D. Service	Single	55.1
	Married	16.4
	Widowed and separated	28.3

working in 1895 were in textiles, foods and specialties, and clothing and cleaning, but in the twelve-year period, the percentage of married women diminished in textiles and clothing while increasing in foods and specialties—35.3% and 32.3% of all married women worked in textiles and clothing and cleaning in 1895, respectively. With foods and specialties, the percentage increased from 15.2% to 19.5%. A suggested explanation for the difference can be found in the methods of work in the three industries. In textiles, home work declined. For women, the reduction was not great, but it was significant enough to account for an over-all loss of married women working. As previously noted, tobacco and clothing experienced decentralization, which increased the proportion of industrial output done by home work.

Yet, where married women were concerned, decentralization did not have the same effect in both industries. Tobacco products manufacture required several persons working together, usually family members assisting in the work process. Domestic tobacco production was normally family work. Where the home worker did not have children to assist, children from other households were often hired a few hours a day to help out.[66] There were only a few instances where the wife did not assist, and for these it was usually because of death or illness. Work procedure in clothing was different. More hands meant more production, but sewing was a job that did not require a collective effort.

The best way to demonstrate the difference between tobacco and clothing in terms of their appeal and accessibility to married women is by including both married and previously married in the profile.[67] Among married and previously married women only 16.5% of the total labor force was in foods and specialties, which constitutes a percentage reduction in this industry's share of women workers from a consideration in which only married are counted. Clothing and cleaning, on the other hand, changes significantly if both married and previously married are considered. While 28.6% of all married women worked in this branch, the figure jumps to 36% if widows and separated women are included. Widows and separated women working alone could not really handle the kinds of tasks peculiar to tobacco production. Clothing and cleaning could be done as solitary employment. Clothing, especially, was a preferred occupation for women who needed to work—a job that could be "picked up" when necessary either in factory or home production. But the more important factor that accounted for the increase was the unusually high concentrations of widows and separated women in cleaning and laundry work.

Most industry branches in 1907 were dominated by single women.[68] In every group except laundry work, single women exceeded half the number employed. Industries with high concentrations of single women were mining, 76%; machines, 76%; fats and soaps, 77%; paper, 74%; and clothing, 77%. The high percentage of single women in clothing is deceptive. The percentage figure confirms that clothing work was predominantly single employment, but because the total number of women in this branch was so large, it must be emphasized that the number of married women exceeded one quarter of the total married working in all industries. The percentage of married women working in foods and specialties, 35%, was the highest in any industry. The reason for the high concentration of married women in this branch was tobacco production, which as previously indicated was a family-based task. The exception among the industry groups was cleaning and laundries. The marital profile is considerably different from other industries. The unusually high percentage of widows and separated women, 31%, seems to indicate that jobs in this industry were not terribly attractive—that mostly women in the direst need sought employment.

To amplify the marital composition of the female labor force in pre-war Germany, an age profile has been computed for five industry groups employing approximately 84% of industrial employed women in the first decade of the twentieth century.[69] The groups used for the age distribution were textiles, foods and specialties, clothing and cleaning, metals, and machines. Overwhelmingly, most women workers were between the ages of twenty and thirty. This was the largest single age category in all five industries. Well over half the number of women working in industry were under thirty years old. The percentage average for these five industries indicated that 65% of all female workers were between fourteen and thirty years of age.

An interesting distinction emerges from the age pattern if the so-called women's industries—textiles, foods and specialties, and clothing and cleaning—are separated from metals and machines. Industries that were new employers of women were significantly more youthful than the traditional groups. The following figures apply to the age category of women workers between twenty and thirty years old: in textiles, 32% of those employed; in foods and specialties, 31.5%; in clothing and cleaning, 32.4%. For metals and machines, the percentages are higher: 33.3% in metals and 38.4% in machines. The difference is even more apparent if the five groups are compared on the basis of workers under thirty years old: 64.4% in textiles were under thirty, 59.5% in foods and specialties, 57.8% in clothing and cleaning, 69.9% in metals, and a significant 74.9% in machines.[70]

Several conclusions can be drawn from these data. First, the age distribution in traditional women's industries was significantly broader, indicating not only that there were jobs women of all ages could do in those industries, but that women could stay on or move in and out with little problem. The broadest age distribution occurred in clothing and cleaning, which employed the highest percentage of women over thirty years old. In fact, approximately 115,000 women were over fifty. The significance of this figure is emphasized by noting that total employment in no other industry except textiles and foods and specialties even came close to the number of women over fifty years of age working in clothing and cleaning. Many were separated or widowed, which partially accounts for the elevated age status.

In addition, clothing and cleaning were ultimately flexible. Jobs could be done by women of all ages at every stage of their lives in either factory or home production. It can be suggested that the tasks were familiar or easily learned. On the other hand, metals and machines were male-dominated industries with relatively high skill requirements. New work experience seemed to call for new workers, girls and young women who probably had not been in industry before. A mature entrant or returning worker was not common. In addition, metals and machines were industries with comparatively little home work. Jobs in domestic industry usually swelled the ranks with older women who were married or previously married.

It is not the intention of this chapter to deny a numerical increase in the number of women working in industrially related jobs, a significant proportion of which were in factory production. However, without examination of the meaning of numerical data, it is too easy to stress change while ignoring the less obvious indications of continuity and stability. The profile of total female employment showed that industry's share of working women actually decreased compared with employment in other occupations. The composition of Germany's industrial labor force remained stable. As industry expanded, more women worked, but women hardly pushed men out of the marketplace, nor did women widely abandon work in other occupations to take on jobs in industry. Most industrially employed women were young and single. Branches where married women worked retained considerable domestic production. A combination of data on marital status and age suggests that women frequently left the work force after marriage, or took up a different form of industrial work.

Consideration of the 1907 census results, which ostensibly marked women and work as a vehicle for social change, really indicated something quite the opposite. The census identified mostly married women working with their families in domestic production during a period of economic depression. The inflation, therefore, confirmed the preservation of an essentially traditional form of women's work and also substantiated the contention that most women's work was a reserve against economic emergency. In an effort to justify an assumption of vast change in the German labor force and in the lives of working women, continuity is easily overlooked. Exploring what remained the same is as challenging as seeking out change, because for German working women continuity predominated.

Persistence in the geographic configuration of women's work indicated that motivation for work was inextricably tied to need. Erosion of regional prosperity translated into more women working to offset the deficit in men's and children's earnings. Distribution of women workers by industry suggests that women were the compensating factor that employers used to tighten or loosen the slack caused by an unpredictable market. Industries that were geared to the consumer market relied primarily on labor-intensive forms of work. Because the work process in many industries did not require factory production, domestic industry expanded in both rural areas and urban centers where there was an ample reserve of female labor. Industry's use of women consigned them to places where women had always been and reinforced traditional work forms. It is precisely for this reason that the obvious numerical changes in industrial employment for women were deceptive.

NOTES

1. Elizabeth Gnauck-Kühne, *Die Deutsche Frau um die Jahrhundertwende* (Berlin: Verlag von Otto Liebmann, 1907), p. 115.

2. Anna Geyer, *Die Frauenerwerbsarbeit in Deutschland* (Jena: Thüringer Verlagsanstalt und Druckerei, 1924), pp. 91, 98.

3. For expanded discussion, see Chapter 6, "Women Home Workers."

4. Frank Tipton, *Regional Variations in the Economic Development of Germany during the Nineteenth Century* (Middletown, Conn.: Wesleyan University Press, 1976), p. 157.

5. *Statistische Beilage des Correspondenzblatt*, Generalkommission der Gewerkschaften Deutschlands, Berlin, Nr. 3 (April 27, 1912), pp. 86–87.

6. Ibid., p. 92.

7. "Zunahme der Frauenarbeit während der Krise," *Tabak-Arbeiter*, Nr. 20 (May 17, 1903).

8. Dora Landé, "Arbeits- und Lohnverhältnisse in der Berliner Maschinenindustrie," *Schriften des Vereins für Sozialpolitik*, Vol. 134 (1910), p. 457.

9. Herberge: Ludwigsstrasse 15, Verein zur Fürsorge für Fabrikarbeiterinnen (1905–1906).

10. *Statistische Beilage des Correspondenzblatt*, computed from table, p. 98.

11. *Statistik des Deutschen Reichs*, Herausgegeben vom Kaiserlichen Statistischen Amte, Berlin, Band 211 (1913), p. 46.

12. *Statistische Beilage des Correspondenzblatt*, p. 92.

13. Ibid., p. 63.

14. Marie Baum, *Drei Klassen von Lohnarbeiterinnen in Industrie und Handel der Stadt Karlsruhe*, Bericht erstattet an das Grossherzogliche Ministerium des Innern und herausgegeben von der Grossherzoglich Badischen Fabrikinspektion (Karlsruhe: Druck und Verlag der G. Braunschen Hofbuchdruckerei, 1906), p. 135.

15. J. Silbermann, "Die Frauenarbeit nach den beiden letzten Berufszählungen," *Schmollers Jahrbuch*, Vol. 35 (1911), p. 232.

16. *Statistische Beilage des Correspondenzblatt*, p. 77.

17. Silbermann, "Die Frauenarbeit," p. 241.

18. Johannes Feig, "Hausgewerbe und Fabrikbetrieb in der Berliner wäscheindustrie," *Staats- und Socialwissenschaftliche Forschungen* (Leipzig: Verlag von Duncker und Humblot, 1896), p. 101.

19. *Statistische Beilage des Correspondenzblatt*, computed from table, p. 63.

20. *Statistik des Deutschen Reichs*, Band 211, p. 46.

21. Tipton, *Regional Variations*, p. 5.

22. Ibid., p. 41.

23. *Statistik des Deutschen Reichs*, Band 211, pp. 161–63.

24. Ibid., p. 163.

25. Ibid., p. 162.

26. Ibid., pp. 161, 163.

27. Ibid., p. 163.

28. Ibid.

29. Ibid., p. 162.

30. Ibid.

31. Ibid., p. 163.

32. Ibid., Band 111 (1899), p. 216.

33. Tipton, *Regional Variations*, p. 95.

34. *Statistik des Deutschen Reichs*, Band 211, p. 139.

35. Ibid., figures compiled from data pp. 164–67.

36. Ibid., p. 46.

37. Erhard Schmidt, *Fabrikbetrieb und Heimarbeit in der Deutschen Konfektionsindustrie* (Stuttgart: Verlag von Ferdinand Enke, 1912), p. 102.

38. Ibid., p. 36.

39. Feig, "Hausgewerbe," p. 30.

40. "Die Heimarbeit in der Berliner Industrie," *Reichs-Arbeitsblatt*, IV Jahrgang, Nr. 12 (1906), pp. 1114–15.

41. Ibid., p. 1113.

42. *Statistik des Deutschen Reichs*, Band 211, p. 23.

43. Ibid., p. 46.

44. E. Jaffé, "Hausindustrie und Fabrikbetrieb in der deutschen Cigarrenfabrikation," *Schriften des Vereins für Sozialpolitik*, Vol. 86 (1899), p. 288.

45. Ibid.

46. *Ergebnisse über die Frauen- und Kinderarbeit in den Fabriken* (Berlin: Carl Heymanns Verlag, 1877), p. 89.

47. Jaffé, "Hausindustrie," p. 306.

48. Ibid., p. 301.

49. *Statistik des Deutschen Reichs*, Band 211, p. 46.

50. Ibid.

51. Tipton, *Regional Variations*, p. 50.

52. E. Neubert, "Die Hausindustrie in den Regierungsbezirken Erfurt und Merseburg," *Schriften des Vereins für Sozialpolitik*, Vol. 40 (1889), p. 119.

53. *Statistik des Deutschen Reichs*, Band 211, p. 23.

54. Ibid., p. 162.

55. "Die Lage der Textilindustrie und ihrer Arbeiter," *Die Neue Zeit*, 19 Jahrgang, Nr. 35 (1900–1901), p. 268.

56. Landé, "Arbeits," p. 462.

57. Ibid.

58. *Statistik des Deutschen Reichs*, Band 211, p. 46.

59. Ibid.

60. Landé, "Arbeits," p. 458.

61. Ibid., p. 460.

62. Elizabeth Altmann-Gottheiner, "Die Entwicklung der Frauenarbeit in der Metallindustrie," *Schriften des ständigen Ausschusses zur Förderung der Arbeiterinnen-Interessen* (Jena: Verlag von Gustav Fischer, 1916), p. 7.

63. *Statistische Beilage des Correspondenzblatt*, p. 92.

64. Ibid., computed from table, p. 92.

65. Ibid., computed from tables, pp. 88–91.

66. Jaffé, "Hausindustrie," p. 313.

67. *Statistische Beilage des Correspondenzblatt*, pp. 88–91.

68. *Statistik des Deutschen Reichs*, Band 211, p., 141.

69. *Statistiche Beilage des Correspondenzblatt*, pp. 88–91.

70. Ibid.

2

Wages, Work Skills, and Job Mobility

" . . . they must reckon in *Pfennigs*"*

Where women worked and what they did, and how they managed their lives, was largely dependent on how industry used the woman worker. Women were a flexible labor supply, dispensable on the personal level, but indispensable in the collective. Low wages, low skill levels, and low job commitment were characteristic of the kind of labor industry required to fill production needs. German firms took shrewd advantage of women. Devaluation of the work performed by women was affirmed in the perception that they were unfitted for the task. In substance, they were ideal.

Objectively considered, low wage potential, poor skill qualifications, and frequent job changes were largely negative. Yet for most women they defined a pattern of existence that allowed them a certain amount of control over the work experience. Elasticity was the important factor. Women in the working class could not and did not expect to be financially independent. There were no real options for them to function on their own economically and no chance for them to build in their own protection for the future. But women were able in a very restricted sense to turn their economic liabilities into assets. They fit-

*Rosa Kempf, "Das Leben der jungen Fabrikmädchen in München, *Schriften des Vereins für Sozialpolitik*, Vol. 135 (Leipzig: Verlag von Duncker und Humblot, 1911), p. 93.

ted into the gears and cogs of the system by negotiating the narrow interstices of the capitalist market. Paradoxically, their strategies for coping turned on the very hindrances that blocked escape from limited opportunity.

Wage differentials between men and women workers had always been broad in Germany. While the gap was diminished somewhat in the decade before World War I, rates by no means approached any degree of gender equality.[1] With the exception of the socialist labor unions, no one believed there was any good reason that they should. The structure of wages for all workers considered both the quantity and quality of work done, but wages also involved myriad cultural and personal factors that defied measurement. The major objection against the concept of equal pay for equal work was the contention that equal work from women was a virtual impossibility. Lower pay for women workers was based on a notion that can loosely be described as "productivity potential." Supported by the fact, and the embellishment of the fact, that most women worked in industry only temporarily in their lifetime, it was generally agreed that they were worth less, or at least would be content with less. Accusations of dilettantism and instability may have been self-serving for employers,[2] but even if the negative connotation of these terms is moderated, it was nevertheless true that women's cycle of employment was different from men's. The concept of commitment to work was hardly specific, yet it involved many factors that did account in most cases for the vast difference between wages for men and women.

Industries where women worked were capital poor and labor rich.[3] Gerhard Bry suggested in his study of German wage structure that capital-intensive heavy industry needed what he described as a "responsible labor supply."[4] Consumer goods industries, textiles, clothing, foods, tobacco, paper—branches with large concentrations of female workers—had different production problems. An elastic market required a flexible labor supply. In determining wages in all industries, performance capacity for women was judged differently from men. Employers could point, with considerable justification, to inadequate preparation, poor skills, inexperience, and job vacillation as bases for lower rates. Yet these were precisely the characteristics of the kind of labor force industry wanted.

Age and experience factors also worked against the woman employee where wages were concerned. Younger women were usually paid less than adult workers. Married women in many industries received more money than single. Just as women reached the peak of their earning capacity, they usually married and left the work force. In addition, there was little consensus among employers regarding the value of the married woman worker. Many employers felt that married women had a stabilizing influence on the younger girls because they were older and more responsible.[5] On the other hand, the employer recognized that the married woman was in the factory because there was no other way to earn enough; most likely she was dividing her time between work, home, and children—responsibilities for which he would have to pay, at least indirectly in lost work time.

All of these factors of training, skill, age, and experience influenced the kind of work women did. It is extremely difficult, if not impossible, in most industries to attempt a comparison between men's and women's wages because men and women performed different operations. Bases for job differences typically incorporated training, skill, age, and experience, with a measure of physical strength added to the mixture for reinforcement. But the argument is more than a circular one. Even in industries where men and women performed similar operations and received similar piece-rate price, it was still unlikely to find women earning as much as the men.[6] To the rather vague concept of commitment there was added the equally subjective notion of propriety. Wages were a social question. Men were superior to women in the social structure; men should earn more.

The argument was bolstered by the important affirmation that the man was the head of the family for whose support he was responsible. This was the theme most frequently used to justify difference in wages where there was no significant difference in capacity or performance.[7] The argument could also be reversed. Equal pay for equal work was disparaged because women did not need the money as much as men. Unfortunately, this contention did not recognize the reason for women's work in the first place. Their earnings were necessary for family survival. But even family survival could be contorted into justification for differential—wages of wives and daughters were only supplemental.[8] Inequality of wages between men and women, whether justified by notions of weak commitment or propriety, made women workers active competitors in the job market.

Systematic data on wages for Germany in the period 1871 to 1914 are not available, but there is sufficient material to develop a sense of what wages for women were by industry and operation. Most existing data were collected at random by the labor unions, especially the socialist trade unions, which sponsored the campaign for equal pay for equal work. Data confirmed that determination of wages was dictated by custom and tradition. A principle of standard rate did not apply, nor were wages determined according to market calculation.[9] Total wages and wage rates varied according to industry's evaluation of both work and worker. Only gradually did determination of wages catch up with "what the traffic would bear."[10] Workers as well as employers adhered to a system based upon hierarchical distinctions in the value of work that were heavily influenced by custom and social status. Pay for women workers was influenced not only by traditional differentials of skill and experience, but also by social prescription of inferior status.

In pre-war Germany, women's wages were approximately half of what men earned.[11] There were examples of sex differentials in every industry including those branches of production that were traditionally heavy employers of women as well as industries where women were newly employed. A survey conducted by the Union of Factory Workers verified a vast discrepancy. Average wages for women were 11.54 M. weekly; those for men were 22.08 M. What was accepted as a normal wage for women was paid only to young boys and incapacitated men.[12]

Top of the wage range for women was at the bottom of the scale for men's earnings. It is immediately apparent that while only 1% of the

Men Workers		Women Workers	
Weekly Wages	Percentage	Weekly Wages	Percentage
- 12 M.	1.12	- 8 M.	8.92
12 - 15	4.71	8 - 10	29.50
15 - 18	17.49	10 - 12	33.80
18 - 21	25.49	12 - 15	20.17
21 - 25	31.12	15 -	7.61
25 - 30	16.40		
30 - 35	2.95		
35 -	.72		

men earned less that 12 M., almost three-quarters of the women fell below 12 M. weekly.

Figures from Stuttgart in 1900 indicate a similar pattern. This information is even richer than data collected by the Union of Factory Workers because wages were listed by industry. Average wages for women were 9.57 M. weekly; those for men were 22 M. Women earned only 43% of men's wages. The following chart indicates the average wages for women and men by industry or job and women's wages expressed in percentage of men's wages:[13]

Occupation	Men's Wages	Women's Wages	% of Men's Wages
Painting and Varnishing	20.53 M.	11.28 M.	55
Shoemaking	18.27	10.89	59
Upholstering	20.75	10.80	52
Day-work	16.72	10.59	63
Sattlers	18.24	10.17	55
Printing	27.64	9.82	35.5
Bookbinding	21.83	9.67	44
Cabinet-making	21.65	9.35	43
Textiles	20.10	9.13	45
Lithography	24.70	9.05	36.6
Goldworking	20.93	9.00	43
Tailoring	18.00	8.91	49
Hand shoemaking	22.06	8.65	39
Tobacco	14.21	8.02	56
Locksmithing	21.30	7.90	37

Jobs where women earned less than half men's wages were skill intensive, artisanal work. Women did assistance labor. Least difference was shown in jobs that were not trade-specific such as the category "day-work," where women and men were more likely to perform similar tasks.

Isolated examples from specific industries further illustrate wide gender differential. Returns from the Wood Workers Union indicated that a difference of 8.10 M. separated men's and women's wages in that industry. Average for men was 19.37 M., for women 11.27 M. weekly.[14] Figures for the brush industry registered a slight gain for women in the first decade of the twentieth century. Average wages for men in 1902 were 18.52 M. and for women, 8.83 M., or 47.6% of men's wages. By 1912, men's wages had increased to 22.18 M., women's to 11.65 M., or 52.5% of men's wages.[15] A conference of unionized textile workers held in Crimmitschau in February, 1910, directed attention to the promotion of equal wages for equal work. Given the focus of the meeting, valuable data on wage differences were collected. Wages for female weavers generally were 80% of men's earnings. In only sixty firms were wages the same for men and women. Rates for men at the same job averaged 50 to 100 *Pfennigs* per piece higher than those for women.

Determination of how wages were paid differed by industry, operation, and employer. Basically, there were two types of wages—time and piece rates. Generally, operation governed rate structure. If a worker was independently responsible for the product, or if she figured importantly in its manufacture, she was usually paid by the piece. Direct labor was customarily piece work; assistance jobs, or indirect labor, normally were hourly. The criterion for distinction was the degree of influence the worker had in the manufacture of the product. Piece work was considered more demanding than time work. Industry wanted urgent performance to increase production and workers understood the relationship between more effort and better wages.

While there were no systematic data on disposition of labor by wage structure, a survey conducted by the Union of Factory Workers in 1909 yielded interesting information. From returns it was learned that 60% of the men polled worked by an hourly rate structure; 40% of the women worked hourly. Twenty-four percent of the men and 40% of the women were in piece work.[16] Women were almost evenly divided between piece and hourly rates, while men workers were largely hourly. There are several suggested explanations for the difference. First, it was more likely that men were employed in heavy industry where an hourly rate was more plausible by virtue of how work was organized.[17] Second, since the Factory Workers Union was not trade-specific, it was probable that men as well as women were employed in indirect labor jobs. However, devaluation of women's work was also a factor. It was believed that men could be trusted to give a fair and adequate performance for time spent. Women were perceived as less predictable. An illustration from the metal industry points up the discrepancy. Beginning women workers were frequently put on piece work even if the job was hourly rated, because it was assumed that women did less work than men.[18]

For women, piece-rate work was consistently better paying, unless the employee was extremely slow or incompetent. Total wages in piece work were usually higher than hourly. In textiles, women weavers and spinners were customarily on piece rate. In Silesia, the wage rate in 1908 for time work was 1 to 1.50 M. a day, which at most averaged out to 9 M. weekly. A woman in piece work could make between 12 and 15 M. and sometimes as much as 18 M. weekly.[19] In tobacco production, the wage system depended on operation. Wrappers, who were almost always men, were paid by the piece. Rolling tobacco, a woman's job, was also piece rated, as were selecting and sorting. Assistance jobs were paid by the week. Translated into money, wrappers, rollers, selectors, and sorters could make between 9 and 12 M. weekly, while helpers were paid 1 to 1.20 M. daily.[20]

Wood products employed women mostly for jobs where technology made possible a finely graduated division of labor. Most women in wood products were on piece work, which averaged about 2 M. higher per week than hourly rate.[21] Average wages for all workers in woods on time rate were 9.43 M. weekly, while the average for piece rate was 11.02 M. in 1909.[22] Brush manufacturing, a division of the woods industry, employed 62% of its work force at piece rate; 68% of the women worked by this wage system.[23] Among the divisions of the paper industry, both systems were used depending on skill required for production and level of mechanization. Carton manufacturing was overwhelmingly piece work.[24] In bookbinding, two-thirds of the women were employed as piece workers, the remainder on time. The majority of workers in fine paper manufacture worked on time, averaging 5 to 10 M. a week in Berlin. For all branches of paper products, lower-paying jobs were usually at time rate.[25]

While it is impossible to draw a neat line connecting wage system with age, there was a relationship. Younger, less skilled, and inexperienced women were more likely to be on a time rate schedule. In some instances, piece work rate could not apply because these less apt workers did not participate directly in product manufacture. They were "helpers." Once a girl acquired knowledge of the job, it was to the employer's advantage to put her on piece work as incentive to greater production. The following chart shows a substantial connection between wage rate system and age.[26]

Wage System	Age Brackets		
	14-15 years	16-17 years	18 years
Hour or day wages	6.22 M.	9.08 M.	9.87 M.
Hour and piece rate		8.25	13.15
Piece work	7.38	10.55	12.20
Weekly wages	5.70	9.80	12.00
Average Wages	6.40	9.54	11.45

The tendency for piece-rate work increased with the age of the worker, paralleling expected improvement in ability and speed. Rates were factory wages. Most of the girls were employed in paper products and foods production. Within each age category, piece work was better paid, with the exception of several adult women working a combination of both systems.

The relationship between wages and age was especially clear in the clothing industry. Women were paid considerably more than girls doing the same job. For example, data from Karlsruhe indicate a vast difference in pay for women over eighteen with the same job definition as other workers. Average weekly wages for sewers over eighteen was 12.04 M.; for younger girls, it was only 4.24 M. For cutters a similar discrepancy was apparent. Adult women earned 11.10 M. weekly; girls under eighteen, 3.43 M.[27]

Different wage scales based on age can readily be justified by the expectation of increased production through experience. What is harder to explain is a difference related to marital status. Given the popularity of the *Herr-im-Haus* concept, married men with families quite commonly earned more than single men. But the same principle was not supposed to apply to women since they were not expected to be the sole support for families. While the evidence is extremely scanty, it does suggest that at least some married women and women who were previously married were favored with higher wages. From a sample of twenty factories in Karlsruhe representing various industries, there was a difference of almost 2 M. between average wages for married women and those for single women over eighteen. Single women earned 11.00 M. weekly; average wages for married were 12.55 M.[28] Differences were especially pronounced in cleaning establishments, where average earnings were 15.32 M. and 11.19 M., and in the polygraph industry, where wages were 13.35 M. weekly for married and 9.93 M. for single.[29] Wage rates for women in Stuttgart also suggested similar variation. Average wages for married women regardless of industry were higher than those for single. Married women earned 10.55 M. weekly, while single workers averaged 9.08 M., signifying a 16% difference in weekly wage.[30] Despite the lack of conclusive evidence on this point, data do confirm the contention that wage rate structure was determined by more than market criteria.

Base wages were subject to both positive and negative alterations that affected total earnings. Regardless of wage structure, individual workers could suffer a reduction in earnings by breaking factory rules. A textile firm in Gera docked its workers 25 *Pfennigs* if they arrived late or left work five or ten minutes early. The same fine was imposed if any worker was caught dirtying factory premises or smoking. Disturbing other workers, mutilating cloth, or altering machines could cost the worker a half-day's pay.[31] Clothing home workers had to buy their own supplies. Outlay for needles, thread, and even machine oil could come to 1 or 2 M. a week.[32]

But there were examples where informality prevailed and worked to the advantage of the employee. For instance, young clothing workers were often provided tea or coffee with bread at the afternoon break. Money wages were so low that the dietary supplement must be considered part of total earnings. Girls in training were frequently treated to a bit of wurst and beer, an apple, or a hot bun at vespers. At Christmas, it was customary for employers to offer a small *Taschengeld* (pocket money) or an item of cloth or clothing as a holiday bonus.[33]

If all the variables that produced the wage differential could be reduced to one point, it would be gender. The woman was perceived as a worker with different capacities and different needs. That those capacities and needs fit the requirements of certain segments of industrial production translated into job access for women. Cost of labor was the most significant variable in the production process. Hiring women assured cost minimization. Perhaps the circle was vicious.[34] If men were paid an adequate wage, women would not have to work. If wages for women increased, industry would have been less anxious to hire them.

But these were the themes of reform, not the conditions of reality. Wages were the single most important factor in industry's selection of the woman worker.

What industry was willing to pay corresponded to what industry expected from women workers. Skill level for most women was low, but industry did not need skilled women workers. Most of the tasks industry set women to do required attention, speed, dexterity, and repetition. A great deal of women's work in factories was related to machine production where watching was as important as doing. Industrial expansion in the late nineteenth century had not meant any increase in skill level for women because mechanization and rationalization decreased need for highly trained workers. Between 1895 and 1907, the number of unskilled in the total labor force grew proportionately larger.[35] Big firms hired more unskilled labor than establishments with fewer employees because the larger factories usually had a more thorough division of labor with more operations done by machine.

Disparagement of women workers because they were poorly skilled came primarily from men, who correctly perceived the threat from such a labor supply. Men in skilled jobs in traditionally artisanal trades were the most hostile. "The woman cannot be acknowledged by her special occupation as men can. One does not recognize her as a driller, miller, stamper, and so on, just simply worker."[36] But industry did not complain, because the "simple worker" filled special needs. Innumerable tasks in factory production just required work, not specific people or specific skills. Women's specialty as labor was flexibility. And flexibility also worked to the advantage of women who needed to work. Low skill did not mean low job qualification. Instead of searching out or waiting for the job that met her skill, the woman worker could get a job just about anywhere. It was clearly a case where the least skilled were the most qualified in terms of access and adjustment.

Clothing was the only industry in which there were more skilled women than men.[37] This was particularly true in needlework and ready-made clothes. Formally, women's training in clothing was a close approximation to a trade apprenticeship. Following the promulgation of the *Handwerk Novelle* in 1908,[38] artisan associations were thrown into confusion over how to define female-run clothing establishments.[39] Only shops run by a master could offer an apprenticeship; credentials of many women in charge of shops where training was offered were suspect. In Munich, the first apprentice qualification under the new law was offered in October, 1909; one woman qualified. The following year, twenty-two women passed.[40] In the spring of 1911, twenty-six artisan associations chose to bring women's tailoring and plain sewing under control of the code, which stipulated an apprenticeship.[41] A three-year training period was considered appropriate for clothing. Data collected by the Artisan Association of Upper Bavaria indicated that according to its formal standards, 90% of the women working in clothing were unqualified; 88% in dress-making, 97% in underclothing, and 97% in ready-made garments.[42] Officials from the association were dismayed by the attitude expressed by most of the girls they questioned; certification was simply not important.[43]

Many girls in training for clothing were little more than servants during their first year, especially in small establishments. In addition to picking up and delivering goods, their duties often included household tasks. It was commonly said that a first year *Lehrmädchen* (apprentice) was hardly more than a *Laufmädchen* (errand-girl), someone at the complete disposal of her mistress. "Some girls never even pick up a needle." [44] Despite the disadvantages of training in a small shop where work relations were informally defined, there were positive aspects. Girls usually acquired more practical experience because there were more opportunities for handling the whole garment at various stages of its assembly. Parents of girls training in large establishments often complained that their daughters knew only one operation and were hardly getting their money's worth from the experience.[45] Families commonly expressed the view that if a girl was not worked hard enough, she learned less, and her potential as an earner diminished.

Generally no wages were paid to girls at the beginning of their training period. There was no hard and fast rule governing the length of training time in clothing; the period without wages could last anywhere from three weeks to two years.[46] Where the relationship between the mistress and her sewers was personal, girls were often given "pocket money." This *Taschengeld* was usually 50 to 60 *Pfennigs* a week for a beginning worker. The gratuity rarely amounted to more than 3 M. a week, and this sum was attainable only after two years with the same mistress.[47] Anything beyond 3 M. was considered wages. A more professional training could be obtained if the family was willing to pay an apprentice fee. Among 720 girls in the Munich clothing industry interviewed on conditions of their work experience, only 3 had paid a *Lehrgeld*. The fee averaged 5 to 8 M. a month for the duration of their training period. And these 3 girls were not from working-class families.[48] Families might be willing to invest time and money in a three-year apprenticeship for boys, but girls were different. Since a daughter would probably marry and leave her job anyway, there was no point in future investment when her wages were needed immediately.

Learning enough to get a job was more important than preparing for a lifetime occupation. Many girls never completed the formal apprentice period. Parents looked upon their daughters' work activity as a "way-station" before marriage, but it was supposed to be a productive way-station for the family. Compensation for lack of skill was figured in terms of the advantage of immediate wages and substitution of job mobility for job security. Sewing had a particular appeal. With relatively little invested in time and energy, girls could manage a salary quickly, as well as anticipate contingencies in the future. "Going for sewing" was seen as insurance against falling on hard times. Sewing was a flexible occupation; it could be picked up and left as necessity demanded. Even families that considered their circumstances to be above the working classes often sent their daughters for training in sewing. For the *Kleinbürgerlich* (lower middle class), facing the disgrace of the factory was unacceptable. "What will our friends and neighbors say if our daughter became a factory girl? With sewing one can always earn her bread, even after marriage."[49] Sewing was versatile; it was respectable and safe.

Training in textiles approximated a trade apprenticeship only for men workers.[50] Job preparation for women consisted primarily of learning the machine. Numbers of skilled women about equaled qualified men workers. In certain operations, women exceeded skilled men. In spinning, winding, thread-twisting, knitting, and crocheting, there were more skilled women than men. Skilled men predominated in weaving.[51] Stretching thread, winding, and reeling were considered semi-skilled jobs. Training usually did not exceed a few days' experience to learn the operation, but further practice was needed to acquire sufficient speed to maintain production. For women reelers, two or three months' experience was required before proficiency levels became acceptable. Winders could reach performance minimum in four to six weeks; a thread stretcher was ready in a few days.[52] Flyspinners, forespinners, and ringspinners were skilled workers. The training period was referred to by the term *Lehrzeit*. During this time the worker learned the machine, increasing her speed and precision. If a girl began training for these operations when she left school at age fourteen, she could acquire skilled status by age sixteen. In other words, training for proficiency normally took two years. In textiles, skilled jobs were usually done by young women who learned the operation as girls. Older women did less skilled and unskilled jobs. Many of these workers were married women who returned to the factory to help support growing families.[53]

Beyond clothing and textiles, most industries were interested in women workers as simply labor rather than as skilled labor. In metals about a quarter of the women employed were skilled. Most of these were concentrated in one branch of the metal industry—gold and silver working. Women satisfied the need for dexterity and precision in the work process.[54] Training in tobacco was a rather informal arrangement. Cigar-making, a large employer of women, required group effort, often with whole families working together. Some states prescribed a training period; others did not. Where formal training was available, on-the-job experience usually lasted for three years.[55] It must be emphasized that large portions of the tobacco industry were domestic production, where requirements were less stringent than factory work. In the paper industry, bookbinding remained heavily hand work, but skilled operations were done by male artisans instead of trained women.[56] There was no formal training period for women in paper products as there was for men. Most women could learn their job well enough to maintain a satisfactory level of production in a couple of weeks. Carton-making employed the largest number of women in the paper industry. It was mostly mass-production machine work. Men were employed only as foremen and as operators on special machines such as the corrugater. Women assembled the boxes.[57]

The question of occupational training for girls reveals the personal and family dimension of wages and job expectations. Why were women workers reluctant to pursue a better wage through better job preparation? The simple fact was that most women perceived little relationship between the two. The real urgency was for immediate earnings. Girls were a source of direct economic return for the family. A daughter in training was hardly an economic asset. In fact, she might constitute a liability if the family had to pay for her training. Most women did not take the time to become skilled workers. Given their intentions and needs, the investment in time, energy, and wage potential was just not practical. In addition, it should be recognized that most women in industry were really little more than children—girls whose contribution to the family was needed immediately, not some vague time in the future when they acquired job status. Parents were reluctant to allow daughters to become involved in a long apprenticeship period. The family was deprived of the additional income, and there was every indication that a commensurate rise in future earning capacity could just as easily be accomplished by a job change.[58]

With little invested in terms of specific training, women did not view work as an opportunity for occupational advancement. Job mobility was the primary means women workers used to improve their situations. Work brought in money; often, when better money was available elsewhere, they moved. But there were numerous personal factors involved with mobility, circumstances that can collectively be described as job satisfaction. The significant point is that women workers did have the opportunity to choose, and the pattern of their work experience proved that they exercised that option. Job changes were frequent; industry changes were not unusual. It was also quite common for women to move from one sector of the economy to another. Occupational mobility was underscored by personal decisions that directed women in and out of the labor force depending on changes in marital status and child care responsibilities. The combination of these factors produced an extremely fluid female labor force.

Commonly, girls from working-class families faced at least ten years of work between the time they left school and marriage.[59] And marriage was no guarantee of rescue. But to equate work time with job consistency is incorrect. Not many girls stayed where they began. In rural areas, girls and women most often combined factory and home work with agriculture. Movement between factory and home work was common. Women who belonged to families where men's earnings were subject to seasonal fluctuation often entered the factory in slack time to compensate for loss of income. Given the nature of most women's work in factories, moving from firm to firm did not necessarily mean a change in the kind of work done. Cleaning and polishing, sorting and packing were similar operations regardless of the product involved. While firms did advertise open positions in newspapers and trade journals, women often heard about work from their friends. A new job was particularly attractive if there was more money available. Several *Pfennigs* a week might be enough inducement to change. One contemporary observer expressed concern that such a meager sum served as sufficient incentive to move. "They abandon friendly relations with their companions for 50 pf. a week. How difficult their lives must be, that they must reckon in *Pfennigs*." [60]

Work biographies of women collected by the factory inspector in Baden define a pattern of occupational and job mobility. The inspector did not pre-select the samples specifically to address the question of job change. Rather, mobility was the prevailing norm. One person, twenty years old, who worked in a paper factory as a set-up girl listed her work history as follows: She had worked three weeks in a wallpaper factory upon leaving school, followed by one and a quarter years as a domestic servant; for one-half year, she was employed in a print shop, and then she carried newspapers, followed by another half year in a different print shop; she had worked at her present job for one and a half years. [61] A twenty-one-year-old girl working as a helper in a paper factory indicated that she had been in domestic service for two years followed by four months as a cooking instructor; she left that position and spent two years in a print shop, and another year in service, followed by one-half year in another print shop; she had worked at her current job for six months; she stated that she preferred domestic service and would return if she found suitable employment. [62] An eighteen-year-old girl in a metal cartridge factory had worked one-half year in agriculture and three months in a factory that she did not identify; she had been at her present job four years, but she was dissatisfied and wanted to take training as a clothes presser. [63]

A twenty-seven-year-old in a paper factory had trained for sewing for one-half year; she spent two years in service in three different households, three months at home when she was unemployed; for one and a half years she worked in the cartridge factory followed by more time at home, and then a half year as a cleaning lady in a hotel; she had worked at her present job a quarter year; she had not been pleased with domestic service and preferred factory work. [64] A twenty-one-year-old worker in the metal cartridge factory had spent two years in a charity home, three months in domestic service, a short time in a paper factory, one and a half years in service in another household, two years in a cartridge factory, and three-quarters of a year in a machine factory; when interviewed she had been at her current job three weeks. [65]

These sketches were the work biographies of women in Karlsruhe. Typical of the employment pattern for women in urban areas was some time spent in domestic service. Similar profiles are quite common for factory-employed women and women working in home industry. In other cities, such as Berlin and Breslau, a ready supply of female labor resulted from girls leaving service. In these two cities domestic industry, especially clothing, absorbed a great deal of the surplus.[66]

What were the circumstances of workers in clothing, an industry where large numbers of girls at least attempted to take training? Clothing also was the one major industry where there were opportunities for occupational advancement since directors were mostly women.[67] While there was less occupational change in the form of girls moving out of the industry, job changes were just as frequent as in other work. Money and mistresses seemed to underlie reasons for most of the decisions. Change was anticipated and considered quite the normal method for either improving circumstances or relieving an unpleasant situation. As in other industries, word of mouth was the principal means of learning about employment. From 250 girls employed in the Munich clothing industry who were asked about placement, only four had obtained their jobs through the employment office.[68]

Incidence of job change by women in textiles was related to age and skill level.[69] Women were more mobile than men.[70] For women workers, most change occurred among those in the seventeen-to-twenty-one-year-old group. Older women were not so eager to move. Many were married and were not so willing to risk losing their earnings. The least skilled also were the most likely to seek improvement by taking another job. Frequency of occupational change was most closely linked to skill level. Workers with the most investment in training and experience might be willing to change factories, but reluctant to retrain for a different job. Among women textile workers, the most stable were skilled weavers and ringspinners in all age groups. Other workers, semi-skilled and unskilled, changed jobs about every two years.[71] As was the case in other industries, women entering textiles at semi-skilled or unskilled levels often came from other occupations. The two most common were agriculture and service.[72] In regions that experienced a decline in opportunities for work in textiles, many women found employment in tobacco products. Since tobacco was heavily domestic industry, the occupational switch might also allow them to remain at home.

Moving in and out of a job, changing occupations, or leaving work entirely for a period of time were indications of individual rhythm in the work experience of women. Within the necessity to work there was a flexibility of choice that suggests an element of personal control. While the choice of working or not working was not a luxury these women enjoyed, they did decide the circumstances of their work experience. Because there was opportunity for employment, instead of passive endurance, women changed jobs to fit the conditions of their lives. Work was a fact of life, but work was a continuum of possibilities that might include agriculture, service, and home work, as well as work in the factory.

Women provided the kind of labor industry required. In most instances, it was inconsequential whether a specific woman stayed on the job or left, because her place could just as easily be filled by someone else. But most women workers did not seek job security. Because they did not pursue work as a life-defining activity or as a lifetime occupation, but rather as a source of ready cash in cases of need or emergency, opportunity for job mobility was more important than job security. If the only jobs available were dependent on skill qualifications and work stability, industry would have been a closed labor market for most women. Instead it was a situation of mutual need which women could utilize for certain advantage.

Employers maneuvered for the most production from least outlay. Because of wage differentials, hiring women was the best way to handle cost minimization, particularly in consumer goods industries where production had to meet and anticipate an elastic market. Factory production expanded the number of jobs women could do, and low wages assured them of job access. The economy of pre-war Germany did not sustain the utopian vision of men at work and women at home. Industry was not that generous. Problematic as the circumstances of the work experience for women appeared, within the narrow constraints of having to work women at least could find a job.

NOTES

1. Gerhard Bry, *Wages in Germany 1871–1945* (Princeton, N.J.: Princeton University Press, 1960), p. 94.
2. Alice Salomon, "Die Ursachen der ungleichen Entlohnung von Männer- und Frauenarbeit," Staats und Socialwissenschaftliche Forschungen, Vol. 122 (Leipzig: Verlag von Duncker und Humblot, 1906), p. 132.
3. Bry, *Wages*, p. 117.
4. Ibid.
5. *Amtliche Mittheilungen. Jahresberichte der Gewerbeaufsichtsbeamten*

und Bergbehörden, Reichsministerium des Innern, Band II (Berlin, 1899), p. 96.

6. Bry, *Wages,* p. 95.

7. Ibid., p. 99.

8. Salomon, "Die Ursachen der ungleichen Entlohnung," p. 18.

9. E. J. Hobsbawm, *Labouring Men* (London: Weidenfeld and Nicolson, 1964), p. 347.

10. Ibid., p. 348.

11. Bry, *Wages,* p. 94.

12. "Statistische Erhebungen über Lohn- und Arbeitsbedingungen der Mitglieder des Verbandes der Fabrikarbeiter Deutschlands," *Reichs-Arbeitsblatt,* VIII Jahrgang, Nr. 9 (1910), p. 680.

13. Theodor Leipart, *Lage der Arbeiter in Stuttgart* (Stuttgart: Verlag von J. H. W. Dietz, 1900), p. 92.

14. "Die Lage der Arbeiterinnen in der Holzindustrie," *Die Gleichheit,* 19 Jahrgang, Nr. 11 (March 1, 1909), p. 169.

15. "Die Arbeiterschaft der Bürsten- und Pinselindustrie," *Die Gleichheit,* 24 Jahrgang, Nr. 4 (November 12, 1913), p. 53.

16. "Statistische Erhebungen," *Reichs-Arbeitsblatt,* p. 680.

17. Dora Landé, "Arbeits- und Lohnverhältnisse in der Berliner Maschinenindustrie," *Schriften des Vereins für Sozialpolitik,* Vol. 134 (1910), p. 467.

18. Ibid., p. 466.

19. Anna Schmidt, "Die Lage der schlesischen Textil- und Tabakarbeiterinnen," *Der Arbeiterpräses,* 4 Jahrgang (February, 1908), p. 52.

20. Ibid., p. 59.

21. "Holzindustrie," *Die Gleichheit,* p. 168.

22. Ibid.

23. "Bürsten- und Pinselindustrie," *Die Gleichheit,* p. 53.

24. Elizabeth Gnauck-Kühne, "Die Lage der Arbeiterinnen in der Berliner Papierwaren Industrie," *Schmollers Jahrbuch,* Vol. 20 (1896), p. 46.

25. Ibid., p. 45.

26. Rosa Kempf, "Das Leben der jungen Fabrikmädchen in München," *Schriften des Vereins für Sozialpolitik,* Vol. 135 (Leipzig: Verlag von Duncker und Humblot, 1911), p. 66.

27. Marie Baum, *Drei Klassen von Lohnarbeiterinnen in Industrie und Handel der Stadt Karlsruhe,* Bericht erstattet an das Grossherzogliche Ministerium des Innern und herausgegeben von der Grossherzoglich Badischen Fabrikinspektion (Karlsruhe: Druck und Verlag der G. Braunschen Hofbuchdruckerei, 1906), p. 107.

28. Ibid., p. 59.

29. Ibid., p. 58.

30. Leipart, *Lage der Arbeiter,* p. 92.

31. "Frauenarbeit in der Geraer Textilindustrie," *Die Gleichheit*, 13 Jahrgang, Nr. 12 (June 3, 1903), p. 90.

32. Johannes Feig, "Hausgewerbe und Fabrikbetrieb in der Berliner wäscheindustrie," *Staats- und Socialwissenschaftliche Forschungen* (Leipzig: Verlag von Duncker und Humblot, 1896), p. 69.

33. Elisabeth Hell, *Jugendliche Schneiderinnen und Näherinnen in München* (Stuttgart: J. G. Cotta'sche Buchhandlung, 1911), p. 92.

34. Landé, "Arbeits- und Lohnverhältnisse," p. 469.

35. *Statistik des Deutschen Reichs*, Band 211 (1913), p. 264.

36. Landé, "Arbeits- und Lohnverhältnisse," p. 463.

37. *Statistik des Deutschen Reichs*, Band 211 (1913), p. 252.

38. The Artisan Ordinance of 1908 tightened regulations on persons practicing trades. The law was part of a series of provisions passed by the Reichstag under pressure from artisan groups urging state protection for a threatened hand work sector.

39. Hell, *Jugendliche*, p. 13.

40. Ibid., p. 24.

41. Ibid., p. 15.

42. Ibid., p. 22.

43. Ibid.

44. Ibid., p. 58.

45. Ibid., p. 61.

46. Ibid., p. 80.

47. Ibid., p. 81.

48. Ibid., p. 80.

49. Ibid., p. 67.

50. Marie Bernays, "Untersuchungen über die Schwankungen Arbeitsintensität während der Arbeitswoche und während des Arbeitstages," *Schriften des Vereins für Sozialpolitik*, Vol. 135 (Leipzig: Verlag von Duncker und Humblot, 1912), p. 191.

51. *Statistik des Deutschen Reichs*, Band 211 (1913), p. 252.

52. Bernays, "Untersuchungen," p. 191.

53. Ibid., p. 195.

54. Otto Hommer, *Die Entwicklung und Tätigkeit des Deutschen Metallarbeiterverbandes* (Berlin: Carl Heymanns Verlag, 1912), p. 42.

55. Anna Schmidt, "Zur Lage der Tabakarbeiterinnen," *Der Arbeiterpräses*, 6 Jahrgang, Nr. 3 (March, 1910), p. 81.

56. Gnauck-Kühne, "Die Lage der Arbeiterinnen," p. 35.

57. Ibid., p. 36.

58. Hell, *Jugendliche*, p. 69.

59. Baum, *Drei Klassen*, p. 48.

60. Kempf, "Das Leben der jungen," p. 93.

61. Baum, *Drei Klassen*, p. 49.
62. Ibid.
63. Ibid., p. 50.
64. Ibid.
65. Ibid., p. 51.
66. Feig, "Hausgewerbe und Fabrikbetrieb," p. 101.
67. Hell, *Jugendliche*, p. 9.
68. Ibid., p. 75.
69. Marie Bernays, "Auslese und Anpassung der Arbeiterschaft der geschlossenen Grossindustrie an den Verhältnissen der Gladbacher Spinnerei und Weberei," *Schriften des Vereins für Sozialpolitik*, Vol. 133 (Leipzig: Verlag von Duncker und Humblot, 1910), pp. 41, 59.
70. Ibid., p. 44.
71. Ibid., p. 142.
72. Ibid., p. 163.

1. Women's factory work, 1900. (Courtesy of Bildarchiv Foto Marburg/Art Resource N.Y.)

2. Women glass polishers, 1910. (Courtesy of Bildarchiv Foto Marburg/Art Resource N.Y.)

3. Women factory workers manufacturing rubber balls, 1900. (Courtesy of Bildarchiv Foto Marburg/Art Resource N.Y.)

3

Classification by Sex: Women as Protected Workers

"a path that departs?"*

Classification by sex was a social and legal reality in Imperial Germany. Women were a public question that entered the political arena with all the moral and religious fervor that policy makers could bring to bear. Industrially employed women challenged and outraged social order at an elemental level. Women working outside the home evoked a cry of danger that converted the personal into the political sphere, private concerns into public issues, and domestic life into civic responsibility. More than just alarmist or disingenuous reaction, public policy reflected deeply felt gender consciousness and an implacable anger toward erosion of cherished ideals. The themes of this resistance focused several interrelated fears: Collapse of the family was imminent and inevitable; industrial work interfered with women's reproductive function; moral perils of the factory compromised modesty and purity; and women's work was a competitive threat to male labor, the implications of which were both substantive and symbolic. The one significant and enduring outcome of the debate about women's employment was to assign to them a legal definition that was based in sex classification. They became protected workers.[1] Once legal limits were placed

*Kenneth Barkin, *The Controversy over German Industrialization 1890–1902* (Chicago: The University of Chicago Press, 1970), p. 89.

on women's employment, legislation became the conduit for all kinds of normative public policy. Protective legislation reinforced the gender division of labor and feminized whole segments of industrial production.

Women's work in late nineteenth-century Germany was perceived as a social problem. In order to understand the reason contemporaries reacted so dramatically to female industrial labor, it must be recognized that conservative political, social, and religious sentiments were particularly strong and vocal in Imperial Germany. Industrialization caused deep and profound conflict among various special-interest groups in the empire which had important implications for society as a whole and definite bearing on the legal prescriptions regarding women's work. Mechanized production in factories was perceived as a threat to the authoritarian, hierarchical order of society. Traditional labor in agriculture and handicraft was glorified as symbolic of strength and stability. Factories disrupted the natural order, and factory workers were perceived as unstable and dangerous. This dramatic conservative resistance to change also had sex implications. It was particularly painful to acknowledge that German women worked in factories. A pervasive ideology of the family said that women's place was in the home. Political parties and various religious and social special-interest groups viewed women and work as a vital concern requiring special attention. This strong conservative resistance to women's factory work reinforced the value of traditional work forms for women in agriculture, domestic industry, and domestic service.

There was strong structural and cultural potential for government intervention into the private sphere in Imperial Germany. The image presented by the term *free enterprise* does not apply in the German case. This is not to say the economy was under state control, but involvement of the state in both industry and agriculture was significant. For example, both industry and agriculture sought state assistance when threatened by reverses in the international market. Minimization of production costs in order to sustain foreign competition was a recurrent theme of economic and political rhetoric in pre-war Germany. Particularly vocal were consumer goods industries such as textiles, clothing, paper, and tobacco products. Whether the constraint was genuine or merely a ploy to increase profits does not really call for closer analysis here. What is important is that industry expected the government to act in its behalf. The obverse of protection from foreign competition was the understanding that government would follow domestic laissez-faire leaving industry free from internal control. Profit motives were submerged in the rhetoric of a strong, national state. Arguments for support were decorated with statements about the Fatherland, the Kaiser, the Church, and the family.[2] Owners and employers intended to maximize production and profit. Industry demanded freedom in handling labor, and the government was slow to intrude on this prerogative.

Yet late nineteenth-century Germany was a society determined to preserve the family as the mainstay of a healthy state. The family could not be abandoned to the needs of industrial production. Explicit in all debate concerning women and work was the assumption that women's working in factories was clearly the cause of a disintegrating social order. Recognition that it was the business of industry to produce, and the fear that the best production circumstances for industry might have disastrous effects on the social fabric, generated voluminous argument. The tension was obvious in the hesitancy with which the state approached legal definition of the women and work issue. Proposals and schemes that were suggested and discarded along the way confirmed the depth of ambivalence surrounding the question. Women workers were treated as the cause of societal illness instead of as a symptom of an unevenly developing economy. In the four decades between unification and World War I, the thrust of the argument moved from prohibition of women's work in the factory to protection for working women.

An important example of the paternalism embedded in Imperial Germany was Bismarck's program of state socialism. Promulgated in the 1880's, it was in part a recognition of the state's responsibility to improve conditions of the working classes. But Bismarck's real intention was to co-opt the nascent worker movement while simultaneously verifying the monarchical state and the values of the traditional patriarchal society. The social policy was aimed at alleviating the worst insecurities of the workers while at the same time defusing the lure of socialism.

The Health Insurance Law of 1883 was the first of three major pieces of legislation in Bismarck's new social policy. Minimum annual income levels were fixed, and workers who fell below minimum were liable to compulsory membership. Sickness benefits were provided beginning on the third day of illness up to a maximum of thirteen weeks.

Contributions and benefits varied, but generally two-thirds of the contribution was paid by the worker and one-third by the employer. The operation of the program was not under any central bureau, but rather was administered through various approved agencies. The most important were the local Health Associations (*Ortskrankenkassen*) which were located in a specific town or region and the Factory Health Associations (*Fabrikkrankenkassen*) based in firms employing over fifty workers.[3] Because of the variety of organizations involved, it is difficult to obtain systematic information on insurance benefits. However, worker budgets and biographies illustrate that payments were hardly sufficient to cover even a minimum level of subsistence and could be considered useful only if supplemented by multiple earnings of women and children.

The Accident Insurance Law was adopted in 1884. Payments went into effect only after the fourteenth week of illness, when the time period covered by health provisions lapsed. Benefits were approximately two-thirds of a worker's average earnings. If the worker was permanently disabled, he could receive a pension or, if deceased, the worker's widow could receive a weekly allowance. Full cost was carried by the employer. Administration of the accident insurance was handled by regionally organized employer cooperatives (*Berufsgenossenschaften*) which imposed annual levies to cover claims.[4] Because the full burden for accident insurance fell on employers, observers commented that at least there were attempts to improve safety conditions in order to reduce probability of claims. The Disability and Old Age Pension Act of 1889 provided disability payment for persons who had made contributions to the fund for at least four years and provided old-age pensions payable at age seventy if there had been twenty-four years of contribution.[5] Funds came from equal contributions from workers and employers with an additional subsidy of 50 M. a year per person supplied by the state.

Implemented more as measures of social control than reform, the various insurance programs were inadequate and generated more resentment than satisfaction.[6] Employers complained about the state's cavalier use of their money. For workers, even modest outlay for contributions created hardship. Socialists, while not actually attacking the scheme as state manipulation, found numerous other grounds for criticism. They described requirements for workers' contribution as enforced reduction in wages.[7] Contributions were too high, benefits hardly sufficient. They claimed that the age designation for pension eligibility was ridiculous because workers hardly ever reached seventy years old.

This considerable broadening of state function into social welfare was an experiment that failed to eradicate the "social question." By the 1890's what to do about the increasing number of industrial workers had become a pressing problem. In the Reichstag various political groups organized for action. Political and social divisions were deep and stubborn. Into this confusion of cross-currents and controversy, the issue of women and work became a vital concern in the larger battle among Germany's special-interest groups because women focused the more general and painful questions about stability and change. Agrarian prophets of doom responded with increasing radicalism. Industrialization was blamed for all Germany's problems. There was talk about national and economic suicide, loss of moral values and sense of duty, evils of urbanization, and destruction of the peasantry. One member of the Free Conservative Party, Kardorff, accused the Chancellor of selling out to the Socialists by ruining the Junkers and the peasantry, the very groups that were vital to the struggle against the working class.[8] One of the most nostalgic statements to come out of the debate appeared in the *Deutsche landwirtschaftliche Presse* in November, 1895:

> Must we really depart from the old Prussia, from the old Germany? Is it definite that Germany will be compelled onto a path that departs from the way which all friends of the fatherland have hitherto judged right?[9]

Similar sentiments were evident in the Catholic Center Party and Catholic social movement. Catholic conservatism was important because the party moved from political ostracism in the 1870's to a position of significant, if not deciding, power in the Reichstag by the first decade of the twentieth century. In the first two decades of its existence the Center was dominated by a backward-looking corporative mentality that aimed at a complete restructuring of the economic and social order. The Center was uncomfortable with industrialization and frightened by industrial workers. In the early period, the party even refused to acknowledge industrial labor, wishing instead to preserve handicraft production by revitalizing the artisan guilds.[10]

By the 1890's, however, encouraged by the new security of a firm place in the Reichstag and directed by new leadership, the Center assumed a less reactionary, more reformist mood. Also provoked into action by the growing strength of socialism among the workers, the party and the Church began to take a more energetic interest in the specific concerns of workers. It was this shift in direction that stimulated the Catholic labor movement. A most sensitive area for the Center, and one that went largely unresolved, was the women's question. The party never really reconciled itself to women's working outside the home. In the first decade of the twentieth century, when corporative slogans were only the ritual bleat of the minority, the party and even the Catholic labor unions maintained that women belonged at home. Because of the pivotal role the party held in the Reichstag, and because most of Germany's Catholic population felt a natural affinity for the Center, the party's position was politically influential.

Social Democrats defined the "social question" in terms of the class struggle. Women workers were central to socialist concerns about capitalist exploitation. By the 1890's Socialists began to advocate protective legislation for women, moving off an ideological commitment for total equality. The positional change represented a realistic acknowledgment that women needed safety from capitalist abuse and recognition that they were doubly burdened in their roles as wives and mothers. The women's question began to take on implications beyond class identification.

In the Reichstag, the Social Democratic Party (SPD), representing an alien and competitive philosophy, remained distinctly outside the political and social consensus. The close alignment between the SPD and the socialist trade unions generated antipathy. Talk about establishing a state within the state and commitment to the international class struggle caused suspicion and fear. A sample of the rhetoric illustrates how far apart the antagonists in the "social question" were and how strident the vocabulary could become. In May, 1904, the Imperial Association against Social Democracy (*Reichsverband gegen die Sozialdemokratie*) was founded, and a representative, Otto Freiherr von Manteuffel, delivered the following remarks to the upper house of the Prussian legislature:

It is not too late to defeat socialism; we must not hesitate any longer to mark Social Democracy as a dangerous disease that eats away at the state organism.

When one finds the cholera germ, measures are taken to exterminate it no matter how harsh they might be . . . just so, we must combat the sickness of Social Democracy.[11]

The intensity and hostility that separated the special-interest groups in German society were not contained within the political arena, but spilled over into the academic and religious communities as well. Germany's industrialization spawned a vigorous debate that taken collectively constitutes a fascinating study of the ideology of economics and the social sciences. Individuals and groups collected data, conducted surveys, and wrote volumes on the effects of industrialization. In the universities, students of the leading economists hurried off in search of information; some of them even went underground, working in factories and shops in order to verify the theories of the masters. Interestingly, it was during the 1890's that women were first accepted as legitimate students in German universities. Many of them who successfully secured places with leading protagonists in the social debate gathered a great deal of material on women workers. For women investigators, the "social question" usually took the form of women and work.

One of the most important organizations involved with social research was the *Verein für Sozialpolitik*. Investigations by the *Verein* during the 1870's and 1880's were of noncontroversial subjects, reflecting the intention to stay away from sensitive political and social topics. Publications totaled in the hundreds of volumes addressing virtually every aspect of the German economy. By the turn of the century, more attention was devoted to the "social question," and surveys about workers multiplied. Among the numerous studies, covering everything from material to moral issues, many focused exclusively on women. Two of the most important were Rosa Kempf's study of Munich factory girls published in 1911, and Marie Bernays' work on the Gladbach textile industry.[12] Kempf worked with Brentano, a liberal at the University of Munich. Information was gathered through interviews and visits with factory girls and their families. Kempf's interest was family life, food, and clothes, rather than conditions of work. Bernays was Max Weber's protégée. She worked in a textile factory incognito for four months before she distributed questionnaires and gathered data; she also had access to factory records. Bernays looked for material on monotony of work and skill differentials, and established a production curve for weekly output of work. These studies were important because it was in part through women investigators that the broader issues of the worker question were focused specifically on working women.

A great deal of the literature regarding women and work was produced as a result of the wider conflict over industrialization. Women's work became the focus of political debates that ranged the spectrum from prohibition to protection. Laws were changed in accordance with society's acknowledgment that women were special and deserved preferential treatment. The effects of industrial work on women's lives, the lives of their children, their health, and even their biology appeared in many scholarly journals dealing with social and economic issues. Women became a vital concern for religious groups that perceived work outside the home as a disruption of the natural order. And Social Democracy embraced women as fundamental to the struggle for freedom and equality.

The first commissioned study of women in industry following unification was the *Ergebnisse über die Frauen- und Kinderarbeit in den Fabriken.*[13] Suggestions for the investigation were made in Reichstag sessions in 1872 and 1873. The petition of April 30, 1873, read as follows: "such collection for the examination into the suitability and necessity for legal protection for factory employed women and children, against Sunday work as well as against excessive employment on any work day."[14] Specifically stated, the suggestion moved toward a proposal for a ten-hour day, prohibition of Sunday work and night work for women, and protection for pregnant workers. Despite the specific and limited nature of the question, the report contained extensive commentary on the whole issue of government regulation in the affairs of industry regarding female employment.

The most volatile question concerning women and work was whether the government should restrict or prohibit factory employment of women. The report was clearly a justification for women's work, moderated by suggestions for protective measures. Proposals included separating men and women in the factory, providing work clothes, strict supervision of machinery, proper ventilation, and recognition of the special concerns of women workers, including changing rooms, and suitable places for eating, and child care facilities.[15] For varying arguments in favor of restriction or prohibition, there were as many refutations reiterating the position that women workers were necessary for the survival of

German industry. "Many industry branches would be ruined by any reduction in women's work." [16]

Conceptualization of the woman worker as a social problem was based on the premise that women had moral and social responsibility as wives and mothers to the *Volk*. [17] Lines of debate drawn in the *Ergebnisse* posed a dilemma that continued to arouse a good deal of sentiment and proselytizing well into the twentieth century. For family life to be preserved, women should not work, yet in most cases where the woman worked, the existence of the family depended on her economic contribution. The Catholic Center Party adopted an aggressive stand in the Reichstag against complete economic freedom for industry. The party was the most important source of agitation for prohibitive and restrictive legislation regarding women's work. Primary concern was always preservation of the family. Representatives of the Center had no difficulty with the solution—women's work must be limited. [18]

The position of the Socialists in the Reichstag was considerably different from that of the Center on the issue of special restriction and special protection for women workers. While the Socialists adamantly favored state protection for workers, discriminatory legislation singling out women was resisted. It was their contention that state concern for protective legislation should apply equally to all workers regardless of sex. The state should actively promote higher wages and a "normal" work day for both men and women. Motivation calling for state intervention was not too far apart from the Center position. Only with provision of adequate wages for men could women stay at home, care for their children, and, most important, eliminate the major source of unfair competition to men workers. [19]

The continuing debate in the Reichstag concerning women's work was fueled by material collected by government-mandated factory inspectors. The first reports were published in 1879. [20] From 1879 until 1881, information on women workers was incorporated with that on child labor. The first entry distinguishing women workers as a separate category appeared in the reports for 1881, underscoring the state's developing interest. [21] Inspectors collected numerical data, but usually there were more important questions under investigation at the direction of the federal authorities. Primarily, information fell into two categories: collection of material as background for suggested legislation regarding women workers, and subsequent recording of the effects of legislation already passed.

Much of the information collected in the 1880's addressed questions and proposals raised by the *Ergebnisse*. For example, the following information was submitted by the factory inspector in Zwickau, Saxony, where women worked in the textile industry. The inspector reported that women did night work particularly in summer, when it was common for work to begin at 6:30 A.M. and continue until 8:30 at night. Separation of women workers from the men was not possible. He observed special attention for married workers in only one establishment—they came to work one hour later in the morning and were allowed extra time at mid-day. Particular concern for pregnancy or sickness in the family was unusual. The inspector isolated one factory for special mention. It was a clothes-bleaching establishment in Langenfeld owned by a Herr Wentzel. Although the official could not report favorably on separation of the sexes or of older workers from young, unmarried women, he was delighted to observe that the owner's wife was particularly interested in cultivating moral and housewifely responsibility among the young girls. The firm employed whole families, and women were allowed extra time with pay at mid-day to prepare meals.[22]

By the late 1880's, focus of concern narrowed on the married woman worker. Although any official investigation was still in the future, attention shifted from women workers in general to protection and restrictions specifically affecting married women.[23] Inspectors asked questions about work-time, break-time, and special consideration for women who had households to run. Inspectors concluded that ousting married women from factories and replacing them with single girls would have disastrous effects on countless families.[24]

Culmination of the Reichstag debates and factory inspectors' investigations was the *Gewerbeordnungsnovelle* of 1891, the most comprehensive law regarding employment in Germany in the pre-war period. The existing legal code had been a collection of Prussian labor regulations that were extended to the Reich in 1871.[25] The new law stipulated general conditions for all workers and mandated specific regulations for children and women. It had taken twenty years for the issues of the *Ergebnisse* to surface in definition of formal provisions. The following regulations pertained to all persons regardless of age or sex: protection for life and health including prescription for work rooms, machinery, light, air space, and ventilation; preservation of morality and decency by providing for a separation of the sexes where the work process allowed, and separate facilities for toilets, washing, and changing. All Sunday and holiday work was prohibited.[26]

Specific provisions regarding children and women were crucial. Child labor under fourteen years old was prohibited. Children had to attend school until fourteen.[27] Work days for persons of both sexes between fourteen and sixteen could not exceed ten hours.[28] The most important issue regarding women was work time. No special treatment was given for married workers. Daily work time for all women could not exceed eleven hours, or ten hours on Saturday or on the day preceding a holiday.[29] On such days, work had to end by 5:30 P.M. Night work between 8:30 P.M. and 5:30 A.M. was prohibited. One hour's rest, usually at mid-day, was mandated. For women who had family responsibilities, break-time could be extended to an hour and a half if requested. Women who wished to return to work after pregnancy could not be employed during the four weeks following delivery without medical permission. Employment in industries where there were special problems of health, safety, or morality could be restricted. Use of women in mining for work underground was prohibited.[30] But the attitude of reluctance toward interfering too closely in the affairs of industry surfaced in the condition that some or all of these provisions could be circumvented if the situation warranted. The law allowed for exceptions in certain industries and seasons due to the demands of production.

Who was to oversee that at least the intention of the law was observed by employers? The task fell to the factory inspectors. Each state appointed its own officials. The following statement was the directive issued for Prussia:

Inspectors should make it their business aided by familiarity with the legal provisions, their technical knowledge, and practical experience to assist by expert advice and friendly mediation in promoting such adjustment of the mutual relations of trade and labor, without burdening the employers with useless sacrifices or needless restrictions, to insure the employees full measure of protection designed by law.[31]

The intention of the directive was clearly not compliance by mandate, but by persuasion. The official role of the inspector was to act as mediator rather than enforcer. The inspectorate was an important link between the working class and public policy. Not only was it their job to implement rules and regulations, they also, by intention and attention, served as vehicles for bourgeois values about the family and women's natural role. In this capacity, they functioned in a prescriptive way.

In 1894, factory inspectors reported on the effects of reduced work time for women. Reactions were mixed. An official from Prussia commented that women he questioned were generally enthusiastic. They used the extra time for household duties. Restrictions on Saturday and pre-holiday work seemed particularly attractive. The inspector quoted one woman worker who stated she previously had to clean and wash late into the night on Saturdays to get the apartment in order for Sunday. Single girls whom he interviewed also praised the extra time at home, indicating that their mothers expected them to help with domestic chores. At least now they had some free time on Sunday. Another woman said she was pleased to be able to devote the extra hour to the garden, where some of the food for the family was grown.[32]

A Dresden inspector wrote about the negative side of reduced work time, particularly about the prohibition of night work. Many women, he reported, were dismissed from factories that required continuous production through the night. Especially affected were those employed in paper and wood products. A large number of these women who were married expressed bitterness over the constraint put upon them with the loss of wages and the time shift, which had previously allowed them to accommodate family responsibilities.[33] In addition, the Dresden official reported that in the textile industry, employers had compensated for the lost hour by increasing the speed of their machines, forcing the women to work at a faster pace to maintain production.[34]

In 1898, the Catholic Center Party sponsored a resolution in the Reichstag calling for a special investigation of the married woman worker.[35] The intention was to gather information that might eventually justify complete prohibition of married women from factory work, or at least a reduction in work time to one-half day. While the results of the investigation did not gloss over instances of hardship, not one report recommended either prohibition or reduced work time. The truth was that married women could not afford even the most benign concern if it meant loss of a job or reduction in wages. "If factory work for women were prohibited or limited, it would mean disaster for many working families. A substitution in the form of higher wage for men or the same wage for reduced work time cannot be expected."[36]

Work time for women was the topic of a special factory inspectors' investigation conducted in 1902.[37] Material collected addressed three questions: reduction of the eleven-hour day to ten hours, extension of the one-hour break to one and a half hours, and a five-and-a-half-hour work day on Saturday and days preceding a holiday.[38] From those employers interviewed, several common themes emerged. Many firms that employed both men and women workers indicated that changing women's work time would result in a similar change for men because the work process required them to work together.[39] Many employers anticipated no significant change in employment or production if such a law was promulgated because they already worked a ten-hour schedule or less per day. But where the ten-hour day had not yet made progress, particularly in textiles, reactions clearly indicated that if such a provision went into effect, employers would not tolerate any reduction in production—pace of work would increase.[40]

The 1902 factory inspection on work time collected the following data, ten years following the imposition of the eleven-hour day. Of the women interviewed, 10.6% worked nine hours or less per day; 42.7% worked nine to ten hours daily; and 46.7% worked more than ten hours. Sixty-five percent of those women whose work time exceeded ten hours were employed in textiles.[41] The following industries (see page 73) are listed in order of increasing percentages of women working over ten hours daily.[42] In the majority of industries about one-third of the female labor force worked more than ten hours daily. Again, the glaring exception was textiles, with almost three-quarters of its women exceeding ten hours. Customary mid-day break was one hour. From the survey, 43.2% of all women polled had one to two hours off.[43] Concerning duration of work on Saturdays and pre-holidays, inspectors noted that about a quarter of the women worked only five and a half hours.[44]

In December, 1908, the Reichstag passed Trade Regulation #137; the provision became effective on January 1, 1910.[45] The most important adjustment concerned the maximum allowable work day. For adult women workers employed in establishments of ten or more persons, a ten-hour day was prescribed. An eight-hour maximum was placed on Saturday work. No action was taken on the extension of the mid-day break. The inspectors had learned that most women were opposed to the extra allowance, favoring early dismissal instead.[46]

Following the promulgation of the 1908 law mandating a ten-hour-day maximum, many firms moved toward adjusting production to meet

Industry	Percentage
Polygraph	3
Machines	15
Leather	22
Chemicals	24
Clothing and cleaning	27
Paper products	28
Metals	31
Fats, oils, and varnish	32
Wood products	33
Foods and tobacco	33
Mining	35
Stone and earth	37
Textiles	71

the new requirements. By 1910, when the law took effect, most establishments were in compliance. The major exceptions were textile firms. An observer from the Catholic Union for Women and Girls commented on the work-time issue in the Silesian textile industry a few months prior to the proclamation of the 1908 restriction. She felt very strongly that despite the direction the Reichstag was taking, Silesian textiles would resist conversion.[47] More favorable results were apparent in other industries. Tobacco manufacturers, excepting home work, generally complied, reducing work time from eleven to ten hours daily.[48] Clothing was an industry that could be within compliance yet circumvent the intention of the law. Because the provision applied only to adult female workers, many firms employing large numbers of girls evaded the change. In addition, so many clothing establishments were small that the ten-person minimum did not apply.[49] While there were no systematic studies made of the results of the 1910 restrictions, it is obvious that many women workers were still not beneficially affected. Large segments of the textile industry pleading competition pressure, big portions of the clothing industry resting beyond the provisions, and all of home industry were not brought into compliance.

As late as 1911, domestic industry remained not only unregulated, but undefined as well. Bringing domestic industry into focus was not an easy task. There were numerous conflicting interests involved, not the least of which were the home workers themselves. Trade unions were especially sensitive about the question of regulating domestic industry because home work was viewed as a competitive source of labor that lay beyond the control of both the state and the unions. National interest in regulation was stimulated by a trade union congress held in Berlin in 1904, the purpose of which was to bring distress in domestic industry into public view.[50] Conference issues were published in a *Protokoll* from which the following statement was taken. Under the sympathetic lament lay a real core of resistance to home industry.

Homework brings many attendant evils in its train which are injurious not only to the out-worker and home worker but also to the consumers and to the welfare of the nation at large. Chief of these evils are the unceasing depression of wages which forces the worker to increase his hours of labor and to make his family work with him, the constant danger in the dwelling from dust and disease and the isolation of his life which makes it impossible for him to meet his fellow workers in a trade union. Low wages offered to home workers react unfavorably upon the wages of workers employed in factories in the same trade who find that the maintenance and elevation of their standard of life is endangered by the existence of home work.[51]

This report of the General Commission of German Trade Unions stimulated interest in domestic industry and directed legislative attention toward identification and regulation. Although proposals concerning the issue of home work regulation were advanced in the Reichstag in 1906, the Home Work Act was not published until 1911.[52] Representatives of most middle-class parties supported legislation for regulation. Social Democrats advocated extreme measures. This was not surprising given the intensity of trade union antagonism to home industry. Their demands included mandating at least twelve cubic meters of air space for each person employed and prohibiting work areas from also being used for cooking or sleeping purposes.[53] Implementing such demands either would have been unenforceable, given the work conditions of most home industry, or would have imposed substantial hardship on persons engaged in domestic production. At the time, it was recognized that adoption of Social Democratic proposals would have a negative effect and would probably bring economic ruin to thousands of workers.[54]

The Act of 1911 stipulated the term *Hausarbeit* for the various systems of production and organization outside the premises of a factory.[55] The act listed regulations and provided for a system of inspection. Regulation was extended to persons working at home and employing members of their families, persons working alone, and persons employed in a non–factory-affiliated workshop. It did not include handicrafts where persons worked directly for customers unless the goods were peddled or sold in the market.[56] Persons who gave out work were obliged to provide account sheets that stated wages and time provisions. Industrial employers were required to keep a list of persons who did home work and to provide the list to the police or industrial inspectors upon demand. There were also provisions regarding conditions of work, but these were written in language that suggested rather than mandated compliance.

Where the nature of employment in certain industrial branches may give rise to dangers to life, health, and morality, competent police authorities may, at the request of the industrial inspector, order certain workshops to comply with . . . requirements.[57]

This whole matter of regulation in domestic industry was approached cautiously. Authorities recognized that compliance with the act's provisions not only could be a nuisance, but would also bring increased economic burden to workers. While material improvement in work places might ease sanitary problems, it was unavoidable that costs to workers would increase, but there were no comparable provisions for a corresponding rise in pay. Wages remained an employer prerogative. A hands-off attitude regarding wage rates virtually assured employers and middlemen exclusive control over the livelihood of their domestic workers. The Reichstag did support a provision in the act that called for posting wage scales for the information of workers in rooms where materials were distributed and collected. It was hoped that publication of wage rates might act as a deterrent to employers who wanted to beat wages down to the lowest possible level. The stipulation for posting wages, however, did not go into effect with the other provisions in 1911. Arrangements were made for the provisions to become legally binding only after investigation confirmed that the industrial concerns involved would not suffer losses.[58] When the war began, the most crucial area of exploitation in domestic industry, wages, was still unregulated.

Changes in Germany's employment and education laws acted to preserve traditional work forms while underscoring industry's need for female labor. In 1891 child labor in factories was prohibited. In addition, children between fourteen and sixteen could only be employed in factories up to a maximum of ten hours daily. Children also were required to attend school for eight years, usually between the ages of six and fourteen. Continuation schools became compulsory until age eighteen. Regulations stipulated that employers had to allow their workers time off to attend. Requirements varied, but generally six to eight hours' attendance a week was prescribed. Textiles and tobacco were particularly affected by the new regulations because both industries employed child labor extensively. Several states chose to circumvent the national law by passing local ordinances permitting the factory employment of children under age fourteen if they had completed the required number of years in school.[59]

Employers and parents of youngsters find the [new law] extremely difficult because thirteen year old children who are finished with school cannot take regular factory employment until fourteen. Older children seem reluctant to take work in the factories, and the parents do not know what to do with their children who are at home and not earning.[60]

There is overwhelming evidence that the major repercussion of the child labor law was expansion of child labor in domestic industry.[61] Factory inspectors noted large numbers of children working in a slipper factory in Zwickau in 1890; after 1891, they disappeared. "The children now work at home; they or their brothers and sisters pick up the cloth at the factory and deliver the finished slippers back."[62] Inspectors in Pirmasens in the Pfalz also reported increased numbers of children working at home. In Arnsberg, most needle manufacture switched from factory to home production. Many times mothers moved into domestic production when their children were forced to leave the factory. "The employment of children in home industry expanded immediately following 1891. Making porcelain doll heads and cartons are now done at home. Mothers and children who were in the factory work at home."[63]

The effect of the law in the tobacco industry was most obvious. The regulation had wide-reaching repercussions in cigar-making because large numbers of children were employed in factories as helpers. "When rollers cannot have their helpers in the factory, they move into home work so as not to lose the cheap labor."[64] There is no precise way to measure the cause-effect relationship between prohibition of child labor and the increased employment of women. Data do indicate that the employment of women between 1895 and 1907 proliferated and that a major share of that expansion was into domestic industry. It can be suggested that the new regulations on child labor and compulsory education pushed children into domestic production and created more dramatic need for women to work to compensate for the deficit caused by loss of earnings.

State regulation did bring moderate gains for women regarding conditions of work. Hours for women factory workers gradually improved during the Reich. From a free-wheeling, industrially dictated climate, by World War I both government and industry had adjusted to the concept of regulation. However, as mentioned previously, the laws were written with such flexibility that it continued to be possible for firms to circumvent the provisions. Despite continuing agitation for greater protective legislation for all women, and despite energetic demands by religious groups for the expulsion of women from factories, "special consideration" in no way diminished the woman worker as a saleable commodity in the labor market. The cautious attitude of the state toward intrusion into the privacy of industry guaranteed a cheap, accessible labor supply.

Justification for the concern over women workers can be explained quite logically on one level by the state's preoccupation with propriety. "The special task of the woman claims for her special attention."[65] Yet underlying preference and special attention was a persistent sex discrimination and anti-feminism that took different forms. The conservative position, which incorporated Catholic and other religious groups, favored complete elimination of women from factory work as the only reliable way of assuring an elevation in men's wages. This contention was supported by a family ideology that confirmed the man as provider, as head of the household. The socialist position called for female equality. Yet the slogan of "equal pay for equal work" really meant different things depending on whether the proponent was a feminist or a male worker trying to preserve his job.

Imperial Germany created an ideology of protected persons to resolve the contradiction of perceived gender inversion. It satisfied many diverse interests. Need for women's work had to be reconciled with what was appropriate for them to do. Industrial work was unwomanly because it too blatantly challenged domesticity, maternity, and male identity. Women were set apart. In order to obtain better conditions, women had to accept special status. Legal insulation acted to institutionalize isolation from the mainstream of labor. Protective legislation was actually used to discriminate against the very group it was designed to protect. In ameliorating some of the abuses of work, regulation at once consigned women to those jobs most susceptible to exploitation. As restrictions increased, women moved further into lightly regulated and unprotected industries, forced there by the need to work and industry's relentless quest for cheap labor. It was an ironic and sad trade-off—a contorted way for women to evade the measures devised to protect them.

NOTES

1. Ann Oakley, *Subject Women* (New York: Pantheon Books, 1981), p. 143.

2. Martin Kitchen, *The Political Economy of Germany 1815–1914* (Montreal: McGill-Queen's University Press, 1978), p. 209.

3. W. O. Henderson, *The Rise of German Industrial Power 1834–1914* (Berkeley and Los Angeles: University of California Press, 1975), p. 231.

4. Kitchen, *The Political Economy*, p. 177.

5. Ibid.

6. Ibid., p. 178.

7. Henderson, *The Rise of German Industrial Power*, p. 233.

8. Ibid., p. 84. The Chancellor at this time was Caprivi.

9. Kenneth Barkin, *The Controversy over German Industrialization 1890–1902* (Chicago: The University of Chicago Press, 1970), p. 89.

10. Ralph Bowen, *German Theories of the Corporative State* (New York: McGraw-Hill Book Company, 1947), p. 94.

11. Ursula Schulz, *Die Deutsche Arbeiterbewegung 1848–1914* (Düsseldorf: Karl Rauch Verlag, 1968), pp. 333–34.

12. Rosa Kempf, "Das Leben der jungen Fabrikmädchen in München," *Schriften des Vereins für Sozialpolitik*, Vol. 135 (Leipzig: Verlag von Duncker und Humblot, 1911). Marie Bernays, "Auslese und Anpassung der Arbeiterschaft der geschlossenen Grossindustrie an den Verhältnissen der Gladbacher Spinnerei und Weberei," *Schriften des Vereins für Sozialpolitik*, Vol. 133 (Leipzig: Verlag von Duncker und Humblot, 1910). Bernays, "Untersuchungen über die Schwankungen der Arbeitsintensität während der Arbeitswoche und während des Arbeitstages," *Schriften des Vereins für Sozialpolitik*, Vol. 135 (Leipzig: Verlag von Duncker und Humblot, 1912).

13. *Ergebnisse über die Frauen- und Kinderarbeit in den Fabriken* auf Beschluss des Bundesraths angestellten Erhebungen, zusammengestellt im Reichskanzler-Amt (Berlin: Carl Heymanns Verlag, 1876).

14. Ibid., p. 1.

15. Ibid., pp. 67–69.

16. Ibid., p. 89.

17. Rose Otto, *Über Fabrikarbeit verheirateter Frauen*, Münchener Volkswirtschaftliche Studien (Stuttgart und Berlin: J. G. Cotta'sche Buchhandlung, 1910), p. 158.

18. Ibid., p. 160.

19. Ibid., p. 137.

20. *Amtliche Mittheilungen. Jahresberichte der Gewerbeaufsichtsbeamten und Bergbehörden*, Reichsministerium des Innern, Band I (Berlin, 1879).

21. Ibid., Band I (1881).

22. Ibid., Band II (1880), pp. 26, 29.

23. A special report on married women in factories was included in the *Amtliche Mittheilungen* in 1899.

24. *Amtliche Mittheilungen*, Band I (1887), p. 65.

25. Alice Salomon, *Labour Laws for Women in Germany*, Women's Industrial Council (Berlin: Adelphi, 1907), p. 3.

26. Ibid., pp. 3, 4.

27. In Bavaria girls could leave school at age thirteen.

28. Salomon, *Labour Laws*, p. 5.

29. Prior to the 1891 law, work time was variable. Individual employers normally set their own hours. Customary work time was a ten- or eleven-hour day beginning at 6:00 A.M. or 7:00 A.M. A major exception was textiles, where a thirteen-hour day was not uncommon; *Ergebnisse*, p. 16.

30. Salomon, *Labour Laws*, p. 5.

31. Ibid., p. 6.

32. *Amtliche Mittheilungen*, Band I (1894), p. 97.

33. Ibid., p. 135.

34. Ibid., p. 141.

35. The investigation was conducted and the report on married women workers was published in the factory inspectors' reports in 1899.

36. *Amtliche Mittheilungen* Band II (1899), p. 897.

37. *Die Arbeitszeit der Fabrikarbeiterinnen*. Nach Berichten der Gewerbeaufsichtsbeamten bearbeitet im Reichsamt des Innern (Berlin, 1905), p. 1.

38. *Arbeitszeit*, pp. 1, 2.

39. Ibid., p. 135.

40. Ibid., p. 143.

41. Ibid., p. 17.

42. Ibid., percentages computed from table, p. 21.

43. Ibid., p. 82.

44. Ibid., p. 93.

45. Elisabeth Hell, *Jugendliche Schneiderinnen und Näherinnen in München* (Stuttgart: J. G. Cotta'sche Buchhandlung, 1911), p. 44.

46. The choice was especially preferred by women who lived too far from the factory to make travel at noon feasible.

47. Anna Schmidt, "Die Lage der schlesischen Textil- und Tabakarbeiterinnen," *Der Arbeiterpräses*, 4 Jahrgang (February, 1908), p. 53.

48. Anna Schmidt, "Zur Lage der Tabakarbeiterinnen," *Der Arbeiterpräses*, 6 Jahrgang, Nr. 3, (March, 1910), p. 81.

49. Hell, *Jugendliche*, p. 44.

50. Heinrich Koch, "The New Homework Act," Office International du Travail à Domicile, Publication #6 (n.d.).

51. "The Central Trade Union Federation of Germany and the Abolition and Regulation of Homework by Trade Union Action," Office International du Travail à Domicile, Publication #6 (n.d.), p. 3.

52. Koch, "The New Homework Act," p. 1.

53. Ibid., p. 7.

54. Ibid.

55. Ibid., p. 2.

56. Ibid., p. 3.

57. "Home Work Act, German Empire, December 20, 1911," Office International du Travail à Domicile, Publication #6 (n.d.), p. 3.

58. Koch, "The New Homework Act," p. 11.

59. *Amtliche Mittheilungen* (1893), p. 56.

60. Ibid., p. 52.

61. In 1903, regulations regarding employment of children in industry were extended to home work. German children under ten years old and foreign children under twelve could not be employed in workshops or commercial estab-

lishments. No child under thirteen who had not completed compulsory schooling could be employed in unhealthy industries. Children could not work before morning school or between 8:00 P.M. and 8:00 A.M. for more than three hours. An hour after school was supposed to be allowed before afternoon work began.

62. *Amtliche Mittheilungen* (1893), p. 57.

63. Ibid., p. 53.

64. Ibid., p. 57.

65. Salomon, *Labour Laws*, p. 11.

4

Intersection of Work and Family

"one cannot know what will happen"*

The expansion and contraction of women's involvement with paid labor marked a pattern of recurrent scarcity. Working-class families could not evade the continuing perils of marginality. The daily, weekly, and yearly struggles with material need were absorbed, only to surface again and again. The patterns that emerge appear as serial interruptions in women's lives reflected most clearly by women's movement in and out of the labor force. These difficult periods were both cyclical and immediate, so families had to have the capacity for long-term endurance as well as the ability to respond to crises. Families lived out the solutions to times of insecurity by selecting options that made each person's contribution useful and manageable. Women's labor was the major discretionary variable. What was possible had to be answered every day. The urgency of economic need left little room for rigidity. How families achieved the degree of flexibility needed for survival depended on the success with which a composite response could be put together.

The family was the best protection against economic vulnerability. As a functioning unit, the family made the difference by collectively

*Rosa Kempf, "Das Leben der jungen Fabrikmädchen in München," *Schriften des Vereins für Sozialpolitik*, Vol. 135 (Leipzig: Verlag von Duncker und Humblot, 1911), p. 201.

augmenting the labor of its individual members and distributing goods and services among them. Families were able to push back against economic uncertainty because they contained the resources necessary for adaptation. In a restricted sense, the family acted as an empowering agent devising strategies appropriate to the time and place of its members. By selecting who worked and by timing the work experience, the family asserted control over its members simultaneously as it came to terms with economic hardship. It is important to view the family as a unit in process, incorporating and responding to needs imposed from the outside as well as those created by internal transitions. The evolving continuum opened up possibilities for various coping configurations. But internal discontinuities also imposed constraints that made the family more susceptible to deprivation at certain times along the life course of its members.[1] Decision-making may not have been a consciously negotiated response to economic variables, but neither was it haphazard or capricious. Relatively simple goals were difficult to accomplish. Persistent insecurity demanded continual reassessment and readjustment. Because families absorbed some of the shock of incessant economic danger, life was made more manageable. The family was the support system that integrated combined efforts and separate needs.

The intersection between the working-class family and economic change was not a collision but a convergence. The family reacted to and modified the work experience by bringing it into coincidence with collective needs and resources. Because most persons interacted with work from their position in families, new conditions could be made to fit without severe disruption. Industrialization broadened the work options open to women. The factory provided another place for gainful employment, a chance to earn higher wages than in the more traditional forms of work in agriculture, domestic service, and domestic industry. There is little to indicate that women used industrial work any differently from other forms of labor. Women continued to do what had always been expected of them; their contributions to the family economy were essential for survival. Work in industry was different, yet women used it as they had other kinds of labor—for supplementary earnings in times of need and emergency. "One cannot know what will happen. . . . I leave my fate in God's hands . . . and I hope everything will be all right."[2] Women's lives belied the trust contained in these words. Few families had the material space to turn things over to God. The shifting movement within families demonstrates that moments of stability were bought with the labor of women. Margins of safety were possible because women exerted extraordinary compensatory effort. The rhythms of work in families trace this process of interaction.

Internal division of labor in the family was contained in the intersection of the life cycles of its individual members. These paths of convergence and divergence presented the framework of constriction and choice within which decisions were made. The principal imperative of economic necessity for women was not the burden of work, but manipulating the work experience to handle both economic need and family responsibility. Focusing on the participation of mothers and daughters illustrates how women integrated the work experience into their lives. If children could be used to supplement family income, their labor and earnings were commonly utilized before mothers went out to work. Women's work experience was intermittent rather than permanent, adjusting to accommodate the demands of changing life circumstances. Although women faced the necessity to work throughout most of their lives, they selected work options that presented the least difficult reconciliation between their productive and reproductive roles. Successful integration meant that the lines of demarcation between work and family could be brought into merger.

Women handled maternity by adjusting the work experience to accommodate child care responsibilities. Children were neither prized nor despised. There is no evidence that couples intentionally produced children to assure an available labor supply. Most parents expressed relief when children were old enough to enter the work force. School-age children were the largest drain on the family economy. After 1891, primary education was compulsory for eight years, usually between the ages of six and fourteen. During this period opportunities for children to contribute to the economy of the family were limited and their life outside the home increased outlay for clothes and supplies as well as fees for school attendance.[3] As children got older, they occupied more space, ate more food, and consumed well over their share of the family's resources if they were not working.[4] Infants and small children created no large problem as extra consumers, but they did limit the mother's options for work.

It is here where data on organization of the German economy become instructive. Although the occupational statistics seem to indicate that women disappeared into marriage, their diminished profile was due to their choosing less visible ways to earn money. Many women left factory jobs when their children were young. Job changes, lay-offs, seasonal and casual employment created some measure of elasticity. It was noted previously that occupational and job mobility were fundamental to the work experience of most women. Child care was the most significant reason for making changes. As long as the structure of work permitted space, there was room for a limited amount of control.

Because women adjusted their work lives to accommodate children when they could, systematic information on fertility related to employment is difficult to obtain. However, worker families continued to produce large numbers of children even after a general decline in fertility became apparent at the end of the nineteenth century.[5] Among women industrially employed, available data show that factory women had significantly fewer children than women working in domestic industry.[6] Not only did factory women have fewer children altogether, but the number having only one child was higher than among home workers. In a survey compiled by the *Gewerkverein der Heimarbeiterinnen* (Union of Women Home Workers), conducted among married workers in 1907, it was determined that almost half the factory women had only one child, while it was common for home workers to have three and four children. This difference was based largely on the fact that women left the factory for other kinds of work when child care became necessary. It was also related to the lower age of factory women compared with home workers. Consequently, the reproductive span among women in factories was shorter and fertility was lower compared with domestic workers.

Pre-marital sex and inadequate or non-existent methods of contraception virtually mandated that for most working women, marriage and maternity were inseparable. Pre-marital sex rather than virginity was more common. In southern Germany, despite Catholic admonitions, the popular notion about "not getting a cat in a bag" prevailed.[7] It was estimated in a review of workers in the Stuttgart Daimler Motor Works that over 50% of worker children were born or conceived before marriage.[8] There is enough evidence from police records concerning illegitimacy elsewhere to suggest that pre-marital sex was not a geographic phenomenon. Information on contraception in worker families is difficult to obtain. Workers' unions had things to say about reproduction. Religious unions urged maternity and solved the problem of possible conflict between womb and work by calling for the expulsion of women from the labor force. Socialist unions urged fewer children in order to assure the health and well-being of the family unit, but pulled back from actually advocating "unnatural" means to accomplish this goal.[9]

So infrequently did real evidence concerning use of contraception and abortion surface that the following survey will be discussed in detail, not for the purpose of telling how many couples were consciously handling their reproduction, but to look into the personal circumstances of those who did. The women questioned were patients of Dr. Max Marcuse, who ran a clinic for skin and sexual diseases in Berlin. No indication of occupational status was asked, although most were wives of workers or, at the time of the visit, living with workers. The doctor conducted his survey over a two-year period and published the results in 1913. Marcuse asked the following questions: "How long have you been married? How many children do you have living? Dead? How many times have you been pregnant? Did you do anything to prevent the birth? What do you or your husband use for protection against having more children?"[10] Of the 100 women questioned, 95 were between 20 and 45 years old; 5 were over 45. Collectively they had produced 118 living children; 46 had died; there were 76 instances of abortion.

The following comments have been excerpted from Marcuse's report.[11] A forty-year-old woman married to a smith had two children. She stated that her husband always took care of such matters. "How?" "I don't know." The twenty-five-year-old wife of a saddler remarked: "My husband bought me a douche, *Mutterspritze*." Another woman indicated that after her fourth pregnancy she had used a douche. When her period was late, she used applications of hot towels and mud packs to bring on the flow, but she had recently switched to a pessary. This person was twenty-eight years old; she had borne eight children in ten years of marriage; five were living. A thirty-three-year-old with two children confided a rather primitive method. "When my flow is late, I jump down hard from chairs and tables to bring it on." Apparently the acrobatics had not worked well because she had had several abortions, and she and her husband were then using coitus interruptus.

A tailor's wife with three children said: "I have a device that was advertised in the newspaper. It cost 5 M. . . . but a child costs a lot more." Another woman in a second marriage who had three children from both unions stated that she always rinsed internally, but when that didn't work, she went to a midwife who took care of it. She aborted several times. A factory worker's wife who was being treated for gonorrhea said that since the birth of her first child she went to the midwife following her period to have a pessary inserted. She stopped using that method when she noticed an infection, and her husband had switched to a condom. One woman indicated that since her last abortion, she and her husband had engaged only in anal intercourse. The following comment came from a forty-seven-year-old woman with three children:

The wife of my husband's friend mixes me a tea. She has been pregnant five times, and it always worked. It always works for me, too. I don't know what's in the tea. The woman keeps it a secret and earns a nice sum for it. She has helped everyone on L Street with it.

Several important observations can be made from Marcuse's information. It is obvious that children were very much present in the lives of these women. This suggests that children did not necessarily mean absence of birth control, but rather ineffective methods of affecting reproduction. Limiting the number of children involved both contraception and pregnancy termination.[12] Because means were hardly optimum, more was done after the fact than before. Another interesting point is that pregnancy and birth opened up access to information and help with reproduction. Midwives played an important role. Friends and neighbors offered remedies and advice. Custom and practice seemed to suggest that women had a much greater chance of controlling subsequent pregnancy than they did in preventing the first experience.

The 1891 *Gewerbeordnungsnovelle* included a maternity clause that prohibited employment in factories during the four weeks following delivery without medical permission.[13] As the law was implemented, it meant that women could be employed if they obtained a doctor's certificate. Factory inspectors observed that large numbers of women falsified information in order to return to work before the termination of the prescribed period. Loss of wages was not the only compulsion: Women feared they would be replaced if they stayed out too long.[14] Some firms compensated lost time due to pregnancy, but there were no indications of how customary this practice was. One textile firm in Leipzig, Stahr and Co., paid 8 M. a week for post-delivery recovery.

However, the woman had to be steadily employed in the firm for at least a year prior to her absence. If the child was born dead or died within the first three weeks, only reduced compensation was given.[15] It appeared as though payment was a bonus for the baby rather than compensation for the mother and that the mother was expected to return to work immediately.

If women with children chose to remain in factory work, relatives were the major providers of child care. Economics precluded sending children out to strangers for most working women. Such arrangements could absorb as much as one-half the weekly wages.[16] Payments differed depending on the age of the child and whether food was provided, but most costs fell between 2 and 4 M. weekly in 1899.[17] Nurseries were not generally available, and most were restrictive. These provisions were stipulated in a nursery ordinance in Alsace-Lorraine:

> No child will be admitted unless the mother fulfills the following conditions— She must come from good background; she must signify that she has worked for the same firm for at least a year. She must certify that her work outside the home is necessary for the well being of her family.[18]

Nurseries and children's homes were not the preferred choice for child care. When family members were not available, arrangements with persons outside the home were usually quite informal.

There are no systematic data on child care arrangements. While factory inspectors included such questions in the 1899 investigation of married women workers, returns were less than satisfactory.[19] Not all districts were included, and factory inspectors were not always careful about recording answers systematically. Where such information was available, between 50% and 70% of children whose mothers were factory employed were cared for by relatives, usually the grandparents. If the grandparents were living in the same household, care was free, but in cases where the children went out of the home or boarded with grandparents, parents had to pay. About 25% of the children whose mothers responded to the questionnaire stayed with non-family members. These persons were usually neighbor women who had children of their own to care for. Children who were left without designated care were almost always school age, generally over ten years old.

Looking only at child care arrangements made by mothers working in factories does not fully address the issue of work and maternity.

The real picture emerges not by isolating factory women as a group, but by observing how women adjusted the work experience to match their circumstances. Women's work patterns suggest that there were greater options to control how they worked than there were possibilities to control fertility. Until more information regarding working-class fertility and contraception is available, tracking working women is a good indicator that women attempted to make the job fit their family circumstances instead of the reverse. This is a primary reason for the continuation of traditional work choices. It is also a fundamental explanation of how women sustained the impact of industrialization without profound disruption. Women's roles as wives and mothers determined and defined their work identity. Decisions were made within this framework governed by a constant attempt to balance family needs with economic needs.

Children were part of the female world, not really part of the continuing responsibility of the male except in an indirect way. Anna Perthen, a socialist activist, told about her childhood with her grandmother:

As the daughter of a textile worker I did not have a rosy childhood. My father's wages were so small that my mother had to work in the factory even though she had nine children. Our grandmother took care of us. It was too far for us to go to the factory while we lived in the country with her, so we did home work. . . . When I was twelve, I moved back [with my parents] to work in the factory.[20]

Daughters were frequently major caretakers if mothers worked outside the home. This Munich family organized its daily routine around the oldest daughter; the mother did factory work.[21] The household consisted of both parents, the daughter, and three school-age children. It was the daughter's job to straighten the apartment because she was the last to leave in the morning. The whole family returned for midday meal. The first child to arrive home made a fire in the stove to warm food. Then the daughter and children together washed the dishes and cleaned up. In the evening the tasks were repeated, only the daughter cooked, making enough extra for the noon meal the following day. Mothers and daughters were available to each other in the caring network. Occasionally responsibility was reversed. Illness bound this Munich factory girl to her family:

I work every day to make sure that my mother who is sick will be taken care of. . . . Everything is so expensive. I have to earn my bread in the factory, so at the end of the week we have something to live on. As long as my mother is alive, all my free time is given to her and the housework. It would be very different for me if my mother were well.[22]

For families whose need required earnings supplementary to the father's income, girls were more valuable than boys in terms of what they contributed to the economy of the unit. Privately, it was not surprising to discover a preference for boys. "Boys are worth more than girls. A boy is a boy; he is better than three girls put together. Girls are to be regretted."[23] Yet if this woman had concentrated on the pocketbook of the family instead of some hazy notions about male superiority, she would have discovered that her daughters stayed at home, turning over their earnings to the family, while her sons enjoyed the privilege of keeping theirs for themselves. Parents were able to realize economic benefit from daughters because most factory girls lived at home. While it would be desirable to register exact numbers or even systematic approximations concerning how many working girls actually lived apart from their families, these data are unavailable. There were many factory girls living alone in rented quarters, but most remained an integral and dependent part of their families. A conservative estimate based on collected impressions ranges from 75% to 90%. Even in large cities where there were great numbers of women working, it must be remembered that many of these women were employed in domestic industry.

In the absence of definite numbers regarding living arrangements of factory girls, a composite profile will be drawn from sources available. In Kempf's group of Munich factory workers, only 10 girls out of 272 lived apart from family: seventy-three percent lived with both parents or a parental surrogate such as a stepmother or stepfather; 17% lived with mothers only; 5% stayed with relatives; 1% lived with fathers only; and 4% roomed with persons outside the family. Three of these stayed with families who were friends and had children about the same age. They paid room and board, but did not have to pay extra for heat and light, and their laundry was done with the family's.[24] Similar living arrangements were evident in a survey of 250 girls employed in the clothing industry in Munich. In all cases, the daughters were an integral part of the family economy. Low wages precluded the possibility of independent accommodations. Girls who did not have parents or whose family lived outside the city stayed with relatives. Only one girl in the group lived away. She had a room in an *Arbeiterinnenheim* (home for working girls) for which she and her roommate paid together 40 M. monthly including board.[25]

The factory inspector in Karlsruhe noted the living arrangements for approximately 1,000 single girls working in factories in the city. Well over three-quarters traveled from surrounding villages to work in Karlsruhe. Many of these girls came from families where agriculture contributed a large share of earnings. It was quite common for the pattern of their yearly employment to fluctuate between factory and field work or home work depending on the season. Only 6% of 900 girls who commuted lived apart from their families. Figures were higher for girls who lived in Karlsruhe: one hundred twenty-five out of 500 took lodging with strangers.[26]

A similar distribution occurred among sewers in Karlsruhe. Single girls from rural homes lived with their families, while about a quarter in the city lived in rented rooms. There was considerable difference between factory girls, and sewers, and the circumstances of girls in Karlsruhe who worked in stores and offices. Regardless of where the family lived, there was greater independence in the third group. About 40% lived apart from their families. Wages were higher, but that did not seem to be the only explanation. Girls who worked at white-collar jobs usually came from single-earner families. Fathers were shopkeepers, artisans, and lower government officials. When questioned, most of these women had a sense of autonomous budgeting. They had experience handling their own money and generally kept most of their pay for themselves.[27]

In Berlin, 939 single girls were interviewed by the factory inspector. While there was a broad range of industries represented, most worked in the paper industry or clothing. Sixty-five percent lived at home; 21% had a *Schlafstelle* (sleeping place); 14% had their own room; and one lived in an *Arbeiterinnenheim*.[28] Regardless of whether the girls lived at home or elsewhere, most had to share accommodations, often with more than one other person.

Examples from the West German textile industry also affirm a pattern of dependence. Most of the female labor in Speyer in the Pfalz came from surrounding villages and small towns.[29] As in other industrial centers located in rural areas, worker families often combined agriculture with factory work. Women, much more so than the men, established a pattern of seasonal employment, often leaving the factory in the spring and returning in winter. The close connection between home and work in Speyer suggests that women lived with their parents. No one lived in a *Schlafstelle* or *Arbeiterinnenheim*. In textile factories in München-Gladbach, about 90% of the single women lived at home.[30] Even Minna Wettstein, who deliberately sought to expose the plight of the factory girl in *3 1/2 Monate Fabrikarbeiterin*, reluctantly admitted that most of them lived at home with their parents.[31]

How money was handled in families where children worked revealed a great deal about the difference in expectations and rewards regarding sons and daughters. Kempf noted in her remarks concerning family income of Munich factory girls that many families could have risen above proletarian level if boys contributed the same proportion of their wages as girls.[32] But sons were allowed more financial freedom. Planning for the future for boys was more important than for the girls in the family. It had to be anticipated that the man would eventually have to support a family of his own. Young men kept more of their earnings for personal use; it was expected that a share of the money would be put into savings for marriage. If the family could provide an apprenticeship, boys got the occupational training instead of girls, even if mothers and daughters had to work to compensate for lack of contribution and additional cost.[33] Although all boys in apprenticeship turned over their entire wages, large numbers of unmarried older brothers living at home kept most of their earnings.

Contributions derived from young men generally paralleled skill level.[34] Men in skilled jobs who were not married and still living at home did not usually turn over their entire earnings to the family. Generally a portion of their wages was given in payment for food. Men with lower skill levels and lower wages were more dependent on the family for services, as well as offering more in support.[35] Frequently they turned over a larger share of earnings in return for which food and clothing including laundry were provided by the mother. Contributions from sons also varied with the skill level of the father. Brothers' share of total income was quite low in families where fathers were skilled, indicating possibly that boys' contributions were being deferred in exchange for a period of apprenticeship.[36]

Interestingly, the skill level of fathers had little effect on contributions from girls. Very few girls could follow their fathers into a trade.

The persistence of a craft mentality was an important notion in the socialization of boys. As industrialization proceeded, the likelihood of a son's following his father's trade diminished.[37] But there is evidence that a generational shift transferred the skill of handicraft production into the factory. Sons opted for higher wages in factory work combined with status derived from skilled qualification.[38] It can be suggested that financial contributions anticipated from sons were related to family expectations for their future occupational status. Boys who were in low-skill jobs or casual labor approximated the high level of expected contribution from daughters, for whom aspirations were traditionally limited.

Girls, even skilled workers, usually turned over their entire wages. Although young men were expected to contribute, they were able to keep a portion of their earnings for personal use. Girls handed in their money and were given a small pocket allowance, *Taschengeld*, to spend on themselves. Substantial purchases such as clothing or shoes were handled by the family.[39] Money for food, if the mid-day meal was taken at work, was usually provided. One factory worker in Karlsruhe remarked that she never had any money of her own; she turned everything over to the family and received no allowance. She was eighteen years old earning 9 M. a week.[40] Another, who was twenty-one, earned 9.6 M.; her mother bought her clothes and provided a mid-day meal on Sundays. From her allowance, which was 1.70 M. weekly, the girl had to buy her meals at work.

One girl who was particularly resourceful saved her Sunday pocket money and eventually was able to purchase a dress from her allowance. She was eighteen years old earning 9 M. a week.[41] Another girl, nineteen, who earned 13.50 M. was given 1.10 M. for carfare to work. Everything else came from the common household.[42] There is no indication that these arrangements changed with age. Getting married or moving out were the only circumstances that altered the daughters' complete integration in the economy of the group.[43] While sons kept all their wage or contributed part of it, they were essentially buying goods and services from the household. Girls did not even have the independence implicit in paying for what they used.

When money was needed, the decision to work was not optional, but there was choice in the kind of work selected. It has already been suggested that the choice did not signify a life-long situation. Most women experienced a variety of jobs, including factory, home work, agriculture, and service in their lifetime, occasioned by both need and circumstance. In worker families, daughters had three major options—industry, agriculture, or domestic service. If the girl was going outside the household for work, the primary choice was a decision between factory and service. A standard theme about women and work in German rhetoric extolled the benefits of a period in service for girls from worker families so that they could acquire domestic skills presumably lost at the factory. Training in service for domestic duties and motherhood was a favorite theme of Catholic writers.[44] Service was also supposed to provide the opportunity for the "less fortunate" to share the delights of a proper life. The uplifting experience was to provide guidelines for the future. Simply put, skills had to be learned; morals had to be protected. Theoretically, a position in service offered a surrogate family, by implication, a substitute that had the potential of transmitting basic social values.

It is obvious that working families did not perceive domestic service in the same way. There are clear indications that parents, most particularly those industrially employed, made conscious decisions about the employment of their daughters. Rejection of service was frequently part of the decision-making process. Service did not fit their life plan, a term used more to describe the present rather than the future. Service was impractical.[45] One consideration was wages. How could a young, inexperienced girl secure a position where she could make as much as in the factory? Employers who paid well did not need inexperienced help. Also, it was recognized that service was a temporary occupation. This did not imply by comparison that factory work was permanent, but rather, industrial work was more flexible. There were more options to take and leave work as situations required. Few girls stayed in service after marriage. Viewed in this way, service was not an opportunity but a dead end.

In addition to economic considerations, there were issues of class involved. It is difficult to discern whether aversion for service was motivated by shame or pride. Perhaps both were present. Workers recognized that persons who hired servants were better situated, and that there was no real sense for their daughters to aspire to such a status in life when circumstances most likely dictated otherwise. Such expectations could only bring bitterness.[46] Also, there was little anticipation for an upwardly mobile marriage. Parents saw only that there were few opportunities for their daughters to meet marriageable men.[47] These considerations offer some explanation for the fact that most servant girls came from rural, agricultural families. Industrial families sought different work options.

Service did not match its nineteenth-century romantic image.[48] Industrial families resisted service as a suitable occupation for daughters. Women frequently left service for jobs in industry for economic and personal reasons. If there had been a geographic move involved in taking a service position, women who changed occupations were then left without even the surrogate family. While this point has not been verified due to lack of data, it can be suggested that many women in *Schlafstellen* and *Arbeiterinnenheime* were domestic servants and former servant girls. This contention mitigates the harsh contemporary attack on the factory as the primary cause for women's living alone in adverse circumstances. Reasons for their living alone must be sought in situations beyond the factory.

What were *Schlafstellen* and *Arbeiterinnenheime?* Although both were accommodations for single women living alone, they were quite dissimilar. Girls' homes were structured living. Order was maintained by regulation and restriction. Most homes were religiously affiliated; some were sponsored by factories employing women workers; a few, particularly in Berlin, were run by women's organizations. *Schlafstellen* were just what the German term describes. They were places to sleep—not single rooms, but shared rooms and even shared beds. Space was rented in a household. Sleeping arrangements were normally with the rest of the family. Beds were in cellars, attics, kitchens, and corridors.[49] *Schlafstellen* were under police regulation, at least in large cities, but since they were in private homes, direct intervention was sporadic and non-productive. Records from factory inspectors indicated that almost 60% of the women living in sleep rooms in Berlin whom they contacted shared accommodations with more than two other people.[50]

Wettstein included vivid descriptions of the sleep rooms she visited. In order to learn more about single accommodations, she placed an ad in a Chemnitz paper requesting a place to stay. She received seventeen replies, some of which were related in detail. "We have a place for you; it is a nice room, but it is not too warm. We have five children, so we must rent. You can come and see it. The price is 2 M. a week with coffee, and you can do your laundry here. There are no men boarders. With regards . . . "[51] When she answered the note, Wettstein found a dilapidated house consisting of two rooms. In one room was a bed and a hammock which she described as a bricklayer's net. She was supposed to share the room with the mother and a four-year-old daughter. The boarder got the hammock. The father, four boys, and a grandfather slept in the other room. Pursuing the remainder of the ads for sleep rooms, she found that cost averaged between 1 and 3 M. weekly. The only rooms that she described as clean and airy were located in the houses and apartments of lower-middle-class families. The cost was 6 to 8 M. a week. Boarders were usually skilled seamstresses and shop girls who could afford the rather steep price.[52]

Arbeiterinnenheime rectified many of the unsavory aspects of sleep rooms by providing clean, if spare, accommodations, food, and orderly surroundings. But discipline was strict and rules were enforced. The intention was to provide working girls with a wholesome, moral family life away from home. Religiously affiliated homes were nondenominational in terms of whom they accepted as long as the girls were willing to comply with prescribed religious observances. House rules for *Das Daheim für Arbeiterinnen* in Leipzig, run by the evangelical sisters, included the following stipulation: "No girl can neglect her duty as a member of this community to go to church and to participate in house prayers."[53] Homes required observance of curfew and prescribed schedules for domestic tasks. Housemothers were constantly in attendance to make sure that all residents observed their responsibilities, both industrial and spiritual.[54] Rooms had to be kept in order daily, and on Saturday afternoons after work, a thorough cleaning was expected. Girls who became ill could not remain in residence; they had to return home or go to a hospital. Girls were charged an insurance fee, the *Krankenhausgeld*, to cover the cost of possible illness. During the summer months, the home in Stuttgart was open from 5 A.M. until 9:30 P.M. In the winter, it opened at 6 and closed at 8:30. No one could leave or enter the house beyond these prescribed hours without special permission. Prayers were recited in common before breakfast and at bedtime. It was the housemother's responsibility to see that the girls occupied their free time profitably with sewing, knitting, or embroidery. Girls were allowed "wholesome" recreation on Sundays.

Cost for lodging and food in the homes was modest. Rooms averaged 1 to 2 M. weekly depending on accommodations. The *Herberge an Ludwigsstrasse* in Stuttgart offered rooms with two or four occupants, but every girl had her own bed, a chair, and a small wash basin;

two girls shared a table and closet.[55] The following menu was posted in the Stuttgart home in 1906: morning coffee with milk and sugar— 8 pf; one roll—3 pf; 1/2 liter of soup—10 pf, with meat—20 pf. The following year the same menu was offered, but the price of meat and vegetables had gone up 5 pf.[56]

Frequently homes required a contract of residency. A three-year period was common. More than just a guarantee of occupancy, it was supposed to be a training period during which the spiritual and moral character of the girls could be molded. The following contract was used in the *Mädchenheim des Diakonievereins Arbeiterinnenfürsorge*, Stühlingen, Baden.[57]

I confirm my entrance in a *Mädchenheim* of the *Diakonievereins Arbeiterinnenfürsorge* in Stühlingen, and I declare that I understand the conditions.

Date   Signature

I understand and comply with all conditions, and leave my daughter for three years in a home of the *Diakonievereins Arbeiterinnenfürsorge*. During this time I am transferring the responsibility for my daughter to the organization and the managing sisters of the home to care for my daughter.

Date   Signature of father or guardian

Application was accompanied by a doctor's certificate indicating general health and capacity to do factory work.

The *Mädchenheim* in Stuttgart did not require a contract of residency, and consequently was more responsive to the immediate needs of the female labor force in the area. House records, which were carefully kept from 1872 when the home opened, indicated a fairly high level of mobility. Occupation, age, marital status, and religion of the residents were registered. The home could accommodate about 150 women, but the actual number in residence varied due to season and demand for female labor in the city's industry. The most mobile were domestic servants. Records showed that during 1877–1878, 101 residents left the home, most of whom were servant girls between positions looking for work.[58] In 1889–1890, the home accommodated 315 unemployed servant girls who remained in residence as long as they needed, some as briefly as overnight.[59] About one-third of the house clients left in the summer. Most of the girls came from neighboring villages. They worked in the factories in winter, but returned to their families in the spring when their labor could more profitably be used in field work.[60] In 1904, a second home was built about three miles away from the Ludwigsstrasse residence to accommodate an increased concentration of industry in that area of the city. About 1,800 women were employed in bookbinding and clothing.[61] In 1910, concern was expressed in the annual report about how to handle the tremendous influx of foreign women, mostly Italians and Austrians, who had migrated to Stuttgart to work in the textile factories.[62]

Without concrete data, it is impossible to determine how many women workers actually lived alone separate from families and just as difficult to discern what kinds of accommodations they occupied. Yet valuable impressions are suggested in the material available. *Schlafstellen* were the ultimate in temporary arrangements. Good accommodations were sheer accident. Because wages for women were not sufficient to support an autonomous existence, women rarely could afford a room of their own. Optimum to be hoped for was lodging in a household where family members were at least cordial. Taking in strangers was not conducive to harmonious living, particularly since privacy was virtually non-existent. Yet, there was one major advantage—no obligation. For women who were already transient, such as domestic servants, perhaps the anonymity of the *Schlafstelle* represented positive choice instead of absence of alternative. The saying "*Stadtluft macht frei*" (city air means freedom) was apparently taken to heart by many disenchanted rural girls.[63] So common was the servant protest against submission and dependence, lack of freedom, and absence of self-will that it is quite plausible that squalor was an acceptable price to pay in exchange for a little leeway.

On the other hand, an *Arbeiterinnenheim* required commitment. Most were extensions of the family, regardless of how well they fulfilled that function. They prescribed a code of behavior, and as can be seen from the contracts, some even required parental sanction. Imposing a minimum residency signified more than lodging facilities. Their mission was reform and, as such, they acted as an educative agency, cultivating virtues of work, order, cleanliness, and morality. The homes were supposed to be havens of safety and sanctity amidst the physical and spiritual abuse of the factory. Living in an *Arbeiterinnenheim* required extra effort. The convent-like existence was clearly a choice either of concerned parents or of the women themselves, who derived security from that kind of structured life.

Focusing on daughters in working-class families shows the extent to which girls as earners were integrated into the family unit. It also illuminates one stage in the female life cycle. As children, girls attended school, tended other children, helped with housework, and deposited their wages with the family. Girls were exposed to multiple demands on their time and energy early in their lives. There was little opportunity to postpone or defer adult responsibilities. The duration of childhood was short, and if work is used as a demarcation, childhood did not exist. The work experience of daughters, especially if it was factory work, tied them closely to the family. Expansion of factory jobs significantly enhanced the family economy because girls could bring in higher wages than were previously available from service in homes and on farms. Factory employment also increased the chances that families could keep girls at home. It was more common for girls in agriculture and service to live away from home than it was for daughters doing factory work. There is every indication that a decision for daughters to take factory work for reasons of wages and residence was part of planned strategies to obtain maximum return from their labor.

With marriage, women's participation in the family economy expanded to incorporate primary responsibility for the household and the almost immediate and inevitable presence of children. Families were a limitation on women's earning capacity, one that they confronted by changing their work lives. Transition into marriage did not mean transition out of the labor force. If it was the man's job to be the economic center for the family, uncertainty compromised that centrality. Yet family strategies were geared toward keeping the mother at home if it was at all possible. Women did not have to be persuaded to don their roles as earners and caretakers because their lives offered no real alternative. The nexus between life cycle and patterns of employment is a model for understanding how women balanced commitment to their reproductive and productive lives.

Relationships of interdependence within families offered a measure of relative security, yet evaluating reciprocity is difficult because internal transitions imposed a variety of burdens on women that changed over time. Women appear to be the recipients of negatively uneven responsibilities and rewards. Were women expected to give more and receive less; who was there for them? The question is worth asking because it helps to capture and clarify the necessity for women to connect into the family economy in a complementary way. Individual choice was circumscribed. Collaboration with the distribution of familial obligations including contributed services and paid labor left little room for personal autonomy. Family responsibilities determined when women worked; they also affected where women worked. Integration in a family called for maximum effort, but it also minimized risk. Women could not choose isolation or independence because in doing so they subverted the very relationship that contained the resources for personal and economic stability. The safety net was the shared dynamic of the family economy.

NOTES

1. Tamara Hareven, *Family Time and Industrial Time: The Relationship between the Family and Work in a New England Industrial Community* (Cambridge, Mass.: Cambridge University Press, 1982), pp. 6–7.

2. Rosa Kempf, "Das Leben der jungen Fabrikmädchen in München," *Schriften des Vereins für Sozialpolitik*, Vol. 135 (Leipzig: Verlag von Duncker und Humblot, 1911), p. 201.

3. Frederic Howe, *Socialized Germany* (New York: Charles Scribner's Sons, 1915), p. 221.

4. Kempf, "Das Leben der jungen," p. 24.

5. John Knodel, *The Decline of Fertility in Germany 1871–1939* (Princeton, N.J.: Princeton University Press, 1974), p. 118.

6. Käthe Gaebel, *Die Heimarbeit* (Jena: Verlag von Gustav Fischer, 1913), p. 36.

7. Fritz Schumann, "Die Arbeiter der Daimler-Motoren Gesellschaft Stuttgart-Untertürkheim," *Schriften des Vereins für Sozialpolitik*, Vol. 135 (1911), p. 103.

8. Ibid., p. 101.

9. R. P. Neuman, "The Sexual Question and Social Democracy in Imperial Germany," *Journal of Social History* (Spring, 1974), p. 278.

10. Max Marcuse, "Zur Frage der Verbreitung und Methodik der willkürlichen Geburtenbeschränkung in Berliner Proletarierkreisen," *Sexual-Probleme. Zeitschrift für Sexualwissenschaft und Sexualpolitik*, Heft 11, 9 Jahrgang (1913), p. 753.

11. Ibid., excerpted from tables, pp. 756–73.

12. Angus McLaren, "Women's Work and Regulation of Family Size: The Question of Abortion in the Nineteenth Century," *History Workshop* (Autumn, 1977).

13. Alice Salomon, *Labour Laws for Women in Germany*, Women's Industrial Council (Berlin: Adelphi, 1907), p. 5.

14. *Amtliche Mittheilungen*. *Jahresberichte der Gewerbeaufsichtsbeamten und Bergbehörden*, Reichsministerium des Innern, Band I (1882), p. 435.

15. Ibid., p. 469.

16. Ibid., Band II, p. 302.

17. Wilhelm Feld, *Die Kinder der in Fabriken arbeitenden Frauen und ihre Verpflegung* (Dresden: Verlag von O. U. Böhmert, 1906), p. 25.

18. *Amtliche Mittheilungen*, Band III (1913), pp. 74–75.

19. Ibid. Survey results reported in Band I–IV (1899).

20. Richard Klucsarits and Friedrich Kürbisch, eds., *Arbeiterinnen Kämpfen um ihr Recht* (Wuppertal: Peter Hammer Verlag, 1975), p. 84.

21. Kempf, "Das Leben der jungen," p. 49.

22. Ibid., pp. 200–201.

23. C. Moszeik, *Aus der Gedankenwelt einer Arbeiter von ihr selbst erzählt* (Berlin: Verlag Edwin Runge in Lichterfelde, 1909), p. 44.

24. Kempf, "Das Leben der jungen," p. 177.

25. Elisabeth Hell, *Jugendliche Schneiderinnen und Näherinnen in München* (Stuttgart: J. G. Cotta'sche Buchhandlung, 1911), p. 163.

26. Marie Baum, *Drei Klassen von Lohnarbeiterinnen in Industrie und Handel der Stadt Karlsruhe*, Bericht erstattet an das Grossherzogliche Ministerium des Innern und herausgegeben von der Grossherzoglich Badischen Fabrikinspektion (Karlsruhe: Druck und Verlag der G. Braunschen Hofbuchdruckerei, 1906), p. 27.

27. Ibid., p. 166.

28. "Die Arbeits- und Lebensverhältnisse der unverheirateten Fabrikarbeiterinnen in Berlin," *Reichs-Arbeitsblatt*, I Jahrgang, Nr. 2 (May 21, 1903), p. 99.

29. Marie Bernays, "Untersuchungen über die Schwankungen der Arbeitsintensität während der Arbeitswoche und während des Arbeitstages," *Schriften des Vereins für Sozialpolitik*, Vol. 135 (Leipzig: Verlag von Duncker und Humblot, 1912), p. 200.

30. Marie Bernays, "Auslese und Anpassung der Arbeiterschaft der geschlossenen Grossindustrie an den Verhältnissen der Gladbacher Spinnerei und Weberei," *Schriften des Vereins für Sozialpolitik*, Vol. 133 (Leipzig: Verlag von Duncker und Humblot, 1910), p. 207.

31. Minna Adelt Wettstein, *3 1/2 Monate Fabrikarbeiterin* (Berlin: Verlag von J. Leiser, 1893), p. 56. Wettstein, a feminist from Berlin, concealed her identity to work in four factories gathering information on women workers. She patterned her project after Paul Göhre, *Drei Monate Fabrikarbeiter und Handwerksbursche*.

32. Kempf, "Das Leben der jungen," p. 129.

33. Hell, *Jugendliche*, pp. 66, 68.

34. Kempf, "Das Leben der jungen," Table 7, pp. 222–28.

35. Ibid.

36. Ibid., pp. 230–33.

37. Peter Stearns, *Lives of Labor* (New York: Holmes and Meier Publishers, 1975), p. 52.

38. Ibid.

39. Baum, *Drei Klassen*, p. 61.

40. Ibid., p. 64.

41. Ibid., p. 65.

42. Ibid.

43. Ibid., p. 61.

44. For discussion of this point see Elizabeth Gnauck-Kühne, *Die Deutsche Frau um die Jahrhundertwende* (Berlin: Verlag von Otto Liebmann, 1907).

45. Kempf, "Das Leben der jungen," p. 60.

46. Ibid.

47. Ibid., p. 61.

48. Ibid., p. 59.

49. *Reichs-Arbeitsblatt*, I Jahrgang, Nr. 2 (May 21, 1903), p. 99.

50. Ibid.

51. Wettstein, *3 1/2 Monate*, p. 61.

52. Ibid., p. 64.

53. *Das Daheim für Arbeiterinnen* (Leipzig: Metzger und Wittig, n.d.).

54. "Hausordnung für die Herberge des Vereins zur Fürsorge für Fabrikarbeiterinnen," Verein zur Fürsorge für Fabrikarbeiterinnen (Stuttgart: Druck von A. Bonz' Erben, 1914).

55. Ibid. (1905–1906), p. 2.

56. Ibid. (1906–1907), p. 2.

57. *Aufnahme-Bedingungen der Mädchenheime des Diakonievereins "Arbeiterinnenfürsorge"* (Stühlingen, Baden, n.d.).

58. Herberge des Vereins zur Fürsorge für Fabrikarbeiterinnen (Stuttgart: 1877–1878), p. 4.

59. Ibid. (1890), p. 4.

60. Ibid., p. 5.

61. Ibid. (1904–1905), p. 6.

62. Ibid. (1906–1907), p. 4.

63. Johannes Feig, "Hausgewerbe und Fabrikbetrieb in der Berliner wäscheindustrie," *Staats- und Socialwissenschaftliche Forschungen* (Leipzig: Verlag von Duncker und Humblot, 1896), p. 101.

5

Economic Need and Family Adjustment

"My husband does not earn enough"*

On a train between Weida and Reichenbach in 1913, two travelers observed a weaver and his family. There were nine children; only two were grown.

They are from my hometown. They are going to Plauen where wages are supposed to be better. Last summer the father butchered 64 cats; some he found, others were brought to him. In our village the people are so desperate that even a stone would show pity.[1]

While the traveler was skeptical about the actual number of cats involved, she was quite certain that need in the textile industry was harsh enough to compel people to face what she distastefully envisioned as cat roast. However, if the prospect of eating cats was repugnant, doing with less or none at all was the accommodation many working families made in order to get by. Numerous indices in pre-war Germany pointed toward improvement in the lives of the working population. Generous opportunity for employment in expanding industry, significant increase in wages, social legislation in the form of sickness, accident, and death

*Amtliche Mittheilungen. Jahresberichte der Gewerbeaufsichtsbeamten und Bergbehörden, Band II (1899), p. 1001.

insurance, and greater options for union participation suggested better times. But for families whose women worked, there was little basis for optimism. The benefits of Germany's industrializing economy were only sporadically distributed.

Wages in industry increased markedly between 1871 and World War I, but along with the ostensibly healthy earnings expansion came a hefty rise in the price of essentials, principally food and housing. Increase in wages did not suggest greater material expectations for many working families, because more money hardly matched the outlay necessary to keep even. In families where women worked, there was little indication that members perceived their combined efforts as productive of a higher standard of living. Neither were women called to work to provide for the future. Concern for savings was rare. The margin of economic safety for families whose women worked was more often too narrow to provide the luxury of plans for the future. An unskilled male worker in the textile industry remarked: "What should the working man hope for, one can rise no further; it is best to hope for a restful old age."[2] Accident, sickness, or death could immediately destroy even these most-tenuous expectations.

Studies addressing the question of the "health" of worker households proliferated in journals and yearbooks beginning in the late 1890's and continued until the war. Scholarly attention was matched by numerous articles in trade papers reacting to an alarming increase in the price of staples and rents. While it can be contended that evidence of worsening conditions was the result of unsophisticated data, nevertheless, similar conclusions from diverse sources, including workers themselves, point to real economic need. "The wife of a worker who must satisfy the necessities of her family and household with a meager weekly wage, feels need more harshly than before."[3] Families bought less and substituted bread and potatoes for meat; fat or margarine was used in place of butter; chicory was brewed instead of coffee.[4] Clothing was mended and handed down; shoes were patched at home. Women and children collected sticks to burn instead of coal.

In 1897, the German Statistics Office, in response to perceived increases in the cost of living, formulated a chart of economic manageability based on a theoretical family of four members. It was determined that 1,300 M. yearly was a minimum level for satisfactory living.[5] Information concerning wages and prices in worker households was compiled from investigations in Berlin, Stuttgart, and Leipzig for the

Annual Income	Level
- 800 M.	insufficient
800 - 1000	very needy
1000 - 1200	needy
1200 - 1300	scanty
1300 - 1500	sufficient
1500 -	satisfactory

two decades at the turn of the century. In Berlin, it was figured that a worker whose wages were 23 M. weekly in 1896 would have to earn at least 26 M. in 1909 to prevent economic deterioration for a family of four. Both these estimates were predicated upon full yearly employment.[6] Between 1890 and 1903, most unskilled labor in Berlin earned less than 1,200 M. a year. In fact, the majority fell below 1,000 M. Even skilled workers faced problems if they were in low-paying consumer industries; skilled male textile workers in Berlin earned less than 1,000 M. annually.[7] If a worker's wages did reach 27 M. weekly in 1910, the condition of the mythical family of four stayed even. More children threw all these estimates out of order.

In Leipzig, cost-of-living estimates including outlay for food and rent rose 175 M. or 22% between 1894 and 1912.[8] Between 1890 and 1910, the price for two rooms in Leipzig rose 24.7%; for three rooms, 10%; and for a four-room apartment, 8%. Smallest accommodations cost the most in terms of rent inflation.[9] Using 1894 as the base year, an index table was computed for food expenditure. The following table (see page 106 top) indicates yearly food expenditures for a normal worker household in Leipzig for the years 1894–1910.[10]

A similar pattern was apparent in Stuttgart. In the families interviewed for that survey, men earners were metal workers. The average increase in wages between 1900 and 1912 was 3.19 M. Weekly expenditures in all cases increased. Using 1890 as the base year, index 100, 1900 expenditures registered decline, index 96, while the index number for 1912 was 122.[11]

Year	Index Number (Base 100)	Year	Index Number (Base 100)
1894	100.0	1903	105.0
1895	97.9	1904	107.1
1896	95.4	1905	108.8
1897	96.9	1906	110.5
1898	101.7	1907	113.2
1899	99.6	1908	116.3
1900	101.5	1909	119.1
1901	103.5	1910	117.0
1902	105.0		

Collectively, these examples suggest a parallel rise in both wages and prices. Yet figures computed by Dr. Carl von Tyszka in 1914 (below) indicate increasing disparity between wage increases and cost-of-living increase. Tyszka attempted computation of real wages. He reached the conclusion that despite substantial improvement in average wages, prices out-paced increases, resulting in diminishing purchasing power.[12]

Not surprisingly, given the lack of information and the not-too-re-

Year	Wages	Cost of Living	Real Wages
Prussia			
1900	100.0	100.0	100.0
1910	104.1	124.5	79.6
1912	116.7	135.8	81.0
Munich			
1900	100.0	100.0	100.0
1910	119.0	118.0	101.0
1912	119.0	122.5	96.5

luctant manipulation of data, other observers reached more favorable conclusions. In July, 1907, the *Tabak-Arbeiter*, a trade newspaper for the tobacco union, carried an optimistic excerpt from a Dresden paper. The Dresden editor reported that workers in industry could anticipate a brighter future because wages were climbing and life would be more satisfactory. "The inquiry by the statistical office will modify the interpretation that the influence of price rise has a damaging effect on the cost of living. Wages since 1903 have risen much higher than prices." [13] An angry rejection appeared in the same article of the *Tabak-Arbeiter* denouncing any predictions of better times. [14] Contemporaries accurately perceived conditions of deepening poverty. The rising cost of living resulted in a steady erosion of real wages. Conditions worsened in 1902, 1907, and 1913, when trade slumps caused widespread unemployment, but no real relief from high prices. Families accommodated by adjusting consumption and utilizing the assistance labor of women and children.

Allowing working women to speak for themselves exposes a wide range of contingencies that individually or in combination forced women into paid labor. Unquestionably, the significant determinant of why women went to work was insufficient income. Economic need was obvious in the case of widows and separated women, especially those who had to provide care for children. [15] But for most German working women, insufficient earnings meant that the man, the head of the household, could not provide adequately for his family. "It is always to be wished that the husband can earn enough alone to provide for his family. This is not always the case. This is especially true if there is no steady employment during the year." [16] Returns in the 1899 factory inspectors' reports investigating married working women were monotonously similar: "My husband does not earn enough." [17] Conditions were far worse for women whose husbands refused to work or drank away their earnings in the local tavern (*Gaststube*). Most women were quite willing to make allowance for beer and tobacco. In fact, very few worker budgets omitted such items. "Beer gives courage; that's why I always gave him money for beer. A man without schnapps is nothing." [18] But men who were reluctant to work were labeled by a rather descriptive German word, *Arbeitsscheu* (work shy). "My husband brings home nothing, and I have two children." [19]

Children placed an especially heavy burden on families. Until such time as children could become earners, more mouths to feed frequently put unmanageable strain on an already fragile existence. Constraints became worse after 1891 when children were prevented from taking factory work before age fourteen. Their contribution could be counted on only in domestic industry.

In the beginning of a marriage, economic need can be handled. Many women leave the factory at marriage. Because so many have been working since leaving school, it is pleasant to stay at home. But with children, need returns, and many go back to the factory.[20]

Accident and sickness could instantly change a family's fortunes. Insurance payments were considerably less than a worker's earnings. If a family could not get by with the father in good health, benefits were hardly sufficient.[21]

I learned about need early in my life. As the daughter of a wagon driver, I had eight years of a comfortable life. When I was 10, my father became ill with lung disease; he did not get well. Those were hard times. My mother did not know how to feed us. When I was 14, I went to the factory. My father died when I was 16. Now my mother also went to the factory. She wanted us both to work in the same place so that we could eat the mid-day meal together and save a little money.[22]

Responses to factory inspectors' questions concerning reasons for work confirm that regardless of the particular contingency, need compelled women to work. These were the responses from 175 women questioned in Württemberg:[23]

115	-	husband does not earn enough
3	-	family is too large
7	-	husband in seasonal employment
12	-	husband is ill
8	-	husband is dead
3	-	provide for old age
3	-	rent too high
1	-	bad luck
23	-	save for emergency

Eight hundred seventy-four women in Oberbayern gave the following reasons:[24]

444	-	insufficient income from man's wage
167	-	widowed, separated
45	-	uncertain income
30	-	sickness
29	-	man cannot work
47	-	large number of children
95	-	family members who do not contribute—parents, relatives
12	-	safety against husband's unemployment
5	-	care for previously married children

In the report from Frankfurt a.O., responses were divided into two groups. Women in the first group had worked before marriage and were then in the factory. The second group comprised women who entered the factory after marriage. Responses were registered in percentages:[25]

employed before marriage

9%	-	death of parents
13%	-	help support family
78%	-	income of parents too low

employed after marriage

31%	-	death of husband
15%	-	husband is sick
2%	-	large number of children
9%	-	live-in relatives
43%	-	husband's wage too low

What constituted need? What was enough to get by? When did it become necessary for women to work? Marriage was often based on economic viability. This was especially true for skilled workers where there was an apparent effort to plan for the future. And the future for workers who had the option to make conscious decisions was directed toward the "normal" family. In other words, the wife did not work. But women's work was not a new phenomenon for many families. For couples who entered marriage by choice, it was recognized by both that the wife would contribute, or at least that she had the capacity to do so. Women did not often bring a nest-egg into the relationship. Savings were difficult to manage because most working girls lived at home with their families before marriage, and they were expected to turn over their wages or at least a large portion of their pay to the household.

While there is no neat formula that can be used to give the precise set of circumstances or the exact level of income determining when women went to work, representative examples both collectively and individually suggest an answer to the question, "What was enough?" It has already been determined that in areas and cities in Germany where there was ample, steady work available for men, the number of employed women was low. Statistics are supported by observation. Paul Göhre, who worked in a factory for three months gathering first-hand impressions of work and workers, remarked in *Three Months in a Workshop*: "If a man earns enough, he doesn't let his wife and children go into the works of his own accord."[26] Göhre had selected a factory making machinery in Chemnitz. The factory employed only men workers, work was steady, and a large number of workers had been employed in the same firm since they were young. In other words, workers could expect good wages.

Similar circumstances were described by the Mannheim factory inspector. In Mannheim, prior to the development of heavy industry, primary activity was consumer goods production, principally tobacco. But the inspector observed that since the development of heavy industry, metals, chemicals, and machines, men could find good employment. " . . . with full justification, they do not allow their women to go to the factories."[27] Sixty percent of the men made between 15 and 27 M. weekly.[28] Very few made below 12 M., and these were usually young and unmarried.[29] In the fifty families interviewed, only seven wives worked.

Selected examples from the Mannheim survey illustrate comparative prosperity levels and family circumstances. Three of the working women were wives of polygraph workers, where wages were considerably lower than average. One worked in a factory in Ludwigshafen, where she earned 9 M. weekly, bringing the combined income to 32.50 M. There were no children, but the couple lived with the husband's parents in two rooms. They paid 7 M. weekly for their share of the rent.[30] The husband of another of the working wives was employed in the paper industry. He earned 16 M. weekly only by including overtime. He and his wife traveled into Mannheim to work by train from Seckenheim at a daily cost of 70 *Pfennigs*. The wife cooked food in the evening to bring to work the next day. They lived in one room without a separate kitchen, for which they paid 80 M. a year. That summer was the first time the woman had gone to work, because the family was having a hard time. She had already decided she was going to stay at home during the winter because she was troubled by leaving her children.[31] Another working wife earned 10 M. a week. Her husband had previously been employed in a chemical factory where he made 20 M. a week. He had suffered considerable injury from industry-related burns and could no longer work. Because the accident insurance payment only amounted to one-third his former wages, the wife went to work.[32]

Those were the exceptions. Most households in the Mannheim survey were single-earner families. Circumstances were considerably better than in households where the wives worked. In most cases the husband earned enough to support everyone; for the remainder, children rather than wives worked. Two selected families illustrate this condition. Both were single-earner families; the husbands worked in metals and machines. Wages were similar, but there was significant difference between the two families due principally to where they lived. The rural family, despite numerous children, was considerably more comfortable. A thirty-three-year-old machine worker, who lived in Mannheim, earned 36.50 M. weekly. There were three children between one and six. The family lived in two rooms with a kitchen, for which they paid 23 M. a month. They enjoyed meat several times a week, but they had no savings. There were seven persons in the second family, including five children. The father was a handformer. His wages were 35 M. weekly. The family supplemented their food budget with homegrown potatoes, some of which were sold for market. They also kept a cow. The family owned their own home, purchased from savings. The man remarked that he would like to save more, but that would have to wait until the children brought home wages.[33]

Collective material summarizes personal instances and confirms that level of prosperity was determined principally by the man's capacity to earn. Berlin metal workers responded that 18.5% of their wives contributed to total earnings.[34] The significance of this figure emerges more clearly if the men are grouped according to skill level, and consequently in the machine industry, by wage-earning capacity. Twenty-four percent of the women married to unskilled workers were employed, while 17% of skilled workers' wives and 19% in the semi-skilled category contributed to family income.[35] The caution that working did not automatically mean factory employment must be reiterated. Over

40% of the women who worked were in domestic industry. Given the significance of home work in Berlin, this figure is not surprising. Almost all of the women in home work had small children to care for. More instances of home work showed up among skilled workers' wives than among the other two categories.[36] Only 17% of the women who worked were in factories, and most of the factory workers were wives of the unskilled. Other women derived earnings from carrying newspapers, delivering lunches, cleaning houses, or taking in boarders.[37] The factory was not the favored choice among work options, particularly if pride and position were involved.

A more comprehensive picture of total family involvement is obvious in a study of Munich factory girls in the first decade of the twentieth century. There were 272 girls interviewed. Most lived with both parents; only 10 did not live at home.[38] Average income of the fathers was 1,233 M. annually; men in skilled jobs earned 1,470 M., unskilled earned 1,106 M. Since the selective criterion for the study was the working daughter, no family depended solely on the earnings of the father. Sixty-three percent of the mothers also worked, but the percentage of income derived from these respective sources indicated that contributions from children greatly exceeded that from mothers in these families. Earnings from fathers averaged 42% of total income, and that from sons and daughters was 43%; mothers contributed an average of about 15%.[39] Interestingly, if the percentage contribution from sons and daughters was broken down, sons contributed only 13%, while daughters' earnings amounted to 30% of the family income. Incidence of mothers working paralleled men's wages. For women who worked full-time, average wages for the father were 21.27 M.; fathers' wages for families where women worked part-time were 24.32 M.; and women who did not work had husbands who earned 25.37 M. weekly.[40]

While daughters who worked in the Munich group were employed in factories, very few of the mothers earned in this manner. This was true even for those women who had previously done factory work. Many derived income from domestic industry, especially those mothers who had done similar work in factories.[41] Another source of income for the working mothers was delivery. Some carried bread, milk, or vegetables door to door; many delivered newspapers, which paid the best in this type of work.[42] Still others cared for children, mostly for other working mothers. Earning in this manner was convenient for those who still had young children or who were already caring for their grandchildren. Many were cleaning women. A few worked full-time, but most went out two or three times a week and at holiday seasons. Pay for cleaning women in Munich in 1910 averaged between 2 M. and 2.50 M. per day depending on whether food was included.[43]

Few of the mothers who worked in factories had pleasant jobs. They worked in tanneries, fur factories, rag works, and brush factories where conditions were smelly and dirty. All were reentry after considerable lay-off. They took work that younger women rejected. "That is only work for old women, no young women would do such work."[44] Only two of the mothers had well-paying factory jobs. One earned 1,000 M. a year running a machine in a saw mill. The woman was fifty years old with twelve children. The other, a tobacco worker, earned 1,400 M. As a child she had worked at home making cigars with her parents. She had gone into the factory after leaving school and had stayed on after marriage to compensate for her "work shy" husband. She eagerly looked forward to better times now that her daughter was working.[45]

From these illustrations, it can be determined that "what was enough" was a highly relative measure. Yet perception of sufficiency was obvious in the decisions for women to work, even more obvious for mothers than daughters. Children's contributions were expected and counted on. Wives, especially mothers, sought employment when there was no other way, and even then the way chosen avoided the factory if possible. It is clear that enough was not extra, but survival.

Daily existence in households where women worked was defined principally in terms of physical labor and material needs, the time and energy required to satisfy the basic requirements for food, clothing, and housing. Women took for granted the burden of housework. They were responsible for the daily routine tasks that kept the household going. Before the war, neither technology nor the consumer economy had penetrated worker households to have any significant ameliorative effect on getting jobs done. Food preparation, cleaning, laundry, mending, and repairs were handled by women. However, fragments emerge from the literature on working-class life that suggest some space in the brutality of everyday existence. One point deals with assumptions about standards of cleanliness and the amount of time devoted to chores. Housework was not the full-time occupation or romanticized preoccupation that it was in bourgeois households where women glorified domesticity. A two-room tenement could hardly be transformed into a monument to purity and tranquility. Tasks may have been ever-present, but one does not sense the relentless pressure for perfection that threads bourgeois prescriptions about the salutary home. Housework resisted conversion into an ideology simply because working women did not have the time or the means to make it more than it was.

Another focus was the social dimension of housework. Neighbors literally bumped into one another drawing water, hanging wash, buying food, using public facilities. Manual labor, having to fetch and carry, put women in touch with one another. Women saw each other frequently and the daily contact both in wage work and housework formed ties that connected women to one another. Within the household, mothers and daughters worked together to do physical labor and to care for younger children. It was a gender and generational link that gave housework a social context and transmitted domestic "skills." Daughters, even full-time factory girls, were socialized to women's work at an early age. Daughters were not asked to help; they were an integral part of the distribution of work in the home. It was expected. Housework was dirty, tiring, and constant, but from necessity, paring it down to essentials and sharing it with others may have made it less onerous.

Expenditures for housing and food formed the major portion of worker budgets. Because little could be done to alter rent costs, food consumption was adjusted to match available funds. Variety was minimal. Fruits and green vegetables were rarely eaten and rarely missed. The bulk of diets consisted of potatoes and bread. Meat was highly prized. It was the best indicator of how well or how poorly a family was doing. Rabbit meat was common. Many workers in rural areas kept a hutch for their own use or sold the animals in the market to shops and in street stalls. In cities, the *Freibank* was a shop that sold inferior cuts and poor-quality meats at lower than market prices. Local butchers sold scraps, and on Fridays, pails of broth in which the shop's sausages were cooked were available if "customers" were quick enough to get there first. Meat usually appeared on worker tables only on Sundays, and then rarely in the form of roast. What little was purchased was made into soup to extend the meager ration.[46]

Custom dictated that the mid-day meal was eaten at home. Many families maintained this schedule even when the wife worked outside the home, providing the factory or workplace was close enough to make commuting feasible. Maintaining this custom was one of the objectives behind the state inquiry into women's work schedules at the turn

of the century. The Reichstag was willing to make a one-and-a-half-
to two-hour break mandatory in order to allow women workers time
to prepare meals. Women rejected this plan. For those who lived close
by, the extra time was not needed, and for those who commuted, the
extra time was useless. Distance from work, not work itself, was the
deciding factor in determining when the main meal was taken.

Various arrangements could be made for the mid-day meal if it was
eaten at the factory. Most frequently, food was taken from home. Not
many workers, men or women, purchased food in public facilities, because cost was prohibitive. Some firms provided food at reduced cost
for their workers. In one Berlin paper factory, workers could purchase
a glass of beer for 10 pf, pickled herring for 10 pf, a boiled egg for 5
pf, and a roll with butter for 5 pf.[47] In other factories where there was
an available heat source, employers allowed workers to use gas jets to
warm coffee and food brought from home. Women also used the heat
from their machines to get a warm meal at mid-day. Separate areas for
eating in factories were unusual. Most workers ate at their machines
or, when the weather was warm, went outdoors.[48] Second breakfast
and vespers break in late afternoon were always taken in the factory.
Again, usually bread was brought from home; employers often fur-
nished coffee or beer at reduced cost. Women who were employed in
sewing rooms and girls in training often got second breakfast and vespers free as part of their total earnings.[49]

A comparison of the weekly menus from two households, both of
which had daughters at work, points up the vast difference in consumption patterns in worker families.[50] One family consisted of ten
persons. The father was an independent printer. Earnings were irregular, but substantial when there was work—about 50 M. a week. There
were savings of 3,000 M., from which the printer withdrew 85 M.
quarterly for the upkeep of his shop. A grown son worked with him.
Both daughters, sixteen and fifteen years old, did sewing, from which
they gave their total earnings of 8.40 M. to the family. The mother
did not work. The family lived in two rooms attached to the shop. The
following was their weekly menu:

The main meal was eaten at mid-day. Breakfast was the same every day: coffee and bread. On Monday: soup with meat, noodles, coffee; in the evening:
wurst, bread, and tea. Tuesday: soup with one pound cooked beef, potatoes,
coffee; evening: cream cheese, bread, and tea. Wednesday: gruel, noodles,

cucumbers, coffee; evening: wurst, bread, and tea. Thursday: soup with meat, cabbage, coffee; evening: cheese, bread, tea. Friday: gruel, noodles, coffee; evening: wurst, bread, tea. Saturday: soup, 1 pound cooked beef, potato salad, coffee; evening: cheese, bread, tea. Sunday: soup with meat, salad, coffee; evening: wurst, bread, tea.

There was no man in the second household. A widow earned 13 to 15 M. weekly sewing curtains at home. A fifteen-year-old daughter also sewed. There was a boy of ten who was still in school. They lived in one room with a kitchen.

First and second breakfast was the same every day: tea without milk, occasionally one or two hot cakes. Monday: soup, meat from the *Freibank*, potatoes, tea; evening: soup and potatoes. Tuesday: wurst and bread; evening: leftovers. Wednesday: milk soup, sauerkraut; evening: soup and potatoes. Thursday: macaroni, bread, soup and wurst in the evening. Friday: cooked meat from the *Freibank*, noodles, bread and tea in the evening. Saturday: noodles and sauerkraut, bread and tea. Sunday: cooked meat and bread; left-overs in the evening.

The limitations of such diets were even further constricted for the women and children in the family. Husbands got first preference. If there was meat available, even meat from soups, men ate. Grown sons also shared more generously in portions and priority. Grown daughters, if they worked, got more than unemployed mothers and small children.[51] Clearly this pattern of preference was the result of both gender and economy in the family. Based solely on economic contribution, working daughters should have been more amply compensated, but boys followed fathers in the hierarchy regardless of how much of their earnings was available to the common household. Food was not merely the reward for monetary contribution, but also represented a complex of tradition and custom that signified disparity in value among members of the family.

Housing in Germany for worker families in the pre-war period could hardly qualify as satisfactory or even adequate. Rents were high and consumed a large portion of annual outlay. Conditions in cities in terms of space and comfort were worse than in rural areas, where at least there was the possibility of occupying a separate dwelling. Company housing for workers was generally available only in places where heavy industry predominated, such as in the Ruhr. Providing workers with a place to live was planned into the economic and social benefits owners expected as return on investment. In 1889, for example, the Bochumer Verein built 1,045 units which housed almost all of its 6,400 workers; there was also a company store and a day nursery.[52] Company housing was used to impart a sense of community as well as to assure a stable, loyal labor force. There were real advantages to workers who got these accommodations. Company houses were cheaper and better maintained than private or public housing, but there was a price to pay. A "good" worker, one who didn't walk off the job or protest, was made aware "when he read his rent contract that his job and his home were not separate and independent of each other."[53] The pattern was similar in Mannheim, where skilled workers in machine and chemical factories quite commonly received free housing as part of their wage package.[54]

For less-privileged workers, housing was persistently dreary and a major uncertainty. Adjustment in housing accommodations was usually downward. More persons in the household—children, relatives, or boarders—seldom prompted a search for more-spacious quarters. Most worker families occupied one or two rooms regardless of numbers living in the household. Very rarely was heat available in every room. Separate areas or rooms for kitchen and toilet facilities were precious and expensive. Cooking, eating, sleeping, and washing were accomplished where necessity dictated. Conditions for home workers were considerably worse since, in addition to the normal routines of life, work had to be done in the same place. Rooms were crowded with people and things because size was small and occupants had to provide for sleeping and eating arrangements in cramped spaces. Sleep rooms were frequently wall-to-wall beds which were shared among family members. Just as there was a hierarchy of distribution for food, fathers were allowed the best accommodations. If possible the men of the household slept alone, leaving mothers to share space with children and boarders.[55] Not all sleep space could properly be called a bed. Sofas, settees, and cots served. Small children slept in carriages and baskets.

Rarely were there indications of improvement in housing conditions. Rather, reports were a litany of shortage and expense. Sanitation was minimal, particularly in old sections of cities. City inspectors noted that in east Munich most workers' quarters were in houses built in the previous century. *Mietkasernen*, tenements, were four and five stories high, containing numerous two-room "apartments." Narrow court-yards were used for hanging wash and airing children. Rooms lacked indoor water and toilet facilities. Water pumps as well as toilets were located in the streets and shared with others. In east Munich, one could purchase a toilet key for about 30 pf. a month.[56] In other sections of the city, toilet access cost about 6 M. a year. Toilet stalls were dark and cramped and city magistrates complained about odors. Even in newly built housing complexes for workers, toilet facilities were shared. It was quite common for four apartments to use one facility.[57]

Despite a low level of personal hygiene, workers cared about their appearance. Regardless of how poorly situated a family was, there was a clear distinction made between work clothes and Sunday dress. Some persons who could afford extra preferred to wear different clothes going back and forth to work from those worn at the work place. Because most factories did not provide dressing rooms, the change was often no more than an outer garment that was considered appropriate for travel.[58] During the week, factory girls wore such similar clothing that dress approximated a uniform, but on Sundays, hats, gloves, even colorful parasols were on display for the weekly stroll (*Spazierenge-hen*). Minna Wettstein, who lived and worked with factory girls in Chemnitz for several months, observed that her companions would go without meat or some other prized food during the week in order to save toward a Sunday dress.[59] While clothes did not have to be new, they did have to be different from what was worn during the week. Clothes were often purchased second-hand. One worker in Leipzig made a clear distinction between his Sunday hat and his "old" hat, even though both were used clothing.[60] Purchasing clothing second-hand was sometimes the only way to get something to wear.

Women who were handy could stretch the family's clothing budget as well as provide extra items of better quality. Women who could sew, knit, or crochet helped a good deal in easing expenditures. Socks were the most common items of homemade clothing. Both wool and cotton yarn could be purchased at considerable savings over ready-made. Girls and women who worked in clothing were often better dressed than factory girls. In addition to being able to make their own clothes, they often received fabrics and other goods as wage supplements which were utilized either for themselves or for other members of the family. Making clothing at home was limited for other kinds of workers be-cause hand-sewing was time consuming, and it was unlikely that a factory worker would be able to purchase a sewing machine for other than production purposes.

Clothes were important to workers. Women were much more sensitive about how they looked than men. Dressing up on Sunday was significant enough to scrimp on other things. Wettstein accused her worker companions of parading around like middle-class ladies on Sundays.[61] But mimicking their "betters" was a shallow explanation for workers' concern for appearance. Wearing a hat on Sunday had more significance than costuming. A young textile worker in München-Gladbach remarked that her landlady rented her a room only after she promised never to emerge from the house without a hat "like a common factory girl."[62] Clothes were not flamboyant display, but rather were symbolic of pride and dignity and public affirmation of personal worth. They also marked a distinction between time spent at work and private time. Both men and women workers wore their separation from the factory with a sense of freedom and control.

Considering the economic restrictions obvious in worker families, it is easy to conclude that their lives were monotonously dull and joyless. But expectations were limited. Comfort was sought in small things: getting the rooms clean, walking outdoors on Sunday, buying a new blouse, going to a dance. Aspirations were narrow; eating well, dressing better, and enjoying a little free time for recreation seemed enough to satisfy. Curiously, there was an absence of anger or resentment. Wishes and hopes were muted. There was a kind of patience that signified a resigned acceptance of the realities of their lives.

I go to my work every day since I left school. I must also help at home because we have many brothers and sisters. My work is no longer difficult because I am used to it. I have been employed in a laundry for three years. I started as a machine girl, but for the last half year I have been pressing. It pleases me that every day I am getting better at my work. If I can learn pressing well, then I could look forward to having a pleasant life, although I can't really think about this now because I have to get better at my work in order to save.[63]

Married working women did not even have the luxury of speculation. Their lives were confined by work and limited by household responsibilities. Saturday afternoons were taken up with cleaning and shopping. One of the real advantages of earlier dismissal on Saturdays and holidays was to allow women time to get to the shops before everything was sold out. Sundays were cleaning days. Chores that could not be done during the week, such as washing and ironing as well as the perpetual knitting, were accomplished on the weekend. Married women stated that their best form of recreation was rest.[64]

Rest was not enough for young people. Because most single girls lived with their families, what they did for entertainment was limited by demands on their time for helping out at home. Sunday was important because it was the only day when recreation and socializing could be enjoyed. The delight of leisure on Sunday was especially anticipated by young working girls, because it was also the only day their families allowed them free time. Money was obviously tight, but it was understood that the few *Pfennigs Taschengeld* they received on the weekend could be spent for their own use. The most popular form of diversion for all workers, young and old alike, was walking.[65] Youngsters joined their friends in the streets and parks or in near-by woods. *Pfennigs* could be spent for a treat along the way. More than a form of exercise, walking allowed young people freedom and privacy from parents where social contacts could be made.[66]

Dancing was popular, but opportunities were limited and costly. At carnival time, many small towns and villages held open dancing. Also at carnival, trade unions held parties where dancing and beer drinking were generously available. Young girls, however, did not attend union functions alone, but were usually accompanied by fathers and brothers who were members.[67] Dance halls were found in most large cities, but there were clear social distinctions among the halls according to price and clientele.

An excellent description of the dance halls in Chemnitz was given by Wettstein, who apparently investigated such places with as much diligence and energy as she devoted to other aspects of her study of factory girls. The most notorious of the dance halls in Chemnitz was the *Kaiserkrone*, which Wettstein described as bestial.[68] The clientele was mostly domestic servant girls and prostitutes who solicited the soldier trade from the Chemnitz barracks. Wettstein related that her companions in the factory stayed away from the *Kaiserkrone* because "no decent girl would go there."[69] In contrast to the *Kaiserkrone*, Wettstein found the *Linde* orderly and the clientele clean and mannerly. This dance hall was frequented mostly by factory men and women. Contacts were easy and expected. Conversation and flirtation could be had for a glass of beer. The hall charged admission as well as an additional fee for each dance. Business was brisk on Sunday evenings.

Level of prosperity in working-class families was linked to the income provided by the head of the household. When that was insufficient or when women were on their own, consumption was adjusted and a variety of earnings strategies were tried. The margin of economic safety was narrow, but because women worked, both as wives and daughters, families coped. Poverty was a relative condition, but subsistence was not. It is important to recognize that the episode of the weaver and his family who were forced to eat cats took place in 1913 in a country that had achieved the pinnacle of industrial development. For many families, grappling with this kind of scarcity was the harsh reality, but the psychic cost of deprivation should be judged in terms of expectations. Distribution of goods and services within families confirms a condition of limited resources and limited aspirations. Getting ahead was not an expressed goal because most multiple-earner families had to struggle just to avert deepening poverty. Dealing with material insecurities dominated their existence and formed the dynamic around which they organized their lives.

NOTES

1. Helene Brandenburg, "Textilarbeiterelend," *Die Gleichheit*, 23 Jahrgang, Nr. 8 (January 8, 1913), p. 117.
2. Marie Bernays, "Auslese und Anpassung der Arbeiterschaft der geschlossenen Grossindustrie an den Verhältnissen der Gladbacher Spinnerei und Weberei," *Schriften des Vereins für Sozialpolitik*, Vol. 133 (Leipzig: Verlag von Duncker und Humblot, 1910), p. 247.
3. "Teure Zeiten," *Die Gleichheit*, 23 Jahrgang, Nr. 17 (May 14, 1913), p. 262.
4. F. Tägtmeyer, "Kosten der Lebenshaltung in Stuttgart, 1890–1912," *Schriften des Vereins für Sozialpolitik*, Vol. 145 (1914), p. 403.
5. Gustav Brutzer, "Die Verteuerung der Lebensmittel in Berlin im Laufe der letzten 30 Jahre," *Schriften des Vereins für Sozialpolitik*, Vol. 138 (1912), p. 67.
6. Ibid., p. 54.
7. Ibid., p. 70.
8. Tägtmeyer, "Die Entwicklung der Lebensmittelpreise in der Stadt Leipzig," *Schriften des Vereins für Sozialpolitik*, Vol. 145 (1914), p. 236.
9. Ibid., p. 259.

122   *At the Very Least She Pays the Rent*

10. Ibid., p. 254.
11. Tägtmeyer, "Stuttgart," p. 409.
12. Carl von Tyszka, "Lebenskosten deutscher und westeuropäscher Arbeiter früher und jetzt," *Schriften des Vereins für Sozialpolitik*, Vol. 145 (1914), p. 287.
13. "Teuerung und Haushalts-Statistiken," *Tabak-Arbeiter*, Nr. 30 (July 28, 1907).
14. Ibid.
15. *Amtliche Mittheilungen. Jahresberichte der Gewerbeaufsichtsbeamten und Bergbehörden*, Reichsministerium des Innern, Band II (1899), p. 103.
16. Ibid., p. 819.
17. Ibid., p. 1001.
18. C. Moszeik, *Aus der Gedankenwelt einer Arbeiterfrau von ihr selbst erzählt* (Berlin: Verlag Edwin Runge in Lichterfelde, 1909), p. 57.
19. *Amtliche Mittheilungen*, Band II (1899), p. 1001.
20. Ibid., Band IV (1899), p. 792.
21. Martin Kitchen, *The Political Economy of Germany 1815–1914* (Montreal: McGill-Queen's University Press, 1978), p. 177.
22. Richard Klucsarits and Friedrich Kürbisch, eds., *Arbeiterinnen Kämpfen um ihr Recht* (Wuppertal: Peter Hammer Verlag, 1975), pp. 137–38.
23. *Amtliche Mittheilungen*, Band II (1899), p. 129.
24. Ibid., p. 47.
25. Ibid., Band I (1899), pp. 76–77.
26. Paul Göhre, *Three Months in a Workshop* (London: Swan Sonnenschein and Co., 1895), p. 116.
27. F. Wörishoffer, *Die sociale Lage der Fabrikarbeiter in Mannheim und dessen nächster Umgebund* (Karlsruhe: Druck und Verlag von Ferd. Thiergarten, 1891), p. 74.
28. These were high wages for the 1890's, available mostly in heavy industry.
29. Wörishoffer, *Fabrikarbeiter in Mannheim*, pp. 104–5.
30. Ibid., pp. 182–83.
31. Ibid., pp. 194–95.
32. Ibid., pp. 182–83.
33. Ibid., pp. 192–93.
34. Two hundred eighty-seven wives out of 1,153 worked.
35. Dora Landé, "Arbeits- und Lohnverhältnisse in der Berliner Maschinenindustrie," *Schriften des Vereins für Sozialpolitik*, Vol. 134 (1910), p. 443.
36. Ibid., p. 448.
37. Ibid.
38. Rosa Kempf, "Das Leben der jungen Fabrikmädchen in München,"

Schriften des Vereins für Sozialpolitik, Vol. 135 (Leipzig: Verlag von Duncker und Humblot, 1911), p. 4.

39. Ibid., p. 123.
40. Ibid., pp. 124–25.
41. Ibid., p. 39.
42. Ibid.
43. Ibid., p. 38.
44. Ibid., p. 40.
45. Ibid., p. 41.
46. Elisabeth Hell, *Jugendliche Schneiderinnen und Näherinnen in München* (Stuttgart: J. G. Cotta'sche Buchhandlung, 1911), p. 118.
47. Elizabeth Gnauck-Kühne, "Die Lage der Arbeiterinnen in der Berliner Papierwaren Industrie," *Schmollers Jahrbuch*, Vol. 20 (1896), p. 81.
48. H. Mehner, "Der Haushalt und die Lebenshaltung einer leipziger Arbeiterfamilie," *Schmollers Jahrbuch*, Vol. 11 (1887), p. 307.
49. Hell, *Jugendliche*, p. 85.
50. Ibid., p. 121.
51. Kempf, "Das Leben der jungen," p. 152.
52. David Crew, *Town in the Ruhr: A Social History of Bochum, 1860–1914* (New York: Columbia University Press, 1979), p. 148.
53. Ibid., p. 151.
54. Wörishoffer, *Fabrikarbeiter in Mannheim*, pp. 178–83.
55. Kempf, "Das Leben der jungen," p. 118.
56. Hell, *Jugendliche*, p. 113.
57. Landé, "Arbeits- und Lohnverhältnisse," p. 438.
58. Mehner, "Der Haushalt und die Lebenshaltung," p. 314.
59. Minna Adelt Wettstein, *3 1/2 Monate Fabrikarbeiterin* (Berlin: Verlag von J. Leiser, 1893), p. 15.
60. Mehner, "Der Haushalt und die Lebenshaltung," p. 315.
61. Wettstein, *3 1/2 Monate*, p. 15.
62. Bernays, "Auslese und Anpassung," p. 227.
63. Kempf, "Das Leben der jungen," p. 201.
64. Hell, *Jugendliche*, p. 171.
65. Bernays, "Auslese und Anpassung," p. 238.
66. Ibid.
67. Hell, *Jugendliche*, p. 170.
68. Wettstein, *3 1/2 Monate*, p. 82.
69. Ibid.

6

Women Home Workers

"the wife belongs at home"*

In Breslau, a mother and her sixteen-year-old daughter worked together sewing petticoats by hand. They earned 11.50 M. a week, but
the work was not steady. A widow who made wicker plaits for straw
hats was paid 50 pf. per 100 meters of plaiting. She worked for the
same firm in Breslau for ten or eleven years. The work season lasted
five months. There were three adults in the household. They lived in
two rooms, one of which was used as the kitchen. In Dorf Niedern-
berg, a nineteen-year-old single girl rented sleeping space from a farm
family. She worked alone sewing vests. In season she worked eleven
hours a day and earned about 13 M. a week. In summer she did agricultural work with the family.[1]

These women and members of their families were employed in German domestic industry. The description of the conditions of their work
experience was recorded in the first decade of the twentieth century.
Factories, which took an increasingly larger share of the production
process, did not squeeze home industry out of existence. Surprisingly,
domestic production survived and in some instances actually thrived.
It was women who made most use of its persistence. Industrial home

*Erhard Schmidt, *Fabrikbetrieb und Heimarbeit in der deutschen Konfektionsindustrie*
(Stuttgart: Verlag von Ferdinand Enke, 1912), p. 160.

work provided an acceptable alternative to factory employment and a supplemental increment to agricultural earnings. The balance and fluidity that persisted between factory and home work preserved women's notions that work, while necessary, could be adjusted and incorporated with the responsibilities of being a wife and mother. The ease with which women could combine a job with domestic duties may have been more important in determining whether they worked than the availability of work or the wages it paid.[2]

However, the idea that women were free to choose their jobs and to regulate the conditions of their work is too idealized a version of domestic industry. Most women worked for reasons of deep economic need, the conditions of their work lives were desperate and confining, and the possibilities for exploitation, including self-exploitation, were ever-present. For women who had to work to live, decorating industrial home work with nostalgic visions of the family workshop is largely historical fiction. Sweatshops and putting-out were sustained in the capitalist economy only because of the extreme hardship produced by inequities in the system itself. The degree of occupational choice women had must be analyzed within the structural margins of their employment options.

Part of the answer to the continuing viability of domestic industry lay in the material advantages it held for the employer. While regulations regarding conditions of employment had been spelled out for factory work in the 1890's, home industry remained virtually beyond the constraints and protections mandated by law into the twentieth century. Compliance with factory regulations for prescribed work space and for hygienic standards including separate work rooms and toilet facilities added to production costs. The many provisions regarding women in factories, particularly the maximum daily work time, cut into the amount of production the employer could expect from a traditionally cheap source of labor. The exclusion of children from factories in 1891 also cut into the profit margin. Children worked even more cheaply than women. Where the directives of the worker-protection laws could be circumvented, employers did so, and home work was an alternate choice.

In addition to the advantages employers sought from the unprotected status of home work, the tasks in some industries were extremely well suited to domestic production, thereby eliminating the cost of maintaining the physical plant. Where production depended more on hand work than on machine, and where decentralization of the work process was more efficient and cheaper than factory concentration, employers preferred home work. Industries that experienced seasonal fluctuation were heavily home work. From the employers' point of view, it was uneconomic to maintain the cost of a work room or factory during the slack period.

Using home workers also freed the employer from having to deal with the trade unions. The Union of German Women Home Workers concluded its first wage settlement with two firms in Kassel in 1905, followed by an agreement in 1906 with two firms in the umbrella industry in Königsberg. These agreements were significant because they were exceptional.[3] Domestic workers were notoriously difficult to organize, a situation the trade unions deplored. But for the employers, the absence of worker organizations virtually assured them unlimited access to an unprotected labor force. As long as home work filled a need in German industry, employers continued to utilize this form of manufacture parallel to or in place of factory production.

While home industry retained a considerable share of the production process for Germany well into the twentieth century, it had always been recognized that home workers were elusive. Domestic industrial workers had always been counted in the national censuses, but they had not been counted accurately. The problem of identifying and recording the extent of home work was complicated both by the mechanics of the German census and by the home workers themselves, either inadvertently or with the full intention of escaping notice. Recognizing this problem is necessary in order to understand that numerical data underrepresents domestic industry.[4]

Of more crucial importance is the "loss" of home workers due to the essential character of domestic production. Examination of these factors will point up the rhythm of home work that made this form of production a kind of escape valve and, in some instances, almost an underground economy. It was inherent in the annual pattern of home work for many workers to go uncounted. The time of year the census was taken contributed in part to the confusion. For a large number of home workers, notably those employed in non-urban areas, domestic industry was a part-time occupation, most usually coupled with agriculture. Since the census was taken in June, there probably was some confusion regarding the identification of major occupation. Mitigating against this situation, however, was the circumstance that individuals were instructed to disregard momentary employment if it differed from the major occupation. Most persons tended to claim industrial rather than agricultural work as the major occupation.[5]

What effect these preferences had on the outcome of the counting is difficult to determine, particularly where women were concerned because many were only part-time family help to begin with. The *Statistik des Deutschen Reichs* noted that even where a man or woman was employed full-time in home work, family helpers probably were not registered.[6] Most likely to be missed were women. The unreliability of numerical data is disappointing. However, it was this very lack of preciseness that reflected most clearly the life style of large numbers of persons, approximately half of whom were women, who moved relatively freely on the edges of more visible and more structured employment.

A tobacco worker from Bremen, Herr Deichmann, reported to the Home Workers' Congress in 1904 that in his perception there were many more persons working in tobacco manufacture at home than the statistics indicated. He suggested this was partly due to the employers' ignorance of the actual number of workers they employed. More importantly, Deichmann believed employers deliberately reported false figures to avoid the mandatory matching payments for workers' insurance. Most likely to go unreported were women—they could be hidden most easily. Employers just neglected to count family members.[7] In many cases it was the workers themselves who intentionally concealed home employment. This was especially true in large cities where the *Hausarbeit* of wives and daughters was deliberately hidden to avoid paying taxes.[8] In addressing this problem of under-representation, the *Statistik des Deutschen Reichs*, which was responsible for the official count, stated that most probably large numbers of persons employed in home work were never identified.[9]

Domestic industry declined in the late nineteenth and early twentieth centuries. The decline was steady and theoretically represented the transfer of production from a predominantly pre-industrial to industrial pattern, that is, from home to factory. In 1882 the number of persons employed in domestic industry was 476,080; in 1895, 457,984; and in 1907, 405,262.[10] Textiles were especially hard hit. According to the *Statistik des Deutschen Reichs* there were 285,102 persons employed in domestic production in the various branches of textile manufacture in 1882. By 1907 that number had diminished to 138,281, a reduction of more than one-half. Expressed in percent—for every 100 persons employed in textiles in 1882, 31.3 were employed in home industry; in 1895, 19.7; and in 1907, 12.7.[11] Home weaving accounted for approximately one-third of the reduction.

Faced with figures like these, it is difficult, at least at first investigation, to contend that *Hausarbeit* persisted as a viable work form. However, these data represent the total picture, and the totals do not tell the same story for men and women. If it is assumed that men and women left textile home industry to work in textile factories, men did so at a much faster and more intense rate than women. There were 182,365 men employed in textile home work in 1882. In 1907, only 56,438 remained, a startling reduction. A very different picture emerges for women. As previously noted, those branches of the textile industry that experienced severe loss of persons employed were concentrated in weaving, and weaving as a home industry was traditionally male-intensive.[12] From a situation where men predominated in home industry in 1882, textiles showed a significant reversal in the gender composition of employment. In 1907 women dominated both numerically and in percentage of the total.[13]

While it is easy to assume a transfer from home work to factory work as was suggested earlier, there is evidence that this contention is not completely true, and is much less true for women. Industries that had traditionally employed large numbers of home workers, old home industry, declined. These industries were mostly textile related and situated in non-urban locations. However, concentration on one, even a very large branch of home industry is misleading. An important exception to the decline in rural home industry was tobacco—cigar and cigarette manufacture. Because of the coincidence of geographic location between textiles and tobacco, many persons left the declining textile industry to take up domestic production in tobacco.[14] Urban home industry expanded, particularly the various branches of clothing manufacture.

The number of persons working in home industry, excluding textiles, increased, and the increase reflected a pattern of adjustment that included both geographic mobility and mobility from one kind of industry to another. Data show that every branch of home industry except textiles experienced an increase in employment. Where gains were indicated, the increase for women was considerably more significant than for men. Industries that were male-intensive showed rather strong percentage increase for women, and industries that had been female-intensive became even more so. Gender reversal occurred in home work in virtually every industry branch, resulting in an increasingly feminized production sector. By the end of the nineteenth century, domestic industry became the domain of women.[15]

Industrial and geographic patterns of domestic industry support the contention that there was ample work for women to do at home. What is significant about German home industry is that it was specialized and localized, similar to the profile for factory work. Areas where industry employed large numbers of women in factories continued to be strong in home work. Women in large cities, where there was little factory employment to absorb available female labor, found places in urban home industry. By 1900 more than one-fourth of Germany's domestic industry was located in large cities, that is, cities with population over 100,000.[16] Twenty-nine percent of the persons employed in domestic production were employed in urban areas in the first decade of the twentieth century. Female home work was even more intensive than the general figures indicate. Of men employed, 23.7% were in large cities, while 32.7% of the female workers were employed in urban domestic industry.

More than one-third of urban domestic industry was concentrated in Berlin.[17] The clothing industry accounted for this concentration, and clothing home industry was female-intensive. Forty-three percent of all urban home industry and 47% of all persons employed in cities were located in Berlin; 48,402 were engaged in clothing manufacture. Breslau followed, with 7,336 establishments and 10,612 persons employed, 80% of whom were women working in the clothing trades. Clothing manufacture and finishing accounted for 74% of all domestic industry in large cities.[18]

Urban centers did not offer women much in the way of industrial employment if factory work alone is considered, but home work provided an opportunity for earning where agriculture and service by either choice or location did not. Factories that were located in cities usually belonged to industrial branches that were heavily male-intensive.[19] In addition, in cities that were centers of heavy industry such as Dortmund, Bochum, Duisberg, and Essen, home workers were scarcely employed.[20] Part of the reason was related to the kinds of jobs avail-

able, and part because wages in heavy industry by the twentieth century were sufficient in most cases for worker families to exist on a single, male, income.

In regions where consumer goods industries prevailed, wages did not
keep pace with the more lucrative jobs in heavy industry. By the turn
of the century, a shift from textiles to metals and machines caused the
eclipse of Saxony as Germany's principal industrial region. It is not
coincidental that 29% of all persons employed in home industry in 1907
were in Saxony. Even more revealing was the pattern of employment
by gender. In Saxony almost 70% of the domestic labor force was female.[21] Men more readily entered factories as textiles mechanized. It
is a major contention of this discussion that the number of women employed in home work was a sensitive indicator of local and regional
prosperity. Where there was ample, steady employment for men, women
did not do industrial work. Increasing living costs coupled with diminishing opportunities for male employment had to be met by women's
work.

Lack of precise figures complicates the problem of arriving at a definite picture of marital status and age category for women working at
home. While married women made up 21% of the total female industrial labor force including both factory and home work in 1907, married women, widows, and separated women made up about half the
number working at home. Because there are fairly accurate figures only
for those women listed as independent home workers, and because only
half the number of women home workers in 1907 listed themselves as
independent, there is a problem in trying to draw conclusions about
the rest. Working family members, as previously noted, eluded the
statistics.

In 1907, 60% of all married women in industry were working as
helpers. Most of these were concentrated in four industry branches—
textiles, foods and tobacco, wood products, and clothing. Seventy-three
percent of all married working women were employed in these four
industries, and industries that had large numbers of family members
assisting were also heavily home work. It can be concluded from these
data that at least half the women working at home were married.[22] The
1895 census indicated that 48% of women over sixteen years old working
at home were married, separated, or widowed.[23] A similar conclusion
can be drawn from a survey of women home workers conducted by
the *Christlicher Gewerkverein der Heimarbeiterinnen Deutschlands*

(Christian Union of Women Home Workers), published in 1906. Most of the women reporting worked in textiles and clothing. Of the 267 women questioned, 56% were married, 24% single, and 19% widowed or separated. The average age of the women taken together was 38.[24]

More definite information regarding marital status and age was available for women listing themselves as independent home workers.[25] More than half the women were married or formerly married in 1907. Forty-two percent were single. While the number and percentage of independent women home workers who were widowed remained constant between 1895 and 1907, there were significant changes in the composition of the work force between single and married women. A decrease in the number of single women was paralleled by an increase in the number of married women working at home. Expressed in percent, in 1895, 53% were single; in 1907, 42%. Age categories for both single and married women remained about the same for both years. While these data may indicate a slightly increased tendency to marry earlier, most probably they reflect the increasing availability of factory work. Young women without family responsibilities could more readily take factory employment. For married women factory work was not so easily handled, and many preferred to remain at home.

Even women who had worked in factories chose to remain at home after marriage when that was possible. Of 1,347 women questioned by the *Gewerkverein der Heimarbeiterinnen* concerning the reason for their employment in domestic industry, 45% reported that the demands of child care necessitated their being at home.[26] This same investigation reported that the number of women in factory work after the birth of a child fell off sharply, while the number of women in home work remained fairly stable with one child and more. The overwhelming reason women chose home work instead of factory work if both were available was intimately related to their family responsibilities.

While it can be estimated that about half the female domestic workers were single, to assume independent living arrangements would be incorrect. The economics of managing rent, food, and clothing on the wages of a home worker virtually demanded participation in a household or family. Wages differed widely by industry and area, yet only rarely was a single wage enough to provide self-support. Sleep rooms, *Schlafstellen*, the cheapest quarters available, were just what the name described—places to sleep, shared rooms, rented beds, shared beds—

not places where home work could be carried out. In Berlin, it was scarcely possible to secure living quarters, one room with some kind of arrangement for cooking, for less than 200 M. a year. An annual income of 600 M. was the barest minimum necessary for a woman providing all costs of living herself. Average annual wages for women in Berlin home industry were closer to 500 M. a year in the mid–1890's.[27] For women trying to earn a living alone by home work in urban areas, the aphorism that they made too little to live and too much to die seemed particularly true.

It was the rhythm and place of work that made *Hausarbeit* acceptable as a form of industrial production for women. Home work cut the time and energy a woman could devote to household tasks, but the intrusion was perceived as less harsh than factory work. Home work was at once flexible and constricting. Because domestic industry generally was seasonal work, it could be combined with agricultural tasks, especially in rural areas. In cities, however, there were periods of unemployment and underemployment when *Pfennigs* had to be stretched over months of lay-off. The seasonal schedule also demanded short periods of rather intense energy when it was not unusual for work to continue for fourteen or fifteen hours a day, often without pause on the weekend. Because of constrictions on time management during season, home workers had to juggle a varied and tight schedule.

The irregularity of home work both allowed and demanded a flexibility in work schedule to take advantage of all chances to earn money. The concept of a one–wage-earner family, relying on a one-job wage is impossible to apply to German home workers in the late nineteenth and early twentieth centuries. Wages in home work were not geared for independence. Perception of an annual wage was difficult for most home workers. Pay was usually reckoned on price per piece, and the intensity of work was a personal thing. Most workers could respond to a question of piece work rates, but when it came to figuring weekly wages, it was not unusual to get approximations and averages. At best, yearly wages could only be estimated because of inconsistent work schedules and seasonal fluctuations. It is not surprising that figures for self-supporting home workers were sparse. Wage data were usually expressed as part of the family economy, testifying to the situation of most female home workers. Earnings of home workers overwhelmingly represented a share of the family wages, and home workers belonged to families that relied on numerous sources of income in order to get by.

In rural areas, domestic industry was usually combined with agriculture, with the husband, wife, and children alternating between farming in the summer and taking in industrial work during the winter months. Only an imprecise notion of primary occupation was possible with these families. Where the husband did not work at home, but in a factory or in construction, the wife and children supplemented the family wages with both home work and farming or gardening. In Baden, while domestic industry was not large, it was diversified and intimately related to agriculture. Rarely was home work the only source of income. Similar circumstances were true for parts of Württemberg. A factory inspector commented on the conditions of home work in his district:

The farming population does home work regularly only in the winter months, in the summer only rarely because all available workers are needed for farm work. Also many women prefer farm work in the summer because they can earn more than with corset sewing.[28]

In Baden, silk winding and wool spinning were jobs done only in the winter months. Women who did silk ribbon weaving worked an average of 200 days a year; chain makers working at home were employed for five months during the winter. Women who worked in the porcelain factory in Freiburg lived in the surrounding countryside; they made up the slack in factory work by sewing on the porcelain doll heads during the winter. This Freiburg factory employed over 1,300 women as home workers. Large numbers of agents went into the countryside to deliver and pick up the finished work. Straw hat workers were hired only in winter, but the brush industry, which employed all year, lost many of its female workers to agriculture in the summer. Brush manufacture in Baden was a revealing example of how an industry was forced to adapt to the pressure of a reluctant labor force. Women would not work in the factories, so plans for further expansion were scrapped in favor of enlarging the network of women working at home.[29]

From a survey taken at the turn of the century of 110 Baden home worker families, it can be determined that in every instance the wife contributed to the total earnings. Average yearly wages for heads of households, most of whom were home workers, was 1,054 M. Average supplement by wives was 233 M., also derived from domestic manufacture. The wife's contribution was necessary and recognized as an important share of the family income. The statement "she at the very least pays the rent"[30] was appropriate commentary on the value placed upon a wife's earning capacity. Costs for housing in Baden averaged about 200 M. a year. Home worker families supplemented both their earnings and their diet with produce from gardens and farms. If the family kept a pig, it could be either slaughtered or sold in the market. Well over half the families had meat at least two or three times a week. However, it was not unusual for families to get by on considerably less quantity and variety of food. Statements such as these were common: "Coffee is the mainstay of our meals"; "Meat does not even come to the table on Sunday."[31]

In cities, domestic industry was no more regular than in rural areas. The kinds of jobs available were seasonal, mostly clothing, and women did home work when men's wages were low or irregular. Women's and children's overcoats in Berlin, for example, offered full employment for eight months during the year; two months were slack and two months there was no work at all.[32] Work season for artificial flower-making in Berlin was eight months a year and for fine feather working six months. In season women worked ten hours a day. Sewing undergarments was generally steadier. Berlin operators usually worked all year averaging about 800 M. annual earnings.[33]

Where unemployment and underemployment brought the family income below subsistence level, home work was frequently the best way for women and children to help out. Men in construction work were especially caught in the bind of good wages during season and no wages or marginal income during the winter months. In Neustadt, a thirty-eight-year-old woman and four of her six children made artificial flowers with the help of her husband, a construction worker who was unemployed. Men very often pitched in to help with home work even if they were primarily employed elsewhere. The six persons working together were able to earn 10 M. 20 pf. for two weeks' work. However, wages were reduced to 4 and 5 M. in the off season.[34]

In another family where the father was employed only six months a year in construction, the wife and children also made artificial flowers. The woman had been a home worker for twelve years. With the help of her two oldest children and two other children whom she hired, the group made 6 M. a week for ten to twelve hours of work daily. The family paid 295 M. rent for a two-room apartment with a kitchen. All of the flower work was done in the kitchen as well as cooking, eating, and washing.[35] A Berlin home worker employed in the highly "style conscious" fine feather industry commented on the rhythm of her work experience:

My husband is a bricklayer and he earns an average of 30 M. weekly in the summer. We have four children from one to six years old and a mother to care for. We pay 270 M. yearly for the apartment which has two rooms and a kitchen. I work in the kitchen. I have worked six years for the same middle-man [*Zwischenmeister*] and earn 3 to 6 M. a week for six or seven hours daily when there is work. . . . There is full work for only four or five months a year. For the rest of the time, there is great difficulty.[36]

In industrial production, factory work blended with home work, creating certain economic options for working-class women. Factories were not alien to home workers. There were close links between home work and factory work that tended to integrate work patterns. Many large establishments maintained a putting-out system for jobs that could better and more cheaply be done at home. A kind of balance between factory and home work formed a line of communication that facilitated a relatively easy transition between the two work settings. More importantly, the work experience of many women included both factory and home production, representing a cycle of employment that paralleled the demands of their lives.

This transition was apparent in industry branches where home work was important. Until 1908, when the practice was forbidden by law, it was possible to take work from the factory to be finished at home. In this way the worker increased his or her earnings with overtime either alone or with the help of other family members. It is difficult to obtain accurate information regarding the number of persons who took work out. Employers were reluctant to divulge these figures to factory inspectors since the first study of the effects of the law took place three years after the prohibition. There are only scattered and conflicting responses concerning the restriction. In Bautzen, single women responded differently from married when questioned about their reactions. Married women welcomed the prohibition, stating that they were no longer under pressure to work at home and could devote more time to taking care of the house. Single women resisted, indicating that they could not understand why they were being prevented from earning a little extra.[37] Württemberg women working in textile and clothing factories reacted to what they claimed was an infringement on their personal freedom to work. They remarked that it was unfair not to be able to use Saturday afternoons and Sundays when the factories were closed to get additional money.[38]

Textiles maintained a fairly substantial putting-out system despite the increase in factory production. In Württemberg, the factory inspector reported that more and more linen cloth weaving was done in factories, but home work was still done by women and children.

The majority of the female home workers are wives and daughters of factory workers, home weavers, and small hand weavers. The young girls are employed for a time in one of the home work related factories and find that they are not suited to the regularity of factory work or for other personal reasons, go over to *Hausarbeit*.[39]

An industry where there were especially close ties between factory and home work was tobacco. Home workers were considered part of the factory establishment to the extent that employers usually did not even separate the two in their records. Where tobacco manufacture was situated in rural areas, factories were often too far to make travel reasonable. In Saxony, Leipzig was a center for tobacco products. To seek out sources of cheap labor, a system of small branch factories, really distribution centers, reached the home workers directly. Sorting was done in the main factory with only minimal manufacturing jobs retained there. In Saxony, the factory also served as the school for training women who took up similar jobs at home after marriage. In Westphalia, where about 26,000 persons were employed in the tobacco industry, training for work was accomplished in the factories, with most workers entering domestic manufacture as soon as they learned enough to do their jobs.[40]

Evidence of the common transition between factory and home work in tobacco was clearly present in comments of women who were questioned about the conditions of their work by the *Christlicher Gewerkverein der Heimarbeiterinnen*. An eighteen-year-old single girl reported that she went into the factory only when she wanted to earn more money. She made inexpensive cigars during the high season between November and February; the rest of the time she worked at home cutting tobacco. Another eighteen year old declared that she worked at home when she was overwhelmed with work at the factory. A twenty-nine-year-old married woman complained about dust in her apartment when she rolled cigarettes at home, indicating she preferred factory work but had to care for her children. Still another married woman, thirty-six, indicated she would return to the factory as soon as her child finished nursing. At the time of the interview, she had worked at home for four years.[41]

In clothing, technology feminized the home sewing industry and formed an important nexus between the capitalist economy and the private household.[42] Both the Singer machine, which was introduced in the 1840's in Berlin, and the Wilson could be purchased on time or rented for home use. By the first decade of the twentieth century, it was possible to purchase a machine for about 150 M., or on time for 1 to 2 M. weekly.[43] The sewing machine brought domestic clothing production up to speed in meeting the demands of an expanding consumer market for ready-made articles. Performed in the home, machine work allowed many women whose talent and dexterity might preclude earning a living by hand the capacity to turn out passable, uniform work.

In Berlin, married women in the clothing industry were the worst-paid home workers. Because they were part of a labor surplus and because their need to earn was a desperate one, they were actually captives in their own homes. Unskilled, turning out cheap articles in bulk, mothers and children sometimes could not earn enough for subsistence. They were at the mercy of their suppliers, the conditions of work were wretched, and the pace of production was frenzied in season. The sewing machine was by no means an instrument of emancipation, but it was a technological innovation that enabled women to remain at home to work.[44]

In clothing there were establishments intermediary to large factories and home work—work rooms, work places (*Werkstätten*), where numbers of women worked for hire for either a middleman or another sewer who had managed to accumulate sufficient savings to purchase machines. A breakdown by marital status for the Berlin clothing industry using a sample of 375 women employed in work rooms and home work revealed opposite concentrations for married and single women. Interestingly, there was no large difference in age. Average age for workroom women was thirty-two; for home workers, thirty-five.[45]

	Work Room Women		Home Workers	
Single	134	56.8%	35	25.3%
Widows	36	15.3%	25	18.1%
Separated	3	1.3%	1	.9%
Married	63	26.6%	77	55.7%
Totals	236		138	

In the choice between work within or outside the home, these work rooms did not seem any more attractive than factories. Most employees were young, unmarried girls who were ostensibly learning the trade; many times they did little more than domestic work for the mistress, such as cooking, cleaning, and running errands. Most of these girls left their apprentice positions and worked at home after marriage.

Work in clothing factories reduced most of the disagreeable features of domestic production: There were opportunities for better training; conditions were cleaner; seasonal fluctuations were less severe; wages were higher; and work time was more regular. Yet home industry expanded while in many instances machines in factories remained idle. Responses to the question of why women did not choose factory work when it alleviated the most negative features of home work ranged from necessity to propriety: "The wife belongs at home."[46] As was the case in the tobacco industry, many women learned the job in the factory or work room, then with marriage or the birth of the first child switched into home work. This cyclical pattern appeared frequently in reports of factory inspectors. In Oberamtsbezirk Baligen, the inspector described the usual cycle of employment in hosiery manufacture:

Most sewers become familiar with hosiery work at an early age. As school children and sometimes even earlier they must help at home, and after Confirmation, with few exceptions, they go to the hosiery factories. Usually when they go back to home work they perform similar jobs often for the same factory where they were employed. In many establishments, there still is a patriarchal relationship between the employer and his people, and the owners of the large factories know their home workers personally.[47]

The following biography clearly illustrates the mobility and flexibility characteristic of the work experience of many German women.[48] Domestic industry was usually part of the cycle. Ottilie Baader moved from Frankfurt to Berlin with her father and family when she was thirteen years old. Her mother was deceased. In Berlin, she did not return to school, but went to work. A journeyman's wife in the neighborhood had a sewing shop where she made dress shirts by hand. Baader worked for a month without pay, learning the job. Then she earned 3 and eventually 5 *Thaler* per month.[49] She worked for this woman for three years. She usually brought work home in order to make extra, putting in a twelve-hour day. Baader and her sister then sought work in a wool factory where she increased her earnings to 2 *Thaler* a week, but she found conditions in the factory quite horrible. After two years, she looked for other work. Baader observed at this point in her life that someone improperly trained for work such as she always had to look out for something better.

At that time in Berlin, there were four or five large firms that used sewing machines in clothing manufacture. Baader learned to sew by machine and went to work in a factory on Spandau Street. There were fifty women working at machines and about the same number doing preparation and finishing by hand. Machine workers were paired with a feeder or helper, and wages were reckoned for both women as a unit. Total wages averaged 7 to 10 *Thaler* a week, which the two women divided after first paying for sewing thread, needles, and other supplies. Despite available work—her employer promised Baader a job as long as she wanted it—she left the factory. Her primary complaint was the pace of factory production. Baader purchased a sewing machine and worked at home. While hours were long, from six in the morning to midnight in season, she remarked that at 4:00 she could stop work, put the apartment in order, and prepare a proper meal. To be in charge of her schedule outweighed whatever material advantages Baader had experienced in the factory.

Women working at home were a barometer, a way of talking about the economic conditions of individual families and about women's place in families. Viewed in this way, women in industrial home work permit a dynamic framework for reaching into the lives of persons who have been previously hidden by generalizations about the working class. Industrial work required adjustments in the personal lives of women, but women came to terms with the necessity to work by imposing an individual irregularity on the work experience. It was an irregularity based in part on the opportunity to select among various forms of work.

Agriculture could be combined with domestic industry, and domestic industry had close ties with factory production. The presence of a large, viable domestic industry in twentieth-century Germany continued to provide women with home-based paid labor options.

Domestic industry did not persist in the German economy for the benefit of women workers. In fact the very opposite is the case; it persisted because women had to work. Therefore, its tenacity should not be read as a sign of economic health, but rather as an indicator of the constraints women faced in combining their work lives with family responsibilities. There was real tension in women's choices. The pressure to work and the pressures of work created personal conflict. Girls hoped marriage meant economic security, but the numbers of women working, especially the increase in the numbers of married women, testified to a reality where not everyone married a public servant, foreman, or master artisan. While marriage and motherhood conferred status in German society, fulfilling women's natural role also provoked economic demotion contained in the heavy weight of the double burden. Because women's choices were limited, they were a vulnerable and accommodating labor source, but women did not respond passively. Wives and mothers resisted outside work whenever they could. They selected ways of earning money that could be made more compatible with household demands.

From the point of view of workers, home industry offered certain advantages. It was in fact an opportunity for gainful employment. The persistence of home industry gave women a way out—a way out of an unmanageable economic situation and a way to circumvent the undesirable and impossible aspects of work in a factory. Although women home workers were not really independent—production demands and seasonal insecurities precluded safety—they were not forced to react on a daily basis to the schedules of industrial time in a factory environment. Decisions to do home work were guided by limited but considered choice, exercised by women who had to make the most out of a bad situation. Industrial home work allowed women a way to control the rhythm of their work lives and to be at least present in the lives of their families. Doing work at home was not utopian. Its very existence denied the rudiments of satisfactory living, but it was an acceptable way for women to integrate work and family.

NOTES

1. C. Heiss and A. Koppel, *Heimarbeit und Hausindustrie in Deutschland* (Berlin: Puttkammer und Muhlbrecht, 1906), pp. 180–229.
2. Tamara Hareven, ed., *Transitions: The Family and the Life Course in Historical Perspective* (New York: Academic Press, 1978), p. 190.
3. Heinrich Koch, "The New Homework Act," Office International du Travail à Domicile. Publication #6 (n.d.), p. 9.
4. Frank Tipton, *Regional Variations in the Economic Development of Germany during the Nineteenth Century* (Middletown, Conn.: Wesleyan University Press, 1976), p. 163.
5. Ibid., p. 162.
6. *Statistik des Deutschen Reichs*, Band 220–221 (1914), p. 163.
7. *Protokoll der Verhandlungen des ersten Allgemeinen Heimarbeiterschutzkongress* (Berlin: Verlag der Generalkommission der Gewerkschaften Deutschlands, 1904), p. 61.
8. *Statistik des Deutschen Reichs*, p. 164.
9. Ibid., p. 163.
10. Ibid., p. 165.
11. Ibid., p. 167.
12. Ibid., p. 169.
13. Ibid., p. 167.
14. E. Jaffé, "Hausindustrie und Fabrikbetrieb in der deutschen Cigarrenfabrikation," *Schriften des Vereins für Sozialpolitik*, Vol. 86 (1899), p. 306.
15. *Statistik des Deutschen Reichs*, p. 167.
16. Ibid., p. 177.
17. Ibid., p. 178.
18. Ibid., pp. 177, 178.
19. Heinrich Koch, *Die deutsche Hausindustrie* (M. Gladbach: Volksvereins-Verlag, 1913), p. 34.
20. Ibid., p. 63.
21. "Das Hausgewerbe in Deutschland nach der gewerblichen Betriebszählung vom Juni 1907," *Reichs-Arbeitsblatt*, VIII Jahrgang, Nr. 2 (1910), p. 110.
22. "Die Frauenerwerbsarbeit im Deutschen Reiche nach den Ergebnissen der Berufszählungen von 1882–1907," *Correspondenzblatt der Generalkommission der Gewerkschaften Deutschland*, Nr. 3 (April 27, 1912), p. 93.
23. *Statistik des Deutschen Reichs*, Band 111 (1899), p. 226.
24. Heiss and Koppel, *Heimarbeit*, computed from charts, pp. 180–229.
25. *Statistik des Deutschen Reichs*, Band 211 (1913), computed from table: "Alters und Familienstandsgliederung der Hausgewerbetreibenden," p. 227.
26. Käthe Gaebel, *Die Heimarbeit* (Jena: Verlag von Gustav Fischer, 1913), p. 36.

27. Hans Grandke, "Die Hausindustrie der Frauen in Berlin," *Schriften des Vereins für Sozialpolitik*, Vol. 85 (1899), p. 250.

28. *Amtliche Mittheilungen. Jahresberichte der Gewerbeaufsichtsbeamten und Bergbehörden*, Reichsministerium des Innern, Band IV (1913), p. 51.

29. "Hausindustrie und Heimarbeit im Grossherzogtum Baden zu Anfang des XX Jahrhunderts," *Reichs-Arbeitsblatt*, V Jahrgang, Nr. 2 (February 21, 1907), p. 125.

30. Karl Bittmann, *Hausindustrie und Heimarbeit im Grossherzogtum Baden*, Bericht an das Grossherzoglich Badische Ministerium des Innern (Karlsruhe: Macklot'sche Druckerei, 1907), p. 1068.

31. Ibid., p. 1071.

32. "Die Heimarbeit in der Berliner Industrie," *Reichs-Arbeitsblatt*, IV Jahrgang, Nr. 12 (December 21, 1906), p. 1114.

33. Ibid., p. 1116.

34. *Protokoll*, p. 24.

35. Ibid.

36. Ibid., p. 191.

37. *Amtliche Mittheilungen*, Band III (1911), p. 24.

38. Ibid., Band IV, p. 33.

39. Ibid., Band IV, (1913), p. 41.

40. Jaffé, "Hausindustrie," p. 311.

41. Heiss and Koppel, *Heimarbeit*, pp. 226–29.

42. Karin Hausen, "Technischer Fortschritt und Frauenarbeit im 19. Jahrhundert. Zur Sozialgeschichte der Nähmaschine," *Geschichte und Gesellschaft*, 4 Jahrgang, Heft 2 (1978), p. 149.

43. Erhard Schmidt, *Fabrikbetrieb und Heimarbeit in der deutschen Konfektionsindustrie* (Stuttgart: Verlag von Ferdinand Enke, 1912), p. 171.

44. Hausen, "Technischer Fortschritt," p. 167.

45. Grandke, "Die Hausindustrie," p. 267.

46. Schmidt, *Fabrikbetrieb und Heimarbeit*, p. 160.

47. *Amtliche Mittheilungen*, Band IV (1913), p. 34.

47. Wolfgang Emmerich, ed., *Proletarische Lebensläufe. Autobiographische Dokumente zur Entstehung der Zweiten Kultur in Deutschland* (Hamburg: Rowohlt Taschenbuch Verlag, 1974), pp. 131–36.

48. A *Thaler* was an old type silver coin worth three Marks.

4. Home hand sewing, Berlin, 1905. (© Archiv für Kunst und Geschichte, Berlin.)

5. Woman home worker making felt slippers, Berlin, 1906. (© Archiv für

6. Father and children making cigars, Berlin, 1910. Their workroom is the kitchen. (© Archiv für Kunst und Geschichte, Berlin.)

7. Mother and school-age children wrapping sweets, Berlin, 1910. (© Archiv für Kunst und Geschichte, Berlin.)

8. Seventy-five-year-old home weaver, Berlin. 1910. (© Archiv für Kunst und Geschichte, Berlin.)

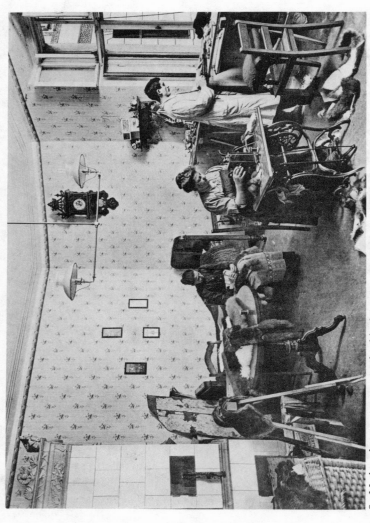

9. Mother, her grown son, and a hired woman stitching pelts, Berlin, 1910.
(© Archiv für Kunst und Geschichte, Berlin.)

10. Home sewing—machine and hand work, Berlin, 1910. (© Archiv für Kunst und Geschichte, Berlin.)

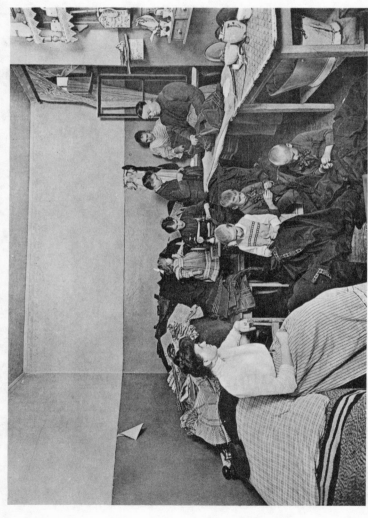

11. Three generations doing laundry work, Berlin, 1912. (© Archiv für Kunst und Geschichte, Berlin.)

12. Widow and her son doing tin plating in a cellar tenement, Berlin, 1912.
(© Archiv für Kunst und Geschichte, Berlin.)

7

Women Workers and the Unions

" . . . unions are important, but not for women"*

At the International Socialist Congress in Stuttgart in August, 1907, Clara Zetkin, a leader in the socialist feminist movement, called for revolutionary change in the position of women in the family and society. She argued that increasing participation in the work force would pave the way for women to free themselves from the confines of the home. Women must demand economic independence from men and from the family.[1] What Zetkin and other feminists did not appreciate was that their admonitions widely missed the real circumstances in the lives of most working women. Zetkin was encouraging women to use union organization to achieve radical change, but most women were neither ready nor willing to make such drastic transformation. Zetkin's promotion of the unions as a means of confronting the exploitation of both men and family was incompatible with the way most women workers perceived their lives.

Organizing women industrial workers was slow and only partially successful in pre-war Germany. Some of the difficulty was due to the competition for membership among the various kinds of labor organizations. The socialist unions began active recruitment among women

*Hilde Lion, *Zur Soziologie der Frauenbewegung: Die sozialistische und die katholische Frauenbewegung* (Berlin: F. A. Herbig Verlagsbuchhandlung, 1926), p. 103.

in the 1890's, followed almost immediately by bids for membership from the Catholic unions and other religiously affiliated organizations. Working women were faced not only with the decision of union participation, but with the conflicting claims of diverse organizations competing for their attention. The messages ranged the spectrum from complete economic emancipation to total expulsion of women from factory work. Another real problem with organizing women lay with the unions themselves. The socialist unions were dominated by men who had ambivalent feelings about inviting women to participate in organization. Religious unions were in the untenable position of arguing for elimination of women's work while simultaneously trying to mobilize women to organize.

The crucial hindrance to organizing women lay in the reasons women sought work and in the conditions of their work experience. Women continued to pursue wage labor with fewer job expectations and less commitment than men workers.[2] Women's approach to work was not conducive to building any strong sense of worker solidarity. The real problem lay in convincing women that membership in a union was the indispensable requirement for improving not only their conditions of work, but the conditions of their lives through work. Participation in a labor organization called for a change in the way women looked upon industrial work. Joining a group to pursue common goals implied some measure of permanence and commitment. Interest in union activity pointed in the direction of regularizing the work experience, but such regularizing was not part of the working life of most women. Work in a factory was supposed to be temporary. Investment in time, money, and energy in union activity was just not seen as especially necessary.

Women gave many reasons for rejecting organization. Some could not be persuaded to the necessity of personal membership in a union: "My husband is organized, why should I!"[3] For others organized effort was viewed with contempt: "Common help! Who has helped me? No one. Why should I help anyone?"[4] Still others could not find time for any activity beyond the demands of work and home: "Tired! I have no time. When I arrive home I must cook dinner and make the beds. My husband is impatient."[5] On the other hand, many organizers saw little to like among the women whose interest they were trying to cultivate. Minna Wettstein, who concealed her identity to learn about working women in factories, commented that factory girls cared nothing about the future and bettering their lives.[6] They knew little about the delights of social democracy and the women's question. She observed with more than a little contempt that even though the girls took newspapers into work and passed them from hand to hand, the only items that held interest were the obituaries: "But it was such a lovely death."[7]

While these comments in no way exhaust the problem of organizing women, they do reveal the kinds of indifference, animosity, and intransigence that limited interest and kept membership low. In the first decade of the twentieth century, Germany had the highest number of organized workers among the states of Western Europe and the United States. However, excluding Hungary and Norway, Germany had the lowest percentage of women organized, falling below Britain, France, and Austria.[8] In 1913 there were 257,236 women organized in unions, which represented 8.5% of total union membership.[9] They belonged to unions affiliated with the three major groups of organized workers: the Socialist Trade Unions (*Freie Gewerkschaften*), the *Hirsch-Duncker Gewerkvereine*, and the Christian unions (*Christliche Gewerkschaften*).

The extent of union membership in the total female work force can be measured for the census years 1895 and 1907. While there are cumulative data on union membership into the war period, absence of new census figures on working women after 1907 precludes a determination of percentage membership in the total female labor force following that date. In 1896, the percentage of working women who belonged to unions was 1.4%, or 12,265 women.[10] In 1907, membership was 169,072 women, or 8% of the female labor force.[11] Comparable figures for men workers indicate that 2,278,369, or about a quarter of the male labor force was organized in 1907.[12] While the numerical increase of women in unions was impressive, it still represented only a fraction of organized labor and a yet smaller percentage of the number of women working.

While attempts to organize workers, even women workers, were tried as early as the 1870's, the German labor movement made no significant progress until the last decade of the nineteenth century. The three groups of labor organizations, the socialist, *Hirsch-Duncker*, and the Christian unions, differed widely on principles of organization and kinds of activity promoted. They were especially far apart on the question of organizing women. The *Hirsch-Duncker Gewerkvereine* were committed to political and religious neutrality and promoted understanding and cooperation between employer and worker. These unions sought to limit factory employment of women, especially young women, because they were the "carriers" and "teachers" of future generations and had to be protected.[13] The *Hirsch-Duncker* unions were never very successful. They secured less than 5% of total union membership and made an even more meager showing among women workers.

Religiously affiliated organizations sought to diminish the inequities between male and female labor by advocating a reduction in women's work. It was hoped that removing women from the labor force would create a condition of labor scarcity which would increase men's chances to earn higher wages. The socialist trade unions were founded on the principles of Marxism, which stressed class conflict, advocated class solidarity, and promoted gender equality. Yet traditional differences between men and women workers created real barriers to full commitment to equality.

Unions faced special problems regarding women. Until 1908 women were forbidden by law in most German states to attend political meetings or to join associations that dealt with political matters. While adherence to the letter of the law varied, it was commonly interpreted that any discussion regarding the "social question," including general conditions of work and wages, constituted political issues. Unions admitting women were put into a vulnerable position and ran the risk of being disbanded by the authorities. The danger of dissolution lessened greatly following the repeal of anti-socialist restrictions in 1890, because authorities no longer needed to use women as an excuse for socialist harassment.[14] Yet, potentially the threat remained in the form of legal proscriptions that could be used against unpopular union activity at the discretion of employers and police.[15]

There was an obvious connection between the newly acquired "freedom" of the socialist unions in the early 1890's and the increase in agitation for membership among women workers. Unions responded primarily to the increased numbers of women in the factory work force. Given the results of the 1895 occupational census, most organizers agreed that the woman worker could no longer be ignored as peripheral to the labor force. Women as workers had to be taken seriously. But the disparity in the value of labor inherent in capitalist industrial growth fostered as much competition among workers as that between workers and employers.

The following chart indicates the numerical and percentage distribution of total membership in the various worker organizations in 1910.[16]

Organization	Membership	Percentage
Socialist unions	2,017,298	58.4
Christian unions	295,129	8.5
Confessional unions	197,840	5.7
Hirsch-Duncker	122,571	3.6
Independent unions	705,942	20.5
National unions	33,284	1.0
Yellow unions	79,991	2.3
	3,452,055	100.0

For the same year using figures for women only, the distribution of membership reveals a considerably different profile (see page 148). The concentration of women in religious unions is treated more fully in Chapter Eight.

Philosophy and emphasis differed among the three kinds of labor organizations, but there was common ground on practical issues. Most unions advocated similar programs; they promoted legal restrictions and protection for women workers. The demands usually incorporated reduction of the work day, a mandated mid-day break, and prohibition of night work and work in unsafe or unsanitary conditions. Unions also agitated for improved wages. The Christian unions promoted "a fair wage" while the socialist organizations demanded "equal wage for equal work." The socialist unions called for the eight-hour day, but other organizations were more moderate on the work-time issue. All unions promoted maternity protection for women workers. Time requested for delivery and recovery ranged from four to eight weeks. And all unions addressed the problem of domestic industry, demanding restrictions and supervision of work done at home. On the personal level, unions collected dues and offered payments for sickness, accident, and unemployment. Socialist unions also offered strike benefits. There were no

Organization	Membership	Percentage
Socialist unions	161,512	64.0
Christian unions	21,833	8.6
Home workers union	8,188*	3.2
Confessional unions	46,049**	18.3
Catholic union for		
domestic servants	8,510	3.3
Hirsch-Duncker	6,097	2.6

* 1912

** This figure includes only major Catholic and Evangelica
organizations and under-represents total confessional
union membership.

strike payments incorporated into the programs of the Christian unions because these organizations frowned upon confrontation in employer-labor relations. Schedules for payments and benefits differed for men and women in all unions. Based on wages and on the traditional view that women's needs were less, there were usually distinct scales for women at considerably lower rates.

The socialist trade unions initiated a campaign to attract women workers to organization in 1892. The First Trade Union Congress, Halberstadt, recognized the importance of female labor in industry and called for energetic recruitment in all branches of production where women were employed.[17] Apparently discouraged with the results, another congress in 1902 demanded a program of regular, planned agitation to enlarge female membership. Fathers, husbands, and brothers in the movement were requested to urge women in their families who worked to join a union.[18] Generally efforts to organize women were disappointing and far less representative of the work put forth.

Much of the inspiration and hard work responsible for organizing women in the *Freie Gewerkschaften* came from socialist feminists within the movement. The most prominent were Luise Zietz, Emma Ihrer, Gertrud Hanna, Ottilie Baader, Lilly Braun, and Clara Zetkin. These women saw in socialism the means of effecting female emancipation. Socialism and feminism were bound together because only through a revolutionary transformation of society could women achieve full equality. Yet the fusion was an uncomfortable one for both the men in the socialist movement and the women themselves, who faced very painful decisions about traditional gender roles.

Although socialist ideology was committed to equality, most men paid little more than lip-service to the idea.[19] Men in the unions supported female membership for much more selfish reasons than ideological commitment to equality. Organized male workers wanted women to join unions because the very presence of women in the factory was perceived not only as the cause of lower wages, but as a potential threat to job security. This was particularly true in industries that were new employers of women. If women could be persuaded to fight for equal or even improved wages, male organizers reasoned that employers would find them less-attractive workers and the competition for jobs would be reduced.

Not only did women activists have to fight against male intransigence, these women also had to resolve real dilemmas related to their position as both socialists and feminists. Working out these problems caused deep rifts among the women in the forefront of the socialist movement. It also forced ideological adjustments to compensate for the incongruity between full equality for women and women's traditional role as wife and mother. Controversy among socialist feminists concerning specific response to gender roles created diversity that encompassed the radicals, Zetkin and Baader, the revisionist Braun, and reformists such as Marie Juchacz.[20]

One of the primary organizational and ideological problems among the women activists was their lack of agreement on the relationship between socialism and other groups fighting for female emancipation. Because most non-socialist feminists and feminist associations were middle-class, socialist women had to choose allegiance. Was the struggle for women's rights more important than the working-class struggle for freedom? Zetkin and Braun were especially far apart on this issue. Somehow the disparity between emancipation of women and emancipation of the working class had to be reconciled. If women's emancipation was primary, then the opponent was men; however, if freedom for the working class was the goal, men and women together had to create class solidarity. Zetkin wanted complete separation from bourgeois influence and subordinated the women's struggle within the working class. She defined emancipation for all women as emancipation from capitalism.[21] Feminists were acutely aware of the contradiction and worried over the ''Janus-character'' of the proletarian women's movement.[22]

Women must promote a class struggle, not a sex struggle . . . it is not women with women against men. The principle of the proletarian women's movement must be proletarian women with proletarian men against capitalism.[23]

Although the feminists believed that work was a vehicle for emancipation, they remained faithful to the ideal of woman as wife and mother.[24] Rapid economic change, they argued, opened opportunities for women to become whole persons instead of passive slaves to men. Despite ideological commitment to liberation, socialist feminists never actually advocated absolute equality. Tradition was too strong. Apart from the rhetoric, socialists argued for reduced work time, better work conditions, and maternity protection for the same reason as the conservative religious unions. Women workers deserved special attention because they were women. Feminists reasoned that women needed preference in order to compensate for past injustice. Perceiving the possibility that women's issues might be submerged in male-dominated unions, women activists addressed the special problems and concerns of the woman worker as separate from her male comrades. The ambiguity was intense. Feminists insisted on equal opportunity not because women were equal, but because they were complementary to men.

Socialist feminists were aware of the dangers in equality and acted in the concrete somewhat differently from theoretical exclamations by promoting special status for women. Within the socialist subculture, itself an ostracized group from mainstream political and economic life in Imperial Germany, absolute adherence to equality would place women into even deeper distress. If restrictive legislation forced women into separatism, activists had to come to terms with the possibility that there might be real benefits hidden away in the prohibitions. Inequality was combined with preference and protection. Political integration that became possible in 1908 revealed deep gender divisions in the socialist labor movement. If socialist women were aware of their intensity before, there was no escaping the reality of sex segregation after 1908; it was discrimination that could no longer be blamed on the laws.

Women recognized that the tenuous advantage they had in promoting female issues could be lost if true merging occurred. There were advantages to maintaining parallel organizations even though they might be subordinate. Socialist women were caught in the paradox of resisting complete equality in order to promote special interests. Once this understanding was grasped, women fought to preserve their own space. At least there was some measure of freedom and autonomy in separation. Winning the battle for political integration may have been an ideological victory, but it rang hollow when women faced a male monopoly in the trade unions.

Many of the women who achieved leadership positions in the socialist movement either were workers themselves or came from working-class families. Because they became public figures, it is relatively easy to trace their origins and involvement with worker organizations. But it is difficult to judge whether their experience can be considered typical for other women who joined labor unions because biographical material for the rank-and-file is sparse. Ottilie Baader, who was born in Frankfurt in 1847, became a sewer in the Berlin garment industry when she was thirteen. She worked at several jobs including both factory and domestic industry.[25] She attended her first public meeting during a protest over the price of yarn. There she made contact with others in the movement, and eventually became a close ally of Zetkin. Between 1900 and 1908 she was a representative to the Central Committee for Social Democratic Women in Germany.[26]

Luise Zietz was the daughter of a home weaver in Hamburg. She worked for a time in domestic service and then entered a tobacco factory at age fourteen. She was introduced to socialism through her husband and joined the Social Democratic Party in 1892.[27] Both Helene Grünberg and Gertrud Hanna joined unions in their trades. Grünberg joined the Tailors Union and took part in a strike in the garment industry in 1896. Hanna became prominent through her activities in the Printers' Aids Union in Berlin.[28] Emma Ihrer founded a union for flower makers in 1901 and mobilized a campaign to eliminate home work in that industry.[29]

Zetkin, perhaps the most influential among the socialist feminists, came from a middle-class background. Born in Saxony in 1857, Zetkin had the unusual opportunity to attend school, the Auguste Schmidt's teachers' seminar.[30] She was influenced toward socialism by her brother and a young man, Ossip Zetkin, with whom she later lived in a common law marriage.[31] She traveled with Zetkin, joining various socialist emigré groups in Europe. Connecting with the socialist network, she made speeches and wrote articles related to women and socialism and was selected to speak before the International Workers' Congress in Paris in 1889. In the talk Zetkin declared: "The question of women's emancipation is ultimately a question of women's work."[32]

The principal organ for socialist feminism was the journal *Die Gleichheit* (Equality). The paper was published bi-weekly. It included theoretical articles on feminism and socialism, but also devoted a great deal of attention to work conditions, the trade unions, and issues pertaining to women and work. In 1905 the paper added a supplement that was a women's section in the most traditional sense. It contained articles on child care and domestic skills, and even included serialized novels. Zetkin was the editor of *Gleichheit* from 1892 until 1917, and through the paper, she exerted a great deal of influence among other women organizers. The subtitle of the journal was "*Zeitschrift für die Interessen der Arbeiterinnen*" (Journal for the Interest of Working Women), but the paper was unpopular with women workers.[33] Vocabulary was difficult and ideological arguments complicated. Criticism that the paper was not reaching women in the factories and was thus falling short of its potential as an organizing tool was answered by Zetkin at the socialist congress in 1896. "*Die Gleichheit* is not for the masses, but for the leaders . . . it is the organ for the avante-garde of the women proletariat."[34] It is no wonder, then, that even an occasional dress pattern, recipe, or serialized novel about the struggle of the working class failed to give the paper a popular base.

What kinds of results did all this commitment and energy bring? Among organized women the socialist unions did well, but within the total female labor force, women just did not embrace unionization. Sixty-eight percent of organized working women belonged to the socialist trade unions. But it would be wrong to conclude that stimulus for membership lay in the ideological appeal of the class struggle as organizers claimed. The pattern of union participation by trade indicated a picture that was more complex than a simple statement of capitalist exploitation or class solidarity. Pressures for organization were material considerations, very often directed by men who pursued the goal of organizing women to reduce job and wage competition. In some industries the sheer size of the female work force gave the appearance of active participation in the representative union. Yet percentage membership in female-intensive industries was low. Women joined unions in proportionally greater numbers in trades where women's work was relatively new, and where male membership was substantial.

Union membership was also subject to fluctuations in the broader marketplace. Union members tended to leave organization when they were out of a job. Unemployment benefits were hardly sufficient compensation for extended periods of lay-off. Women were the least compensated. Elaborate scales of payment benefits that made significant distinction among married men with children, married men without children, and single men put women at the bottom of the list. In addition, most unions required a long period of dues payment before benefits were available. There was an immediate and sharp reduction in male membership in the trade unions between 1907 and 1908 in response to a depressed economy.[35] Female membership began to experience the effects of unemployment a year later. Because their labor was cheaper, women were kept on longer.

The largest numbers of women organized in the socialist unions were in the textile union. In 1897 female membership was 3,314. But this figure represented only 1% of the total number of women working in that industry. In the metal industry, 4.7% of the women employed were organized; 9.8% in the book binders' union.[36] There was little change in the pattern of membership in the first decade of the twentieth century. Numbers increased but the percentage divergence between employment and membership remained large. Three trade-specific unions eventually achieved membership exceeding 10,000 women: textiles, tobacco, and metals. Textiles remained the most significant numerically, but organized women represented less than 10% of the total female work force in the industry. Of the three trade-specific organizations, textiles had the smallest percentage of unionized women. Twelve and a half percent of women tobacco workers were organized. The most dramatic figures were in the metal industry: 20% were organized.[37] Textiles and tobacco employed large numbers of women, and both industries continued to have substantial home work production. Significantly fewer women were employed in the metal trades. In 1907 only 6% of the work force was female, while in textiles and tobacco, women workers comprised about 50% and 25% of the labor force, respectively.[38] Total union membership in textiles and tobacco for both sexes was low, but the metal union consistently produced the largest membership of all the trades.[39]

All trade unions identified the same problems regarding female workers and hindrances to organization. They blamed poor wages and work conditions on women. Lamenting the low persistence among women on the job and the lack of consistency in their commitment to union solidarity, the *Textilarbeiterverband* (Textile Workers Union) complained that women were ideal workers, ideal from the employer's point of view. They were willing to work long hours for little pay. Women were less demanding. They were an elastic source of labor— they gave the employer too much power.[40] Exhortations to organization were similar in the tobacco industry. Here conditions were aggravated by a substantial increase in the number of women employed due to decentralization, which was reflected in more home work. Statements about nicotine dust and lung disease only superficially camouflaged the real reason for increased agitation among women workers. "In Germany, as long as the cigar industry exists, women's work will exist."[41] The *Tabakarbeiterverband* (Tobacco Workers Union) intensified its program for recruitment in 1903 with some small positive results.[42] Organization was seen as the only way to improve conditions. A major target of the tobacco union was the elimination of domestic industry because home workers were perceived as competition for jobs and wages.

"Blessed" with many fewer women workers and much less home work than textiles and tobacco, men in the metal industry fought to preserve the power of exclusivity. Women in the metal industry were a relatively new phenomenon. The implications were clear: Women were a threat.

The small desire of women to belong to an organization is in part due to their fearful nature—they dread they will be dismissed, and in part because so many are young girls who look upon their work in industry as temporary—they believe their future is marriage.[43]

Even more deprecating were union attitudes toward women's ability to do the job. Members of the metal union were convinced that women workers were so poorly skilled that it made no difference which industry employed them. The criticism tended to be an exaggeration. A quarter of the women in metals were skilled workers.[44] The union did not neglect an attack on domestic industry. Here the threat was more perceived than real. Two percent of the total employed in metals in 1907 were in home production.[45] Disparaging women's motivation and ability to work, the *Metallarbeiterverband* (Metal Workers Union) urged organization as the means of preventing the worse effects of having women in the industry.

Drawing on the example of the metal union, it would be easy to conclude a direct relationship between union membership and skill level. However, a comparison between the number of skilled workers in an industry and participation in a union does not reveal such a neat picture. There is support for the contention for men, especially in industries with strong artisanal tradition, but not for women. In textiles, where there were large numbers of both men and women unskilled workers, male union participation was twice that of women. In tobacco there was no wide difference in skill levels between men and women, but men again doubled female participation. Skill qualifications in tailoring were about the same for men and women, yet only 2.8% of the women were organized compared with 22% for the men. Bookbinding was a real anomaly. Men workers were skill-intensive while skilled women workers were hardly in evidence, yet there were proportionally more women organized than men.[46] Organizers attributed the positive results to intensive agitation in that industry to recruit women workers. However, closer examination reveals that bookbinding was overwhelmingly factory labor. Rather than skill level being the key to intensity of unionization, the crucial factor was domestic industry. Industries that retained high concentrations of home work yielded fewer organized workers.

Two critical determinants of women's participation in labor organization within specific industries were the proportion of the production process maintained in domestic industry and the number of married women working. These factors were interrelated. Marriage precluded persistence. Married women either left the factory entirely for home work or took other kinds of jobs. If they remained, the further restrictions on time and energy in attending to household tasks and children constituted prohibitive limitations to union activity. Although the reasons for resistance to organization were complex, most union activists acknowledged the fact that marriage imposed responsibilities on women that were vastly different from men's. For some married women the financial burden was difficult, especially if their husbands were already paying dues to a union. Lack of leisure prevented most women from taking time to attend union functions. And although difficult to pinpoint exactly, most married women were oriented toward family rather than work. As previously noted, even the most radical socialist feminists believed that women's domestic role was just as important a contribution to society as her work outside the home. Supportive of the connection between unionization, married workers, and domestic industry was the large number of married women in those industries where union involvement was proportionally low. These were also the industries that retained a sizable share of the production process in domestic work.

Home work presented a constantly nagging problem for the unions. The socialist unions sought to organize home workers by trade, bringing both factory and home workers into a common organization. Because domestic industry constituted competition, the unions demanded legal restrictions on home work and actually went so far as to demand its abolition. Unions argued for increased restrictions in order to eliminate competition or at least to make domestic industry less attractive to employers.

Agitation to organize home workers by the socialist unions occurred simultaneously with stepped-up efforts in the early 1890's to unionize women generally. But success was minimal. The German Tailors and Seamstresses Union was especially interested in restricting home work because the garment industry experienced heavy expansion in both home work and female labor. The following observation was made by the president of the Tailors Union:

It appears that the easiest home workers to organize are the skilled men whose number is limited and who cannot be replaced very easily. It is more difficult to carry on agitation among even skilled women, and the most difficult thing of all is to organize women who make cheap goods in gross.[47]

There was only one large protest movement among garment workers in pre-war Germany. The strike occurred in 1896 and affected workers in Berlin, Breslau, and Erfurt. It was a strike that simultaneously called for restricting work done at home and also demanded higher wages for home work. The protest called attention to conditions in domestic industry. Wage demands were partially met, but requests for restrictions on home production went unheeded. Union participation fell off almost immediately after the strike; women left in much greater numbers than men.[48] The trade unions did not seem to be consciously aware of the contradiction in their demands. They were asking home workers to contribute to their own elimination. Women knew implicitly that home work had to be preserved to hold on to a margin of economic safety.

Die Gleichheit ran a series of articles at the turn of the century evaluating the progress of unionization among women. The journal stated that one of the most difficult obstacles to overcome was the fact that industries where most women worked were experiencing increases in home work. Textiles and clothing were the worst, but expanding home work in metals and porcelain products was linked to the increase in female labor in these industries. *Gleichheit* also noted a relationship between wages, hours of work, and incidence of organization. In locations where women received comparatively higher wages and worked shorter hours, unions had more success. But ultimately *Gleichheit* had to fall back on less precise reasoning for women's failure to organize.

It is most difficult to reach the woman worker. Difficulty that is due in part to backward social development of women and their peculiarity as women that gives them double responsibilities; in part through a false perception of work as merely an interim station before marriage.[49]

Despite energetic campaigns for recruitment, labor unions achieved only limited success with women in Imperial Germany. The ambiguity inherent in organizing women was reflected in the conflicting claims of the various labor unions. Unions became the focus for competing ideologies—religious associations struggling with socialist organizations to win worker loyalties. Unions in Germany were more than labor oganizations. They represented a complex of attitudes toward life and society, and served to illuminate the broader political and social issues that permeated the whole question of working women.

Unions promoted the notion that women could begin to control the conditions of work and the circumstances of their lives through organization. Yet the nature of women's work precluded using the unions as instruments for transformation. Until women defined work as more than a temporary experience, traditional attitudes against full participation of women in organizations and society would continue to permeate the consciousness of both men and women. "Yes, I believe unions are important, but not for women. Men do such things."[50] Before the war the circle of constraints that bound women to industrial work would not be altered. That they were largely unskilled and low-paid diminished potential for mobilization. The episodic nature of women's work did not support commitment to organization. Farfetched indeed were Clara Zetkin's exhortations for women to use work as a vehicle for emancipation.

Limitations to mobilizing women also could not be surmounted because the gender contradictions embedded in male dominance in union organizations were too strong. Even socialist unions, committed to egalitarian principles, could not move very far beyond a traditional definition of women as properly wives, mothers, and economic helpmates. It was a dilemma that plagued both men and women in the movement. At the core of gender consciousness, political and economic activism for women was simply unacceptable. In order to push back against this disparity, women in the socialist labor movement created a separate space for themselves—it was a theoretical and tactical arrangement that reinforced their isolation and diminished their strength. Ironically, the solution allowed men a way to justify and reaffirm their anti-feminism toward women generally and their strong resistance to women as equal partners in the workplace. Women working with women gave an illusion of power without conferring the ideological and operational strength required to impact significantly on the socialist movement or to alter the constraints of the work experience. The labor movement produced a contradictory legacy where women were concerned. Unions both opened up opportunity for activism and at the same time reinforced potential restrictions for the advancement of feminist issues.

NOTES

1. Clara Zetkin, "Der Kampf um das Frauenwahlrecht soll die Proletarierin zum klassenbewussten politischen Leben erwecken," *Arbeiterbewegung und Frauenemanzipation 1889 bis 1933*, Band 3 (Frankfurt/Main: Verlag Marxistische Blätter, 1973), p. 15.

2. Peter Stearns, *Lives of Labor* (New York: Holmes and Meier Publishers, 1975), p. 60.

3. Hilde Lion, *Zur Soziologie der Frauenbewegung. Die sozialistische und*

die katholische Frauenbewegung (Berlin: F. A. Herbig Verlagsbuchhandlung, 1926), p. 102.

4. Ibid.

5. Ibid.

6. Minna Adelt Wettstein, *3 1/2 Monate Fabrikarbeiterin* (Berlin: Verlag von J. Leiser, 1893), p. 71.

7. Ibid., p. 72.

8. "Die internationale Gewerkschaftsbewegung im Jahre 1907," *Reichs-Arbeitsblatt*, VII Jahrgang, Nr. 9 (1909), p. 691.

9. *Zentralblatt der Christlichen Gewerkschaften Deutschlands*, 14 Jahrgang (Krefeld: von Acken Buchdruckerei, 1914), pp. 342–43.

10. *Correspondenzblatt der Generalkommission der Gewerkschaften Deutschlands*, 9 Jahrgang, Nr. 33 (Hamburg: August 28, 1899), pp. 202–3.

11. *Statistische Beilage des Correspondenzblatt*, Nr. 3 (April 27, 1912), p. 63, computed from tables. Lilly Hauff, *Die Deutschen Arbeiterinnen-Organisationen* (Halle a S.: Ehrhardt Karras Verlag, 1912), p. 122.

12. *Correspondenzblatt*, Nr. 3 (April 27, 1912), p. 63, computed from tables. "Die internationale Gewerkschaftsbewegung im Jahre 1907," *Reichs-Arbeitsblatt*, VII Jahrgang, Nr. 9 (1909), p. 691.

13. Hauff, *Arbeiterinnen-Organisationen*, p. 110.

14. Between 1878 and 1890 public socialist activity was suppressed.

15. Gertrud Hanna, "Women in the German Trade Union Movement," *International Labour Review*, Vol. VIII, No. 1 (July, 1923), p. 22.

16. "Die deutschen Arbeitnehmerorganisationen im Jahre 1910," *Reichs-Arbeitsblatt*, IX Jahrgang, Nr. 9 (1911), p. 691. Data for women computed from "Arbeitnehmerorganisationen," *Reichs-Arbeitsblatt*, p. 690. *Zentralblatt der Christlichen Gewerkschaften Deutschlands*, p. 343. Hauff, *Arbeiterinnen-Organisationen*, p. 122.

17. Hauff, *Arbeiterinnen-Organisationen*, p. 15.

18. "Die Arbeiterinnen in den deutschen Gewerkschaftsorganisationen im Jahre 1900," *Die Gleichheit*, 11 Jahrgang, Nr. 19 (September 11, 1901), p. 147.

19. Jean H. Quataert, "The German Socialist Women's Movement 1890–1918," unpublished dissertation (University of California, 1974), p. 148.

20. Jean H. Quataert, *Reluctant Feminists in German Social Democracy, 1885–1917* (Princeton, N.J.: Princeton University Press, 1979), p. 56.

21. Lion, *Zur Soziologie*, p. 30.

22. Ibid., p. 50.

23. Ibid., pp. 49–50.

24. Quataert, "Socialist Women's Movement," p. 387.

25. Richard Klucsarits and Friedrich Kürbisch, eds., *Arbeiterinnen Kämpfen um ihr Recht* (Wuppertal: Peter Hammer Verlag, 1975), p. 377.

26. Ibid.

160   *At the Very Least She Pays the Rent*

27. Quataert, "Socialist Women's Movement," pp. 92, 94.
28. Ibid., pp. 99–100.
29. Quataert, *Reluctant Feminists*, p. 173.
30. Ibid., p. 65.
31. Ibid., p. 66. Zetkin's family name was Eissner.
32. Zetkin, *Arbeiterbewegung und Frauenemanzipation*, p. 7.
33. Lion, *Zur Soziologie*, p. 93.
34. Ibid.
35. "Arbeitnehmerorganisationen," *Reichs-Arbeitsblatt* (1911), p. 683.
36. *Correspondenzblatt* (August 28, 1899), pp. 196–97.
37. Figures for the three unions were computed from *Reichs-Arbeitsblatt* (1909), p. 681, *Correspondenzblatt* (1912), p 73, and *Statistik des Deutschen Reichs*, Band 211 (1913), p. 46.
38. *Statistik des Deutschen Reichs*, Band 211 (1913), p. 46.
39. *Zentralblatt der Christlichen Gewerkschaften Deutschlands* (1914), p. 342.
40. "Die Lage der Textilindustrie und ihrer Arbeiter," *Die Neue Zeit*, 19 Jahrgang, Nr. 35 (1900–1901), p. 270.
41. Walther Frisch, "Die Organisationsbestrebungen der Arbeiter in der deutschen Tabakindustrie," *Staats- und Socialwissenschaftliche Forschungen*, Band 24, Heft 3 (Leipzig: Verlag von Duncker und Humblot, 1905), p. 247.
42. "Der deutsche Tabakarbeiterverband im Jahre 1904," *Beilage zum Tabak-Arbeiter*, Nr. 31 (Leipzig: July 30, 1905), p. 1.
43. Otto Hommer, *Die Entwicklung und Tätigkeit des Deutschen Metallarbeiterverbandes* (Berlin: Carl Heymanns Verlag, 1912), p. 43.
44. Ibid., p. 42.
45. "Die Hausindustrie nach den Angaben der Hausgewerbetreibenden," *Statistik des Deutschen Reichs*, Band 220–221 (1914), p. 166.
46. Hauff, *Arbeiterinnen-Organisationen*, pp. 128–29.
47. Office International du Travail à Domicile, "The Abolition and Regulation of Homework by Trade Union Action," Publication #6 (n.d.), p. 12.
48. Quataert, "Socialist Women's Movement," p. 176.
49. *Die Gleichheit*, (September 11, 1901), p. 146.
50. Lion, *Zur Soziologie*, p. 103.

8

The Christian Labor Organizations

"The worker question is a moral problem . . . "*

In grouping the various labor organizations, the term *Christliche Gewerkschaften* was used rather indefinitely by contemporaries to distinguish the religious organizations from the socialist trade unions and the *Hirsch-Duncker* unions. The Christian movement incorporated both the confessional unions, the Catholic and Evangelical, and the interconfessional, which were committed to Christian principles and open to persons from various religious faiths. While the socialist unions talked about equality, the Christian unions stressed separate organizations for women where that was possible. This emphasis reflected what the unions called the special problems of women workers.[1] Concern for women was directly related to religious visions of a patriarchal society. They talked about home and family and offered comfort and reassurance to working women. They encouraged young girls to marry and encouraged married women to have children. Union membership was promoted with the sanction of the churches and the energy of missionary zeal. The unions brought belonging to a labor organization within the bounds of propriety because association with church and Christian values lent an aura of legitimacy to organization.

*"Die Katholische Arbeiterorganisation und die Sozialdemokratie," *Der Arbeiterpräses*, 8 Jahrgang, Nr. 6 (June, 1912), p. 173.

The Christian unions began with the premise that the religious and moral well-being of their members was as important as, if not more important than, concerns for the material conditions of work. Christian unions faced a real dilemma regarding women. On the one hand, they were committed to the sanctity of the home and family. On the other, they had to face the reality of women's working outside the home. Christian unions consistently attempted to reconcile the irreconcilable. Women did not really belong in factories. This phenomenon upset the natural order of things. Yet, to promote the goal of a better family life, the unions had to meet the woman where they found her—on the job.

Despite the contradictory messages sent out by the religious unions, they apparently made more sense to women than to men. In the first decade of the twentieth century, distribution of membership among the three major groups of organized workers indicated a much heavier concentration of women than men in religiously affiliated organizations. Over 30% of organized women workers belonged to religious unions compared with about 15% in total union membership. There were about 22,000 women organized in the *Christliche Gewerkschaften*, the interconfessional associations, in 1910; 87% were employed in two industries—textiles, tobacco, and in domestic industry.[2] Reference to the extraordinary success the Christian unions had among home workers and domestic servants is expanded later in this chapter.

In 1910 there were about 2,000 women organized in the *Verband der Evangelischen Arbeiterinnenvereine*, Deutschlands (Association of Evangelical Working Women's Organizations). The *Verband der Katholischen Vereine der Erwerbstätigen Frauen und Mädchen*, Deutschlands, Berlin (Association of Catholic Organizations of Employed Women and Girls) had a membership of 28,500 and the *Verband Süddeutscher Katholischer Arbeiterinnenvereine* Munich (Association of South German Catholic Working Women's Organizations) totaled 15,500 women.[3] The numbers in part reflected the religious composition of the work force in specific regions and cities. Religious unions competed successfully with the socialist trade unions in west Germany and the south. Many religious organizations were locally based and served a specifically targeted constituency, that is, Catholic and Evangelical workers in the immediate geographic area.

While membership was divided among confessional and interconfessional organizations, religious unions together represented almost one-third of the women's labor movement. It is crucial, therefore, to understand why the religious unions held such appeal for women. It can be argued that the anti-feminist and anti-capitalist patriarchal society emphasized by the Christian unions provided the very image women needed for safety in changing times. To be defined as a wife and mother first and only secondarily as a worker fit women's perception of themselves. Given the chance to retain traditional values without apology or threat allowed a substantial number of women at least partial resolution to the insecurities of role conflict. It also served to mollify male fears of female intrusion or escape into the world of work. Churches reassured men that women would remain in their proper place.

The church was a link that helped women adapt to an industrial environment. It harmonized the woman's primary responsibility in the family with the necessity to work, even if that job was in a factory setting. This communication was especially true for women who were new to the labor force. Feelings of separation and alienation among young women who came into the cities from farms or small towns were ameliorated somewhat by having a familiar institution ease the way. The church functioned as both a religious and social center. It provided a ready-made circle of contacts and friends. The religious unions, closely affiliated as they were with the institutional churches, connected women's economic life with their personal and family life. Intending to serve in a moderate and supportive way, the unions organized social activities, offered advice, and safeguarded the spiritual well-being of their members.

It should be noted also that the philosophy of the religious unions was compatible with the paternalistic orientation of many German industrial firms. This vision of work relations helped clarify and make more acceptable the conditions to which women were exposed in an industrial environment. The Christian unions, especially the Catholic organizations, were committed to social peace.[4] In *Rerum Novarum*, the papal encyclical on The Condition of Labor, the Catholic position on the relationship and responsibilities of workers and employers was clearly articulated.

. . . religion teaches the laboring man and the workman to carry out honestly and well all equitable agreements freely made, never to injure capital, not to outrage the person of an employer, never to use violence in representing his own cause, nor to engage in riot or disorder and to have nothing to do with men of evil practices, who work upon the people with artful promises and raise foolish hopes which usually end in disaster. . . .[5]

While it may appear from this statement that the Church was urging the laborer to accept his lot without question, there is more than just a message of submission contained in the encyclical. The Catholic Church believed in mutuality; in a very real sense the worker entered into an understanding with the employer. Steady, peaceful, useful labor was expected from the worker in order to fulfill his side of the work relationship. But the church also taught that the employer had just as binding an obligation to his workers. Labor was not to be exploited—workers were not slaves, but human beings with dignity and deserving of respect "if we listen to right reason and to Christian philosophy." [6]

Catholicism saw the employer as a patriarchal father having the right to authority over his children to be sure, but also as a benevolent parent with responsibilities and obligations for stewardship. Thus respect for authority was an important component of Catholic ideology extended into the workplace. Catholic workers, especially women, were predisposed to compliance with their bosses' right to respect and obedience.[7] This sense of order and obligation coincided with the workers' own perception of responsibility and discipline. Obedience to someone in authority on a higher social level was part of the accepted order.[8] The unions reinforced and legitimated the relationship between worker and employer. Contained in an explication of the program of the Catholic worker movement was the following statement: It is in the interest of all for the worker to fulfill his duty . . . not only on the job, but also in urging other workers to organize.[9]

Religious labor unions, especially those designed exclusively for women, facilitated women's transition to work. Christian unions maintained that there was a place of refuge for women who had to work. They legitimated paid labor, validated the relationship with employers, provided social services, and offered spiritual comfort. It was a practical and religious program that spoke to the needs of many women. The message of the religious unions was very different from socialist demands for equality and freedom. It must be recognized that such demands in early twentieth-century German society were viewed as strident and threatening by many women. The reality of women's lives called for reinforcement of traditional components instead of a complete restructuring of family and society. The shelter of the churches and the religious unions gave women something to hang on to in the midst of a sometimes unmanageable life. The patriarchy was familiar.

It structured society and family relationships, and could easily be extended into the world of work, as the Christian unions sought to do. The goal of the religious unions was to unite all non-socialist workers.[10] Yet parochialism among the Christian organizations created some measure of confusion and doubt and tended to divide workers who wanted to join religiously oriented groups. The Catholic unions were especially adamant on the issue of exclusivity. Despite the fact that Catholics did join the interconfessional unions, the practice was frowned upon by the Church. Formal permission allowing Catholics to join such unions was not granted until the papal encyclical, *Singulari Quadam*, in 1912, and even then, workers were supposed to request formal permission from their bishops.[11] Considering the fragmentation that exclusivity produced, it is even more remarkable that the Christian unions were so successful among women workers. Instead of acting as a deterrent, the close connection between the institutional church and the labor organizations was a distinctive means for active recruitment.

The last established and least successful among the three types of Christian organizations were the Evangelical unions. In 1910, these unions claimed only 159,990 members, of which 2,130 were women organized in the *Verband der Evangelischen Arbeiterinnenvereine*, Deutschlands, Hannover, founded in 1908.[12] Impetus for organization was primarily a reaction to both the socialist and Catholic unions, but progress was limited. The Evangelical groups lacked the cohesion and encouragement to reach out to women that was present in the Catholic hierarchy. Also, they entered competition for membership well after other organizations were established.

Primary concern of the Evangelical unions was the promotion of religion among women workers. Only secondarily were economic matters considered.[13] The union congress in 1908 listed the three major goals of the organization: They included strengthening Evangelical and religious principles among working women, promoting Evangelical and Christian values in the life of the nation, and promoting the economic and social interests of working women and women in the working class.[14] High on the list of priorities concerning practical matters was the initiation of programs for teaching domestic skills to working girls. In the first year of its operation, the union established courses in sewing, cooking, and home management in twelve of its fifteen affiliates.[15]

Evangelical unions sponsored a newspaper called *Die Deutsche Ar-beiterin* (The German Working Woman), which was directed toward the special concerns of working women. Not surprisingly, very few articles addressed issues related to conditions of work. *Die Deutsche Arbeiterin* stressed women's domestic role.

We often speak in our union about marriage, a topic of interest for our young girls . . . our joy is very great when one of ours enters marriage . . . yet we hear often "no children or at most only one child." . . . But think, German women, on you rest the hope, the future, and the might of the people [*Volk*] and the blessing of heaven.[16]

The title of the paper was rendered as an illumination depicting two female figures. The figure to the left represented woman at work; that to the right—woman at rest. The woman at rest gracefully held a newspaper which read, "Leisure Hours." An aura of calm and contentment prevailed; even the dove perched on the Bible between the two figures had the hint of a smile. *Die Deutsche Arbeiterin* stated flatly: "We are an organization for Christian principles, not a trade union."[17]

The acute distress of the Christian organizations in grappling with the problem of women workers was most obvious in the torturous path taken by the Catholic unions. The energy and success of the Socialists pressured the Catholic hierarchy into a more aggressive social policy. In the face of the reality of women in industry, Catholic organizers proceeded from identification of the factory as enemy to identification of socialism as evil adversary. Priests and bishops provided leadership. In 1869, von Ketteler, the Bishop of Mainz, called for the exclusion of all children and married women from factory production.[18] Another priest, Franz Christoph Moufang, in the 1880's, described what he believed was the cause of social disintegration in the working class.

One recognizes that income increases when women and children also go into the factory to work. It is not right because the more women and children come the less the man can earn. The man should earn the bread by working, the wife should tend to the house and children, then they will both be fully employed.[19]

Despite the approval of the Pope, who encouraged Catholic labor unions to reach out to women workers, the nagging doubt regarding the propriety of women in factories persisted.

The papal encyclical *Rerum Novarum* launched the Catholic worker movement in 1891. There were numerous limitations both ideological and practical which needed resolution before the Catholic movement could deal effectively with the material concerns of its workers. Preoccupation with the "socialist danger" generated a great deal of rhetoric, but little substantial action. Commitment to an ideological position of spiritual enrichment glossed over more practical matters. Only gradually did the Catholic unions develop economic and political goals directed toward reform in the conditions of work. All this foot-dragging was much more obvious as the unions began to deal with working women.

A major purpose of the Catholic movement was to rescue workers from socialism. By 1905, it was common to read in the Catholic worker press about delivering "our" women from atheism, materialism, class struggle, and revolution.[20] Directives were peppered with the word *Weltanschauung*, literally "world view." Socialism was not only a political and economic movement, but an opposing philosophy of life. "Socialism is a unified *Weltanschauung* based on false principles of historical materialism and atheism. . . . Before all else a *Weltanschauung* must incorporate the relationship of man to God. Social Democracy is anti-religion and anti-Church."[21] Clearly the Catholic hierarchy was ready to do ideological battle. The worker question was translated into a moral issue, and the Catholic worker movement took a militant stand against what was labeled the "atheistic worker movement under the flag of Social Democracy."[22] Because the worker question was placed within the framework of morality, the Church claimed absolute right to dictate policy. "The worker question is a moral problem and the Church has the last word to say on the subject."[23]

The slogan "marching separately, fighting together" characterized the attitude of the Catholic labor movement toward mixed unions.[24] Women could be protected best in a single-sex organization. It was unfortunate enough that women had to work side by side with men in the factory. Only further damage would result from their being paired together in a labor union. Organizers claimed that worker problems were not the same as women worker problems; mixed unions would be dominated by men, thereby diminishing attention to the special concerns of women. Women's natural modesty, *Schamhaftigkeit*, demanded the privacy and community of other women.[25] Ultimately, it was not the economic aspects of the woman's life that occupied attention, but preservation of her religious and moral well-being.[26]

Catholic unions found it difficult to address worker problems related to women purely on economic or class terms. Abrasive work conditions had to be mitigated principally because woman's primary function was wife and mother. Catholic unions, with the support of political representatives in the Center Party, the party for political Catholicism, promoted preferential and protective policies regarding women, especially married women. Justification for preference was based on the woman's double burden, *Doppelberuf*. She was both woman (wife and mother) and worker. The Catholic worker movement was absorbed with the preservation of the family. More important than the burdens the factory imposed on the working woman herself, the Catholic hierarchy feared the devastating effects work would have on the home and children. Authority in the family would break down. Children would become immoral because the factory had separated the mother from her child. Who would be responsible for the religious training of the children?[27]

In order to assure the integrity of the family, organizers even admonished their representatives in the unions that too much worker solidarity was harmful. Leaders were urged to keep meetings to a minimum. Workers who spent evening after evening drinking beer and smoking cigars at union meetings were bringing ruin to the family as well as to the Catholic labor movement. If the wife also worked and belonged to another organization, these separate evenings would surely bring resentment and discord. Family nights were suggested to assure women that the union was not eroding family life.[28]

In 1898, the Center Party promoted a resolution in the Reichstag calling for an investigation into the peculiar problems of married working women. It resulted in extensive information on work conditions compiled in factory inspectors' reports.[29] Demands to establish different work schedules for married women sponsored by the Center with the support of the Catholic unions were not realized because both industry and working women balked at the idea. Some officials in the Catholic worker movement were slow to grasp the consequences of the work/time issue for the woman worker. Motivation for the study of married working women had broader and potentially more devastating implications. The more conservative members of the party hoped that the investigation would turn up sufficient justification to support legal abolition of women from factory work. Blundering on, certain officials could not be dissuaded from pursuing demands to exclude married women entirely. The Catholic worker press, *Der Arbeiterpräses*, had great praise for employers who refused to hire married women and urged others to follow the example.[30] This observation was made in 1908.

Thank God that there are still today many employers who will not hire married women in their factories; in this regard certain Catholic employers in western Germany deserve the highest praise. In Düsseldorf alone there are 314 factories in which there is fundamentally no married female labor.[31]

As late as 1910, the leader of the Catholic Organization of Working Women and Girls, Amalie von Schalscha, argued for the expulsion of women from the "chains of the factory." "No, it is not too late. I want to alert the whole world of women that they must share in this holy delivery."[32]

Despite the persistence of an anti-work ideology regarding women, the Catholic unions recognized the need to go beyond rhetoric. When the interconfessional unions adopted a program with more emphasis on economic issues in 1902, Catholic organizations modified their position also.[33] The resolution of the congress of Christian unions included numerous provisions related to legal changes in work conditions for women. The Christian unions sponsored the reduction of maximum work time to a nine-hour day and a one-and-a-half-hour mid-day break and the prohibition of female labor in mining and other industries where conditions were unhealthy or hazardous; they supported the extension of the labor laws regarding women and children to cover domestic industry and the prohibition of take-out work from factories after hours; they proposed maternity protection for a period of eight to ten weeks and called for reduced work time to one-half day for married women and women who had child care responsibilities.

The Catholic unions adopted a new statement of purpose in 1905 which reflected greater concern for practical issues, but remained basically parochial in direction. The statement included seven provisions: promotion of religious life; preparation for domestic life; education in religious and social questions; protection in time of need, sickness and death; instruction about labor laws for women; information about union organization; and commitment to closer social ties among members.[34] Procedure for implementation of these proposals was drafted in a nine-point program that emphasized common prayer and participation in the sacraments. Cooking, sewing, and ironing classes were organized, as well as Sunday afternoon meetings featuring plays, lectures, and singing. Several statements in the program were directed more toward women as workers. The unions encouraged participation in the social insurance funds and membership in savings plans, and called for better factory inspection.[35] It is obvious from these statements that the Catholic program was only a hesitant excursion into the world of work. References to insurance funds and factory inspection were practically submerged under a continued preoccupation with religious and domestic concerns.

Important insight into women's response to religious unions can be gained from a study of the labor movement in Düsseldorf.[36] In a city dominated by heavy industry and male labor, women workers were economically marginal.[37] They worked in the declining textile industry, in clothing, and in new places in chemical and paper factories doing mostly unskilled labor.[38] Not only did women accept the miserable conditions of insecure jobs and poor pay, they chose not to respond to socialist solutions for improvement.[39] Two-thirds of the working class in Düsseldorf had migrated to the city from the Rhineland and Westphalia. In 1907, 73% of these workers were Catholic.[40] The traditional role of women as wives and mothers was strong, supported by both men and women in the working class. Women workers were family oriented; they perceived themselves as helping even when they had fulltime factory jobs. The patriarchal definition of women's place promoted by the Catholic Church served to underscore social attitudes that were part of the working-class culture. The power of the Church and political Catholicism permeated the Catholic working class, structuring its values and organizing attitudes toward family, gender, and work.

Further, women were closely bound to the Church.[41] Priests had wide influence in their lives. Condemnation of socialism combined with simultaneous advocacy of Catholic organizations produced results. More women than men maintained formal ties with the Church. They accepted its authority and listened to its teaching. Being active in the Church both religiously and socially reduced women's need to seek connections in other, less-compatible associations. Verified by religion and sanctioned by authority, working women joined Catholic organizations. Not only did women accept the conditions of their domestic and economic lives, their anti-feminism was as strong as that of the men.[42] Catholicism taught that family and religion were private, that a woman's work life was tangential to her primary function. Politicizing work, as socialists sought to do, was further proof that the Church's warnings about unfriendly persons and "evil practices" in the marketplace were true.

In München-Gladbach, a textile city in west Germany, the Catholic Church ran a home for factory girls who had moved into the city for work in the mills. On Sundays there were small parties where the girls could meet and socialize. Marie Bernays, who investigated the textile industry, observed that the Catholic Church was the single most important cultural component in workers' lives.[43] Estranged from the public and political life of the community, struggling with feelings of dependence and vulnerability, workers looked to the Church for security. Bernays sincerely believed that workers did not respond to the Church out of ignorance, but because there was a vitality in religion that satisfied their longing for joy in life. Faced with the dreariness of daily work, Sundays allowed them time to enjoy the peace and safety of Church services.

Sunday mass in the big cathedral, surrounded by beautiful paintings and beautiful music, connected the workers to a thousand year old culture that clasped and enveloped them in familiar traditions.[44]

The Catholic Church talked explicitly about women's pain, not in abstract terms, but in the suffering and survival of everyday life. A religion that embraced sinners and misery also held out hope for redemption and freedom and made endurance possible. It was a message working women understood in the deepest part of their being. Spirituality promised an end to suffering.

By investing work with value, religious unions allowed women a way to verify themselves both as women and as workers. Religious unions had extraordinary success among women in domestic industry and domestic service. Both areas of women's work were particularly resistant to unionization. In part the limitations came from the isolation of the work experience. More importantly, unionization was impeded by the traditional nature of women's work and by the gender consciousness of the labor force. In neither area did women workers see the religious unions as functioning in opposition to their best interests. The negative approach of the socialist unions implicitly labeled women in home work and domestic service as competitive anachronisms somehow unfit for the class struggle. What set the religious unions apart and almost guaranteed them greater access was their capacity and willingness to address the issues of women in traditional work forms. A sense of identification and mutuality effected a viable connection.

Compared with socialist unions, Christian associations were much more successful with home workers. The concept of separate unions for women provided a ready structure for a separate organization for women home workers.[45] Attempts by the *Christlicher Textilarbeiterverband* (Christian Textile Workers Union) to incorporate home workers into a mixed union failed to produce results. It was assumed that organization in textiles would prove fruitful given the extensive amount of home work in the industry. But by 1907 only 67 home workers had joined the union.[46] A special organization proved much more successful. The Christian Union of Women Home Workers was established in Breslau in 1900 as an independent women's organization.[47] Instead of encouraging homogenization of workers by trade, the union concentrated on the special problems of the woman home worker. The program included extending sickness and accident insurance coverage to domestic clothing workers; promoting wage lists to minimize disparity; sponsoring improved work conditions through inspection of homes and apartments where domestic production took place; calling for more female officials to supervise inspection; and restricting take-out work from factories.[48]

The organization was based on the theory of self-help. Members paid weekly dues ranging from 10 to 40 *Pfennigs* depending on individual wages. Death insurance could be obtained for a monthly payment.[49] Between 1900 and 1913, the organization achieved a membership of 8,385; it accounted for 30% of the female membership in the Christian unions.[50] The Christian Union of Women Home Workers was one of the few unions that did not experience significant fluctuation in membership in the thirteen years of its existence before the war. Membership consistently increased. Gains were even sharper in depression years. Union membership jumped from 5,917 to 6,476 in 1908–1909 and continued to make important progress until the war.[51] The relative success of the Christian Union of Women Home Workers indicated a great deal about the broader problem of organizing women. Apparently they felt more comfortable in single-sex unions or separate organizations that were designed specifically for them.

Among domestic servants, the Catholic Church became the self-appointed guardian to preserve a patriarchal relationship between servant and employer.[52] The Church contended that traditional values associated with a surrogate family were being compromised by increasing depersonalization. Whether real or perceived, the Catholic hierarchy believed that young, impressionable girls living apart from their families were in spiritual danger.[53] The impetus for confessional unions was above all a religious one, and the close relationship with the Church was intentional. The Catholic movement to organize domestic servant women produced significant results. In 1899 there were 70 associations with 40 hospices supported by the unions and the Church.[54] A special effort was made in south Germany to combat socialist activism there. The *Verband Katholischer Dienstmädchen– und Hausangestelltenvereine* (Association of Catholic Servant Girls and Domestics Organizations), Munich, was founded in 1907. In addition to religious concerns the *Verband* incorporated reference to the "economic and social interests" of servant girls. Membership expanded rapidly. In 1908, there were 4,300 members; by 1911, the *Verband* had attracted 10,208 women.[55]

Catholic associations for domestic servants did not directly confront such worker issues as wages and shortening the work day, but rather communicated a set of shared values articulated by the Church. Receptivity to religious supplications had a great deal to do with feelings of estrangement. There apparently was a need to preserve the notion that the employer was indeed a surrogate family, that the domestic was not just a wage earner devoid of involvement with her substitute household and undeserving of care and solicitude. Catholic unions articulated mutual respect and obligation and thereby transmitted a sense of security and belonging that was painfully absent from the harshness of the socialist vision of capitalist exploitation.[56] Joining life and work experience was an important coupling—one that offered comfort even when the ideal fell short of realization.

Religious unions were vehicles for the transmission of traditional values into the economic sphere. They formed an important bond between the churches and the experience of work. Emphasis on patriarchy, family, and women's proper role replicated the hierarchical order of organized religion. Extending these principles into society provided a way to structure economic variables that may have been unfamiliar or threatening. Institutional response to new economic and social conditions permitted many women the opportunity to express feelings of dissension and dissatisfaction through a confessional organization while at the same time giving them a way to identify fully with their inherited religion.[57] Religion was an empowering agent for women, giving them psychic protection against economic vulnerability.

How is it possible to reconcile the anti-feminist, anti-work ideology of the religious unions with women's positive response to them? Demands for elimination of women from the factory and even demands for reduced work time did little to improve the material conditions of families whose women had to work. Curiously the ambivalence of the Christian unions in this regard was matched by the paradoxical position of the woman worker. Emphasis on religious and domestic concerns served a need among women. In times of uncertainty, the presence of the church and its affiliated organizations was a constant that acted to reduce the strains of individual and social transition. Religious and moral principles were firm and consistent. Defining women as wives and mothers validated perceptions that were part of working-class culture. Recognizing women's work as necessary was affirmed in organizations created for the purpose of supporting them in their economic role. This act of acknowledgment fostered unity.

Religious unions facilitated adaptation to change. They offered legitimacy to working women by being spiritually and materially accessible. They helped women handle the real problems of their lives. At least women perceived that such help was available to them in organizations that stressed familiar values and provided tangible proof that women were special and important. The programs of the religious unions reified a longing for a society that honored women and separate gender roles. Connecting the home and family with work was the significant integrative factor in the lives of women workers—one that explains a great deal about the appeal of the religious unions.

Women's response to religiously affiliated unions is an important way to gain access to how many women defined themselves in Imperial Germany. The unions focused a broad spectrum of feelings comprising elements of anxiety, resistance, and rightness. It should not be assumed that women workers who joined the Catholic and Evangelical unions were merely willing collaborators in their own victimization. Such an explanation ignores the deep gender consciousness of many women who were forced to somehow combine the contradictions of ideology and reality. In a real sense, religious unions allowed women to express this contradiction and to take action toward its resolution. Economic change may have created "women out of proper place, out of proper role, outside the natural order,"[58] but economic necessity required that they come to terms with its dislocation. An ideology of patriarchy and politics of the family was the framework that invoked a system of right and wrong and preserved absolutes in a time of uncertainty.

NOTES

1. Lilly Hauff, *Die Deutschen Arbeiterinnen-Organisationen* (Halle a S.: Ehrhardt Karras Verlag, 1912), p. 71.

2. "Die deutschen Arbeitnehmerorganisationen im Jahre 1910," *Reichs-Arbeitsblatt*, IX Jahrgang, Nr. 9 (Berlin, 1911), p. 685.

3. Ibid., p. 690.

4. August Erdmann, *Die Christliche Arbeiterbewegung in Deutschland* (Stuttgart: Verlag von J. H. W. Dietz Nachf, 1909), p. 507.

5. "*Rerum Novarum*: The Condition of Labor, 1891," in *Social Wellsprings*, Fourteen Epochal Documents by Pope Leo XIII (Milwaukee: The Bruce Publishing Co., 1940), p. 177.

6. Ibid., p. 178.

7. Tamara Hareven, *Family Time and Industrial Time: The Relationship between the Family and Work in a New England Industrial Community* (Cambridge, Mass.: Cambridge University Press, 1982), p. 133.

8. Ibid.

9. "Soziale Fragen," *Der Arbeiterpräses*, 1 Jahrgang (1905), p. 45.

10. Erdmann, *Christliche Arbeiterbewegung*, p. 320.

11. *Singulari Quadam*, Encyclical Letter of Our Holy Father Pius X to Our Beloved Son, George Kopp, Cardinal Priest of the Holy Roman Church, Bishop of Breslau and to the Other Archbishops of Germany, September 24, 1912; in *All Things in Christ*, Encyclicals and Selected Documents of Saint Pius X (Westminster, Md.: The Newman Press, 1954), p. 188.

12. "Arbeitnehmerorganisationen," *Reichs-Arbeitsblatt* (1911), p. 690.

13. Hauff, *Arbeiterinnen-Organisationen*, p. 167.

14. "Was will und was muss der Verband Evangelischer Arbeiterinnenvereine Deutschlands?" *Die Deutsche Arbeiterin*, 6 Jahrgang, Nr. 1 (January 4, 1914), p. 1.

15. Hauff, *Arbeiterinnen-Organisationen*, p. 169.

16. "Viel Kinder, viel Segen," *Die Deutsche Arbeiterin*, 5 Jahrgang, Nr. 14 (April 6, 1913), p. 241.

17. "Was will . . . ?" ibid. (January 4, 1914), p. 1.

18. Erdmann, *Christliche Arbeiterbewegung*, p. 39.

19. Ibid., p. 52.

20. "Was auf sozialdemokratischer Seite für Arbeiterinnenbewegung im Jahre 1903 geschah," *Der Arbeiterpräses*, 1 Jahrgang (1905), p. 31.

21. "Die Katholische Arbeiterorganisation und die Sozialdemokratie," ibid., 8 Jahrgang, Nr. 6 (June, 1912), p. 171.

22. Ibid., p. 172.

23. Ibid., p. 173.

24. "Getrennt Marschieren, Vereint Schlagen," ibid., 3 Jahrgang (1907), p. 65.

25. "Sittliche Gefahren für die gewerbliche Arbeiterin," ibid., 1 Jahrgang (1905), p. 284.

26. "Arbeiter und Arbeiterin," ibid., p. 189.

27. "Die Differenzierung der Arbeitszeit verheirateter und unverheirateter Arbeiterinnen," ibid., 4 Jahrgang (December, 1908), p. 368–69.

28. "Arbeiterverein und Familie," ibid., 1 Jahrgang (1905), p. 165.

29. For discussion concerning factory inspectors see Chapter 3, "Classification by Sex: Women as Protected Workers."

30. "Differenzierung der Arbeitszeit," *Der Arbeiterpräses*, p. 376.

31. Ibid.

32. "Die Arbeiterinnenfrage," ibid., 6 Jahrgang (March, 1910), p. 119.

33. Hauff, *Arbeiterinnen-Organisationen*, p. 132.

34. Ibid., p. 133.

35. Ibid.

36. Molly Nolan, "Proletarischer Anti-Feminismus. Dargestellt am Beispiel der SPD-Ortsgruppe Düsseldorf, 1890 bis 1914," *Frauen und Wissenschaft*. Beiträge zur Berliner Sommeruniversität für Frauen, Juli, 1976 (Berlin: Courage Verlag, 1977).

37. Ibid., p. 361.

38. Ibid., p. 365.

39. Ibid., p. 361.

40. Ibid., p. 363.

41. Ibid., p. 361.

42. Ibid., p. 366.

43. Marie Bernays, "Auslese und Anpassung der Arbeiterschaft der geschlossenen Grossindustrie an den Verhältnissen der Gladbacher Spinnerei und Weberei," *Schriften des Vereins für Sozialpolitik*, Vol. 133 (Leipzig: Verlag von Duncker und Humblot, 1910), p. 240.

44. Ibid.

45. Hauff, *Arbeiterinnen-Organisationen*, p. 71.

46. Ibid., p. 69.

47. Ibid., p. 71.

48. Ibid., p. 73.
49. Heinrich Koch, *Die Deutsche Hausindustrie* (M. Gladbach: Volksver-eins-Verlag, 1913), p. 201.
50. *Zentralblatt der Christlichen Gewerkschaften Deutschlands*, 14 Jahrgang (Krefeld: von Acken Buchdruckerei, 1914), p. 343.
51. Hauff, *Arbeiterinnen-Organisationen*, p. 72.
52. Uta Ottmüller, *Die Dienstbotenfrage. Zur Sozialgeschichte der doppelten Ausnutzung von Dienstmädchen im deutschen Kaiserreich* (Münster: Verlag Frauenpolitik, 1978), p. 117.
53. Ibid.
54. Ibid.
55. Ibid., p. 119.
56. Ibid., p. 121.
57. Vernon Lidtke, *The Outlawed Party: Social Democracy in Germany, 1878–1890* (Princeton, N.J.: Princeton University Press, 1966), p. 300.
58. Jane De Hart Mathews and Donald Mathews, "The Threat of Equality: The Equal Rights Amendment and the Myth of Female Solidarity," unpublished paper, Brown University (April, 1982), p. 9.

Conclusion

In order to assess the impact of economic change on women, we must ascertain what resources were available to them and reconstruct a sense of women's interests and opportunities. Women's personal, familial, and societal position in Imperial Gemany was marked by paradox. The dilemma lay in resolving the contradictions embedded in the structures and institutions that at once created the options and constraints of their lives. The basic determinants within which they functioned incorporated the organization of work and the composition of the family. These elemental components influenced the manner in which women constructed coping responses on which their survival depended. How successful they were in accomplishing integration of the conflicting demands imposed on them by economic needs and family needs decided their well-being.

The pressures required constant attention. Women responded by moving back and forth across the boundaries of their public and private spheres. While the economic dimension of their lives was large in its urgency and privation, women attempted to improve their life chances by exercising control over the narrow choices available to them. Although the severity of limitations may give the impression of powerlessness, the perception of weakness is misleading. Working women were disadvantaged, but their accommodations functioned to maximize their constricted options.

The burdens of adaptation required to achieve a relative measure of safety were borne primarily by women. They used the spaces in the organization of work and the resources contained in the family to ward off the dangers of economic debilitation. Structural dependency accentuated the detrimental effects of economic development. Women's assignment to domestic labor had broad implications for their lives outside the home. Division of labor in the family and the attitudes that underlay and perpetuated it influenced women's labor market expectations, their participation with work, and the returns they received for their efforts. The sexual division of labor was not just culturally determined, but responsive to material conditions of production. The undervaluation of female labor reflected the general subordination of women which industry used to its benefit in the form of sex-segregated jobs and lower wages.

Women were multiply jeopardized. The linkages between familial and economic spheres, whereby sexual inequalities in the familial division of labor helped to perpetuate sexual inequality in the labor market, had an overlapping and depressant effect on their economic activity. Domestic labor, household work, and child care impinged negatively on productivity and work commitment. Since there were few replacements for women's labor in the household, paid labor outside the home or involvement with domestic industry required that they expend extra effort. There was almost no redistribution of tasks in the domestic division of labor with women's entrance into the labor force. The process of adjustment was a costly one because gender inequities built into the social and economic system demanded that women negotiate their dependencies for advantage. This was the essential dilemma of women's work.

What were the acceptable and practical solutions? There was stored "wealth" in women's labor. Both industry and women recognized its value and both sought to expand opportunities for remunerative employment. But this was a difficult accomplishment in a society that insisted that women belonged at home simultaneously as industry's appetite for female labor became more prodigious. The doctrine of capitalist expansion, validated by economic progress, competed with an equally aggressive ideology of the family that could not allow women and children to become part of the human sludge of the system. Discrimination served to blunt the edges of the problem. Differential treatment of women in the labor force lowered their visibility and lessened their competition with men. Social and political recitals and resolutions struggled to talk women back into the home with ideological prescriptions and to legislate women to their proper role with protective laws. Movements for substantive reform of industrial abuses were impressed with normative messages. The penalties women paid for all this attention were isolation and exploitation.

Germany had a long history of resistance to advanced forms of factory development and the urbanization that this often entailed. Even in the late nineteenth century social and political pressures against factory industrialization were still powerful. This resistance constituted another reason, apart from economics, that employers preferred to rely on older methods of manufacturing organized outside a formal factory setting, often at a distance from the large cities as well. It was also part of the reason capitalism relied so heavily on women's labor, which was less likely to be union organized and therefore more easily controlled. It was not only because female labor was cheap, but because it was tractable, that capitalist development followed up on its use along the paths of least resistance.

Keeping female labor plentiful and cheap served important industrial needs. Despite the societal premise that men were primary providers, in many instances men's wages were unreliable and inadequate for family support. Indirectly, industry held women captive through the economic uncertainty of men. Women and children had to be available as compensatory labor. That they were present in large numbers in specific regions and cities in Germany testified to both the vagaries of the capitalist market and the unevenness of capitalist development. Associating low pay with women's work brought economic dividends for industry. Embellishing the assumption that family demands impinged on job performance, industry treated women as less reliable workers. Claims about labor instability, buttressed by custom and tradition and the sexual division of labor, justified lower wages. Because women worked from necessity, in many cases just eking out subsistence, they were economically vulnerable. They accepted poor wages because there were no viable alternatives. Designating jobs as women's work sanctioned lower pay and assured industry of a cheap supply of ready labor. Men sought higher wages when they could, leaving whole industries and large segments of selected industries feminized. The circle became self-justifying.

Women struggled to accommodate need for earnings with attention to the tasks of daily life, the most important of which was child care. If the factory system facilitated a reward structure that promoted continuous employment and long and relatively inflexible working hours, women had to reverse this rigidity or at least modify it to make it handleable. There were limits on the extent to which they had control over decision-making because their private lives were bound into the social and economic system. Their choices were narrow, but the rhythm of their interaction with paid labor indicates effort to bring work under control. They sought jobs that they perceived as least intrusive with family responsibilities and most coincident with the variety of demands created by changing circumstances in their lives. The life cycle of these women always included work, but the timing of work and the tasks performed were marked by high-mobility jobs with easy entry and exit that could be used for income in response to immediate conditions. Interaction with work was intermittent, occasionally punctuated by linear interruptions in one trade, but more frequently a composite of a variety of occupations that existed on the fringes of regular employment. High transience meant that women used the flexibility inherent in marginal work to create some economic space.

Most women, both as wives and as daughters, engaged work as part of a family unit. Expansion of factory production in the period between 1871 and 1914 appeared in the form of a work choice for women at one stage in their life cycle. As opportunities for factory work grew, daughters, young single women, took places in industry with higher frequency and in greater numbers than their mothers. Factory work expanded options for paid labor and was incorporated into a woman's work life at a time when domestic responsibilities left her relatively free to meet the regularity and constrictions of a factory schedule. The interaction and exchange of labor in the family among mothers and daughters illustrates women's connection to the family economy and their attempts to space paid labor in congruence with domestic activities for the welfare of the group.

The presence of extensive domestic industry in pre-war Germany at once affirmed industry's search for cheap, available labor and women's need for a work form that preserved a modicum of manageability. Protective legislation that placed restrictions on women's work in factories and prohibited child labor caused greater economic scarcity, increased hardship and further retreat into domestic industry as a way of maximizing the labor of the family unit. Domestic industry became the domain of women and children by the first decade of the twentieth century. In this regard, social policies that intended redress of abuses also carried prescriptive messages. Women and children belonged at home, but practical concerns made it impossible for them to afford to stay there without working. Protective legislation generated change, but there were unanticipated negative effects on the economic well-being of those persons in the target groups. Preservation of traditional work forms further isolated women, yet domestic industry was at least in part remedial because it permitted women to remain at home. The fit was by no means satisfactory, but women continued to validate their life experience with their work choices.

If women's participation in labor unions is used as a measure of active intervention in the work experience, women chose informal controls rather than organizational ones. Formal articulation of demands for better work conditions and improved wages was only vaguely understood and considerably removed from women's immediate economic goals. Women's vulnerability was replicated and aggravated in labor unions dominated by men. The authenticity of egalitarian sentiments expressed by the socialist trade unions was suspect as men intended to impose regulation on women's work in factories and at home to shrink their presence in the labor market. Disincentives to union activity were contained in the ambivalence of the men in organization and in the reluctance of women to validate work through organized activity. Their central commitment was elsewhere. Women's relatively favorable response to religiously affiliated labor organizations tells a great deal about how women perceived themselves. Supporting patriarchy and advocating the family, Catholic unions, especially, connected with the needs of their religious constituency. The Church followed women into the world of work, and working women achieved some comfort in its protection.

Cultural, intellectual, and religious dimensions in the history of Imperial Germany are just beginning to include perspectives of women. Public policy issues and the process of their implementation catch some of these themes. Women were the targets of both praise and criticism in German society, and working-class women were especially visible. Women's place was implicitly understood, yet we know very little about the social dynamics of class and gender that contributed to working women's perception of themselves and the prescriptions that governed the female role.

More needs to be done with the influence of religion among women in both its spiritual and organizational function. It is clear that established religions showed great interest in working-class women. But because biographical material is scant, it is difficult to make statements about religion as a regulating agency or inspirational presence on the personal level. Conservatives condemned socialism as anti-religious, yet it is not at all clear how salient this criticism was to workers. Organized churches and their leadership provide an important focus for locating the connections between religion as a political and moral force in German society and its impact as both a conservative and activist social agency.

Because this study looked at women who worked, women and their families came into view when they were engaged in some form of productive labor. It would be useful to discover how the fortunes of individual families changed over time, and how those changed circumstances altered occupational and educational expectations for both sons and daughters. Local studies will add considerably to our knowledge of generational mobility. Clarifying the organization of time and resources within families would yield valuable insight into how persons perceived the options open to them. Discovering evidence that family time and resources were manipulated to anticipate preparation for the future would point up the kinds of avenues Imperial German society offered for upward mobility. It would be important to know if these opportunities were widely enough available to inspire family strategies to accomplish them. The conservative influence most worker families exerted on their members, particularly the daughters, may have acted to miss chances for upward mobility because of preoccupation with immediate circumstances. Certainly in most families whose women worked in industry, there was little sense of manipulating resources for anything more than getting by.

Following up the themes of this study would also provide historical perspective for the topic of women in Weimar and Nazi Germany. We must validate women's history in Germany by excising the presence of the anachronistic imperative that tends to filter the past through the experience of National Socialism. The Nazi image of womanhood projected backward is a sterile construct, one that imposes an artificial constraint on the past and diminishes appreciation of women's place in their own time. It would be important to discover if the dislocation of the war years and the vastly altered circumstances of the Third Reich had significant impact on working women. Identifying similarities and specifying differences would speak again to the issue raised in this text regarding the relationship between external economic and political circumstances and the kinds of choices women made to handle their lives.

Failure to recognize the economic activities of women implies failure to consider factors affecting their contributions to society, the ways in which they were prepared for their tasks, the techniques both emotional and practical that they used, and the efficacy of their efforts. This study of German working women permits an important way of redressing the silences of invisibility. How women located themselves in their own personal space and time encompasses more than their work experience. Traditional determinants of behavior persisted under the impact of significantly altered economic conditions. Family responsibilities were unchanging despite women's presence in the labor force. Women had to draw on deep personal resources in order to combine work and family. Historians may be forcing the issue in searching for dramatic change for women in the process of industrialization. Dignifying women without romanticizing them requires that we identify and understand their own perceptions and aspirations within the context of the cultural and structural conditions that influenced their lives. The dominant theme of this study is the adaptive strengths and strategies women generated as they engaged a system in economic transition. Women's work in Germany has dramatic implications that need to be evaluated in the broader context of European history and the history of women.

Selected Bibliography

The following selected bibliography lists primary materials and secondary sources. Many of the secondary citations are in English and are readily available in large libraries. Primary materials include government publications, periodicals, and separate entries for sources for which there are title and author. Detailed references for government materials and journal articles appear in the notes for each chapter.

PRIMARY MATERIALS

Government Publications

Amtliche Mittheilungen. Jahresberichte der Gewerbeaufsichtsbeamten und Bergbehörden, Reichsministerium des Innern, Berlin, 1879–1919.

Beschäftigung verheiratheter Frauen in Fabriken für das Jahr 1899. Nach Berichten der Gewerbeaufsichtsbeamten bearbeitet im Reichsamt des Innern, Berlin, 1901.

Die Arbeitszeit der Fabrikarbeiterinnen. Nach Berichten der Gewerbeaufsichtsbeamten bearbeitet im Reichsamt des Innern, Berlin, 1905.

Ergebnisse über die Frauen- und Kinderarbeit in den Fabriken auf Beschluss des Bundesraths angestellten Erhebungen, zusammengestellt im Reichskanzler-Amt, Berlin: Carl Heymanns Verlag, 1876.

Reichs-Arbeitsblatt, Kaiserlichen Statistischen Amt. Abteilung für Arbeiterstatistik, Berlin, 1903–1914.

Statistik des Deutschen Reichs, Herausgegeben vom Kaiserlichen Statistischen Amte, Berlin, 1872–1917.

Journals

Blätter für das Armenwesen. Zentralleitung des Wohltägtigkeitsvereins in Württemberg.

Der Arbeiterpräses. Herausgegeben vom Verbande der Katholischen Arbeiter-Vereine, Berlin, 1905–1914.

Die Deutsche Arbeiterin. Organ des Verbandes Evangelischer Arbeiterinnen-Vereine Deutschlands, Hannover.

Die Gleichheit. Zeitschrift für die Interessen der Arbeiterinnen, Stuttgart, 1892–1914.

Die Neue Zeit. Wochenschrift der Deutschen Sozialdemokratie, 1890–1914.

Schmoller, Gustav. *Jahrbuch für Gesetzgebung, Verwaltung und Volkswirtschaft im Deutschen Reich,* Leipzig: Verlag von Duncker und Humblot, 1877–1919.

Schriften des Vereins für Sozialpolitik, Band 1–188, Leipzig und Berlin: Verlag von Duncker und Humblot, 1873–1939.

Staats- und Socialwissenschaftliche Forschungen, Gustav Schmoller, ed. (with M. Sering), Leipzig: Duncker und Humblot, 1878–1916.

Published Sources

Altmann-Gottheiner, Elizabeth. "Die Entwicklung der Frauenarbeit in der Metallindustrie," *Schriften des ständigen Ausschusses zur Förderung der Arbeiterinnen-Interessen,* Jena: Verlag von Gustav Fischer, 1916.

————. (Gottheiner, Elizabeth.) "Studien über die Wuppertaler Textilindustrie und ihre Arbeiter in den letzten zwanzig Jahren," *Staats- und Socialwissenschaftliche Forschungen,* 1903.

Aufnahme-Bedingungen der Mädchenheime des Diakonievereins "Arbeiterinnenfürsorge," Stühlingen, Baden, n.d.

Baum, Marie. *Drei Klassen von Lohnarbeiterinnen in Industrie und Handel der Stadt Karlsruhe,* Bericht erstattet an das Grossherzogliche Ministerium des Innern und herausgegeben von der Grossherzoglich Badischen Fabrikinspektion (Karlsruhe: Druck und Verlag der G. Braunschen Hofbuchdruckerei, 1906.)

Bebel, August. *Die Frau und der Sozialismus,* Stuttgart: J. H. W. Dietz, 1893.

Bernays, Marie. "Auslese und Anpassung der Arbeiterschaft der geschlossenen Grossindustrie an den Verhältnissen der Gladbacher Spinnerei und Weberei," *Schriften des Vereins für Sozialpolitik,* Vol. 133, Leipzig: Verlag von Duncker und Humblot, 1910.

————. "Untersuchungen über die Schwankungen der Arbeitsintensität während der Arbeitswoche und während des Arbeitstages," *Schriften des Vereins für Sozialpolitik,* Vol. 135, Leipzig: Verlag von Duncker und Humblot, 1912.

————. *Untersuchungen über den Zusammenhang von Frauenfabrikarbeit und Geburtenhäufigkeit in Deutschland*, Berlin: W. Moeser Buchhandlung, 1916.

Bittmann, Karl. *Hausindustrie und Heimarbeit im Grossherzogtum Baden*, Bericht an das Grossherzoglich Badische Ministerium des Innern, Karlsruhe: Macklot'sche Druckerei, 1907.

Braun, Adolf. *Die Arbeiterinnen und die Gewerkschaften*, Sozialdemokratische Frauenbibliothek, Berlin: Buchhandlung Vorwärts, 1913.

Brutzer, Gustav. "Die Verteuerung der Lebensmittel in Berlin im Laufe der Letzen 30 Jahre," *Schriften des Vereins für Sozialpolitik*, Vol. 138, 1912.

Correspondenzblatt der Generalkommission der Gewerkschaften Deutschlands, 9 Jahrgang, Nr. 33, Hamburg, August 28, 1899.

Das Daheim für Arbeiterinnen, Leipzig: Metzger und Willig, n.d.

Dyhrenfurth, Gertrud. "Die hausindustriellen Arbeiterinnen in der Berliner Blusen-, Unterrock-, Schürzen- und Tricotkonfektion," *Staats- und Socialwissenschaftliche Forschungen*, 1898.

————. "Heimarbeit und Lohnfrage," *Schriften des ständigen Ausschusses zur Förderung des Arbeiterinneninteressen*, 1909.

Erdmann, August. *Die Christliche Arbeiterbewegung in Deutschland*, Stuttgart: Verlag von J. H. W. Dietz Nachf, 1909.

Feig, Johannes. "Hausgewerbe und Fabrikbetrieb in der Berliner wäscheindustrie," *Staats- und Socialwissenschaftliche Forschungen*, Leipzig: Verlag von Duncker und Humblot, 1896.

Feld, Wilhelm. *Die Kinder der in Fabriken arbeitenden Frauen und ihre Verpflegung*, Dresden: Verlag von O. U. Böhmert, 1906.

Fischer, Edmund. *Frauenarbeit und Familie*, Berlin: Springer Verlag, 1914.

Frankenstein, Kuno. "Die Lage der Fabrikarbeiterinnen in den Deutschen Grossstädten," *Schmollers Jahrbuch*, 1888.

Frisch, Walther. "Die Organisationsbestrebungen der Arbeiter in der deutschen Tabakindustrie," *Staats- und Socialwissenschaftliche Forschungen*, Leipzig: Verlag von Duncker und Humblot, 1905.

Gaebel, Käthe. *Die Heimarbeit*, Jena: Verlag von Gustav Fischer, 1913.

Geyer, Anna. *Die Frauenerwerbsarbeit in Deutschland*, Jena: Thüringer Verlagsanstalt und Druckerei, 1924.

Gnauck-Kühne, Elizabeth. *Die deutsche Frau um die Jahrhundertwende*, Berlin: Verlag von Otto Liebmann, 1907.

————. "Die Lage der Arbeiterinnen in der Berliner Papierwaren Industrie," *Schmollers Jahrbuch*, Vol. 20, 1896.

Göhre, Paul. *Three Months in a Workshop*, London: Swan Sonnenschein and Co., 1895.

Grandke, Hans. "Die Hausindustrie der Frauen in Berlin," *Schriften des Vereins für Sozialpolitik*, Vol. 85, 1899.

Hanna, Gertrud. "Women in the German Trade Union Movement." *International Labour Review*, Vol. VIII, No. 1, July, 1923.

Hauff, Lilly. *Die Deutschen Arbeiterinnen-Organisationen*, Halle a S.: Ehrhardt Karras Verlag, 1912.

"Hausordnung für Herberge des Vereins zur Fürsorge für Fabrikarbeiterinnen," Verein zur Fürsorge für Fabrikarbeiterinnen, Stuttgart: Druck von A. Bonz' Erben, 1879–1914. Druck der J. B. Metzler'schen, 1872–1879.

Heiss, C., and Koppel, A. *Heimarbeit und Hausindustrie in Deutschland*, Berlin: Puttkammer und Muhlbrecht, 1906.

Hell, Elisabeth. *Jugendliche Schneiderinnen und Näherinnen in München*, Stuttgart: J. G. Cotta'sche Buchhandlung, 1911.

Herberge: Ludwigsstrasse 15, Verein zur Fürsorge für Fabrikarbeiterinnen, 1905–1906.

Herkner, Heinrich. "Probleme der Arbeiterpsychologie," *Schriften des Vereins für Sozialpolitik*, Vol. 138, 1912.

Hirsch, Max. "Frauenarbeit und Frauenkrankheiten," *Biologie und Pathologie des Weibes*, Berlin, 1924.

———. "Die Gefahren der Frauenerwerbsarbeit für Schwangerschaft, Geburt, Wochenbett, und Kinderaufzucht," *Archiv für Frauenkunde und Konstitutionsforschung*, Leipzig, 1925.

Hirschberg, Ernst. *Die Soziale Lage der Arbeitenden Klassen in Berlin*, Berlin, 1897.

Hommer, Otto. *Die Entwicklung und Tätigkeit des Deutschen Metallarbeiterverbandes*, Berlin: Carl Heymanns Verlag, 1912.

Jaffé, E. "Hausindustrie und Fabrikbetrieb in der deutschen Cigarrenfabrikation," *Schriften des Vereins für Sozialpolitik*, Vol. 86, 1899.

Kaempfe, Eugen. *Die Lage der industriell thätigen Arbeiterinnen in Deutschland*, Leipzig: Druck von A. T. Engelhardt, 1899.

Kampffmeyer, Paul. *Die Prostitution als soziale Klassenerscheinung und ihre sozialpolitische Bekämpfung*, Berlin: Verlag Buchhandlung Vorwärts, 1905.

Kempf, Rosa. "Das Leben der jungen Fabrikmädchen in München," *Schriften des Vereins für Sozialpolitik*, Vol. 135, Leipzig: Verlag von Duncker und Humblot, 1911.

Koch, Heinrich. *Die deutsche Hausindustrie*, M. Gladbach: Volksvereins-Verlag, 1913.

———. "The New Homework Act," Office International du Travail à Domicile. Publication #6, n.d.

Krukenberg, Elsbeth. *Die Frauenbewegung, ihre Ziele und ihre Bedeutung*, Tubingen: J. C. D. Mohn, 1905.

Landé, Dora. "Arbeits- und Lohnverhältnisse in der Berliner Maschinenindustrie," *Schriften des Vereins für Sozialpolitik*, Vol. 134, 1910.

Lange, Gustav. "Die Hausindustrie Schlesiens," *Schriften des Vereins für Sozialpolitik*, Vol. 42, 1890.

Lange, Helene. *Die Frauenbewegung in ihren modernen Problemen*, Leipzig: Quelle und Meyer, 1908.

Leidigkeit, Hans. *Die Fabrikarbeit verheirateter Frau*, Greifswald: n.p., 1919.

Leipart, Theodor. *Lage der Arbeiter in Stuttgart*, Stuttgart: Verlag von J. H. W. Dietz, 1900.

Lion, Hilde. *Zur Soziologie der Frauenbewegung. Die sozialistische und die katholische Frauenbewegung*, Berlin: F. A. Herbig Verlagsbuchhandlung, 1926.

Marcuse, Max. "Zur Frage der Verbreitung und Methodik der willkürlichen Geburtenbeschränkung in Berliner Proletarierkreisen," *Sexual Probleme. Zeitschrift für Sexualwissenschaft und Sexualpolitik*, Heft 11, 9 Jahrgang, 1913.

May, Max. *Wie der Arbeiter Lebt*, Berlin: Carl Heymanns Verlag, 1897.

Meher, A. "Die geheime und offentliche Prostitution in Stuttgart, Karlsruhe, und München," *Görres-Gesellschaft zur Pflege der Wissenschaft im katholischen Deutschland*, Heft 11, 1912.

Mehner, H. "Der Haushalt und die Lebenshaltung einer leipziger Arbeiterfamilie," *Schmollers Jahrbuch*, Vol. 11, 1887.

Moszeik, C. *Aus der Gedankenwelt einer Arbeiterfrau von ihr selbst erzählt*, Berlin: Verlag Edwin Runge in Lichterfelde, 1909.

Müller, Klaus. *Die unehelichen Geburten in München*, Friedberg: K. Wendelsteinsche Buchdruckerei, 1914.

Neubert, E. "Die Hausindustrie in den Regierungsbezirken Erfurt und Merseburg," *Schriften des Vereins für Sozialpolitik*, Vol. 40. 1889.

Office International du Travail à Domicile, "The Central Trade Union Federation of Germany and the Abolition and Regulation of Homework by Trade Union Action," Publication #6, n.d.

———. "Home Work Act, German Empire, December 20, 1911," Publication #6, n.d.

Otto, Rose. *Über Fabrikarbeit verheirateter Frauen*, Münchener Volkswirtschaftliche Studien, Stuttgart und Berlin: J. G. Cotta'sche Buchhandlung, 1910.

Pappritz, Anna. *Einführung in das Studium der Prostitutionsfrage*, Leipzig: Verlag von Johann Ambrosius Barth, 1919.

Pohle, Ludwig. "Die Erhebungen der Gewerbe-Aufsichtsbeamten über die Fabrikarbeit verheirateter Frauen," *Schmollers Jahrbuch*, 1902.

———. *Frauenfabrikarbeit und Frauenfrage*, Leipzig: Veit and Co., 1900.

192   *Selected Bibliography*

Popp, Adelheid. *Autobiography of a Working Woman*, Chicago: F. G. Browne, 1913.

Protokoll der Verhandlungen des ersten Allgemeinen Heimarbeiterschutzkongress, Berlin: Verlag der Generalkommission der Gewerkschaften Deutschlands, 1904.

Rauchberg, Heinrich. "Die Hausindustrie des Deutschen Reichs nach der Berufs- und Gewerbezählung," *Schriften des Vereins für Sozialpolitik*, Vol. 84, 1899.

Rost, Hans. "Beiträge zur Moralstatistik," *Görres-Gesellschaft zur Pflege der Wissenschaft im katholischen Deutschland*, Heft 18, 1913.

Salomon, Alice. "Die Ursachen der ungleichen Entlohnung von Männer- und Frauenarbeit, Staats- und Socialwissenschaftliche Forschungen, Vol. 122, Leipzig: Verlag von Duncker und Humblot, 1906.

————. *Labour Laws for Women in Germany*, Women's Industrial Council, Berlin: Adelphi, 1907.

Schmidt, Erhard. *Fabrikbetrieb und Heimarbeit in der deutschen Konfektionsindustrie*, Stuttgart: Verlag von Ferdinand Enke, 1912.

Schumann, Fritz. "Die Arbeiter der Daimler-Motoren Gesellschaft Stuttgart-Untertürkheim," *Schriften des Vereins für Sozialpolitik*, Vol. 135, 1911.

Silbermann, J. "Die Frauenarbeit nach den beiden letzten Berufszählungen," *Schmollers Jahrbuch*, Vol. 35, 1911.

Simon, Helene. *Der Anteil der Frauen an der deutschen Industrie nach den Ergebnissen der Berufszählung von 1907*, Jena: Verlag von Gustav Fischer, 1910.

Spann, Othmar. "Die Geschlechtlich-sittlichen Verhältnisse im Dienstboten und Arbeiterinnenstande," *Zeitschrift für Sozialwissenschaft*, Vol. 7, Berlin, 1904.

Statistische Beilage des Correspondenzblatt, Generalkommission der Gewerkschaften Deutschlands, Berlin, Nr. 3, April 27, 1912.

Stieda, Wilhelm. "Grossstädtische Berufsverhältnisse," *Schmollers Jahrbuch*, Vol. 9, 1885.

Stillich, Oscar. "Die Sittlichkeit der Dienstboten," *Mutterschutz-Zeitschrift zur Reform der sexuellen Ethik*, 3 Jahrgang, 1907.

Tägtmeyer, F. "Die Entwicklung der Lebensmittelpreise in der Stadt Leipzig," *Schriften des Vereins für Sozialpolitik*, Vol. 145, 1914.

————. "Kosten der Lebenshaltung in Stuttgart, 1890–1912," *Schriften des Vereins für Sozialpolitik*, Vol. 145, 1914.

Tyszka, Carl von. "Lebenskosten deutscher und westeuropäscher Arbeiter früher und jetzt," *Schriften des Vereins für Sozialpolitik*, Vol. 145, 1914.

Wettstein, Minna Adelt. *3 1/2 Monate Fabrikarbeiterin*, Berlin: Verlag von J. Leiser, 1893.

Wörishoffer, F. *Die sociale Lage der Fabrikarbeiter in Mannheim und dessen nächster Umgebund*, Karlsruhe: Druck und Verlag von Ferd. Thiergarten, 1891.

Zentralblatt der Christlichen Gewerkschaften Deutschlands, 14 Jahrgang, Krefeld: von Acken Buchdruckerei, 1914.

SECONDARY SOURCES

Alexander, Sally. "Women's Work in Nineteenth-Century London; A Study of the Years 1820–50," in *The Rights and Wrongs of Women*, Juliet Mitchell and Ann Oakley, eds., Harmondsworth, Middlesex, England: Penguin Books, 1976.

All Things in Christ, Encyclicals and Selected Documents of Saint Pius X, Westminster, Md.: The Newman Press, 1954.

Barkin, Kenneth. *The Controversy over German Industrialization 1890–1902*, Chicago: The University of Chicago Press, 1970.

Beier, Rosemarie. *Frauenarbeit und Frauenalltag im Deutschen Kaiserreich. Heimarbeiterinnen in der Berliner Bekleidungsindustrie 1880–1914*, Band 348, Frankfurt/Main: Campus Verlag, 1983.

Blackborn, David. "The Problem of Democratisation: German Catholics and the Role of the Centre Party," in *Society and Politics in Wilhelmine Germany*, Richard Evans, ed., New York: Barnes and Noble Books, 1978.

Blewett, Mary H. "Work, Gender and the Artisan Tradition in New England Shoemaking, 1780–1860," *Journal of Social History*, Vol. 17, No. 2 (Winter, 1983).

Borchardt, Knut. *The Industrial Revolution in Germany 1700–1914*, London: The Fontana Economic History of Europe, Vol. IV, 1972.

Bowen, Ralph. *German Theories of the Corporative State*, New York: McGraw-Hill Book Company, 1947.

Boxer, Marilyn J. "Women in Industrial Homework: The Flowermakers of Paris in the Belle Époque," *French Historical Studies*, Vol. XII, No. 3 (Spring, 1982).

Boxer, Marilyn J., and Quataert, Jean H., eds. *Socialist Women: European Socialist Feminism in the Nineteenth and Early Twentieth Centuries*, New York: Elsevier North-Holland Inc., 1978.

Branca, Patricia. *Silent Sisterhood: Middle Class Women in the Victorian Home*, London: Croom Helm, 1975.

———. *Women in Europe since 1750*, London: Croom Helm, 1978.

Bridenthal, Renate. "Beyond Kinder, Küche, Kirche: Weimar Women at Work," *Central European History*, Vol. VI, No. 2 (June, 1973).

———. "The Effects of Women's History on Traditional Historiography with

Specific Reference to 20th Century Europe." Paper read at the Berkshire Conference on the History of Women, October 27, 1974.

Brownlee, W. Elliot, and Brownlee, Mary M. *Women in the American Economy: A Documentary History, 1675 to 1929*, New Haven: Yale University Press, 1976.

Bry, Gerhard. *Wages in Germany 1871–1945*, Princeton, N.J.: Princeton University Press, 1960.

Cantor, Milton, and Laurie, Bruce, eds. *Class, Sex, and the Woman Worker*, Westport, Conn.: Greenwood Press, 1977.

Chafe, William H. *The American Woman: Her Changing Social, Economic, and Political Roles, 1920–1970*, New York: Oxford University Press, 1972.

Clapham, J. H. *The Economic Development of France and Germany 1815–1914*, Cambridge, Mass.: Cambridge University Press, 1955.

Conze, Werner, ed. *Sozialgeschichte der Familie in der Neuzeit Europas*, Stuttgart: Ernst Klett Verlag, 1976.

Crew, David. *Town in the Ruhr: A Social History of Bochum, 1860–1914*, New York: Columbia University Press, 1979.

Dahrendorf, Ralf. *Society and Democracy in Germany*, New York: Doubleday and Company, 1967.

Davis, Natalie Zemon. "Women's History in Transition: The European Case," *Feminist Studies*, No. 3/4 (Spring/Summer, 1976).

Dawson, William. *The Evolution of Modern Germany*, New York: Charles Scribner's Sons, 1908.

Degler, Carl. *At Odds: Women and the Family in America from the Revolution to the Present*, New York: Oxford University Press, 1980.

Desai, Ashok. *Real Wages in Germany 1871–1913*, Oxford: Clarendon Press, 1968.

Dublin, Thomas. *Women at Work: The Transformation of Work and Community in Lowell, Mass. 1826–1860*, New York: Columbia University Press, 1979.

Eisler, Benita, ed. *The Lowell Offering: Writings by New England Mill Women 1840–1845*, New York: Harper and Row Publishers, 1977.

Emmerich, Wolfgang, ed. *Proletarische Lebensläufe. Autobiographische Dokumente zur Entstehung der Zweiten Kultur in Deutschland*, Hamburg: Rowohlt Taschenbuch Verlag, 1974.

Engelsing, Rolf. "Das Häusliche Personal in der Epoche der Industrialisierung," *Zur Sozialgeschichte deutscher Mittel- und Unterschichten*, Göttingen: Vandenhoeck und Ruprecht, 1973.

Evans, Richard. "Feminism and Female Emancipation in Germany 1870–1945: Sources, Methods, and Problems of Research," *Central European History*, Vol. IX, No. 4 (December, 1976).

————. *The Feminist Movement in Germany 1894–1933*, London: Sage Publishers, 1976.

Evans, Richard, and Lee, W. R., eds. *The German Family*, Totowa, N.J.: Barnes and Noble Books, 1981.

Gillis, John. *Youth and History*, New York: Academic Press, 1974.

Graves, Pam, and White, Joseph. " 'An Army of Redressers': The Recent Historiography of British Working Class Women,'' *International Labor and Working Class History*, No. 17 (Spring, 1980).

Grebling, Helga. *Geschichte der deutschen Arbeiterbewegung*, München: Deutscher Taschenbuch Verlag, 1966.

Hamerow, Theodore. *Restoration, Revolution, Reaction*, Princeton, N.J.: Princeton University Press, 1958.

————. *The Social Foundations of German Unification*, Princeton, N.J.: Princeton University Press, 1972.

Hareven, Tamara. *Family Time and Industrial Time: The Relationship between the Family and Work in a New England Industrial Community*, Cambridge, Mass.: Cambridge University Press, 1982.

Hareven, Tamara, ed. *Transitions: The Family and the Life Course in Historical Perspective*, New York: Academic Press, 1978.

Hareven, Tamara, and Langenbach, Randolph. *Amoskeag: Life and Work in an American Factory-City*, New York: Pantheon Books, 1978.

Hareven, Tamara, and Vinovskis, Maris, eds. *Family and Population in Nineteenth-Century America*, Princeton, N.J.: Princeton University Press, 1978.

Hartman, Mary S., and Banner, Lois, eds. *Clio's Consciousness Raised*, New York: Harper Torchbooks, 1974.

Hartmann, Heidi I. "The Family as the Locus of Gender, Class, and Political Struggle: The Example of Housework,'' *Signs*, Vol. 6, No. 2 (Spring, 1981).

Hausen, Karin. "Technischer Fortschritt und Frauenarbeit im 19. Jahrhundert. Zur Sozialgeschichte der Nähmaschine,'' *Geschichte und Gesellschaft*, 4 Jahrgang, Heft 2 (1978).

Hausen, Karin, ed. *Frauen suchen ihre Geschichte: historische Studien zum 19. und 20. Jahrhundert*, München: Beck'sche schwarze Reihe, 1983.

Henderson, W. O. *The Rise of German Industrial Power 1834–1914*, Berkeley and Los Angeles: University of California Press, 1975.

Hewitt, Margaret. *Wives and Mothers in Victorian Industry*, London: Rockcliff, 1958.

Hinterhof, Keller und Mansarde. Einblicke in Berliner Wohnungselend 1901–1920, Hamburg: Rowohlt Taschenbuch Verlag, GmbH, 1982.

Hobsbawm, E. J. *Labouring Men*, London: Weidenfeld and Nicolson, 1964.

Hoffmann, Walther. *Das Wachstum der deutschen Wirtschaft seit der Mitte des 19. Jahrhunderts*, Berlin: Springer Verlag, 1965.

Honeycutt, Karen. "Clara Zetkin: A Socialist Approach to the Problem of Women's Oppression," *Feminist Studies*, Vol. 3, No. 3/4 (Spring/Summer, 1976).

Howe, Frederick. *Socialized Germany*, New York: Charles Scribner's Sons, 1915.

Kaelble, Hartmut. "Der Mythos von der rapiden Industrialisierung in Deutschland," *Geschichte und Gesellschaft*, 9 Jahrgang, Heft 1, (1983).

Kennedy, Susan Estabrook. *If All We Did Was to Weep at Home: A History of White Working-Class Women in America*, Bloomington: Indiana University Press, 1979.

Kessler-Harris, Alice. *Out to Work: A History of Wage-Earning Women in the United States*, New York: Oxford University Press, 1982.

Kirkpatrick, Clifford. *Nazi Germany: Its Women and Family Life*, New York: The Bobbs-Merrill Co., 1938.

Kitchen, Martin. *The Political Economy of Germany 1815–1914*, Montreal: McGill-Queen's University Press, 1978.

Klucsarits, Richard, and Kürbisch, Friedrich, eds. *Arbeiterinnen kämpfen um ihr Recht*, Wuppertal: Peter Hammer Verlag, 1975.

Knodel, John. "Aussichten für die historische demographische Forschung," *Mitteilungen der deutschen Gesellschaft für Bevolkerungswissenschaft* (April, 1968).

———. *The Decline of Fertility in Germany 1871–1939*, Princeton, N.J.: Princeton University Press, 1974.

———. "Demographic Transition in German Villages." Paper prepared for the Summary Conference on European Fertility, Princeton, New Jersey (July 23–27, 1979).

———. "Infant Mortality and Fertility in Three Bavarian Villages: An Analysis of Family Histories from the 19th Century," *Population Studies*, Vol. 22 (November, 1968).

———. "Ortssippenbücher als Daten für die historische Demographie," *Geschichte und Gesellschaft* (1975).

———. "Two and a Half Centuries of Demographic History in a Bavarian Village," *Population Studies*, Vol. 24 (November, 1970).

Knodel, John, and Shorter, Edward. "The Reliability of Family Reconstitution Data in German Village Genealogies (Ortssippenbücher)," *Annales de Demographie Historique* (1976).

Köbele, Albert. *Ortssippenbuch der Gemeinden Binzen und Rummingen*. Landkreis Lorrach in Baden, Band 38, Baden: Selbstverlag des Herausgebens Grafenhausen, 1967.

Kocka, Jürgen, et al. *Familie und soziale Plazierung.* Studien zum Verhältnis von Familie, sozialer Mobilität und Heiratsverhalten an westfälischen Beispielen im späten 18. und 19. Jahrhundert, Opladen: Westdeutscher Verlag, 1980.

Kuczynski, Jürgen. *Die Geschichte der Lage der Arbeiter unter dem Kapitalismus. Studien zur Geschichte der Lage der Arbeiterin in Deutschland von 1700 bis zur Gegenwart,* Band 18, Berlin: Akademie Verlag, 1963.

Lambi, Ivo Nikolai. *Free Trade and Protection in Germany 1868–1879,* Wiesbaden: Franz Steiner Verlag, 1963.

Langewiesche, Dieter, and Schönhoven, Klaus, eds. *Arbeiter in Deutschland. Studien zur Lebensweise der Arbeiterschaft im Zeitalter der Industrialisierung,* Paderborn: Ferdinand Schöningh, 1981.

Lebovics, Herman. "Agrarians versus Industrialists," *International Review of Social History,* Vol. 12, No. 1 (1967).

Lerner, Gerda. "Placing Women in History: Definitions and Challenges," *Feminist Studies,* No. 1/2 (Fall, 1975).

Lidtke, Vernon. *The Outlawed Party: Social Democracy in Germany, 1878–1890,* Princeton, N.J.: Princeton University Press, 1966.

McBride, Theresa. *The Domestic Revolution: The Modernization of Household Service in England and France 1820–1920,* London: Croom Helm, 1976.

McLaren, Angus. "Women's Work and Regulation of Family Size: The Question of Abortion in the Nineteenth Century," *History Workshop* (Autumn, 1977).

Mason, Tim. "Women in Germany 1925–1940: Family, Welfare and Work," *History Workshop* (Spring, 1976).

Mathews, Jane De Hart, and Mathews, Donald. "The Threat of Equality: The Equal Rights Amendment and the Myth of Female Solidarity." Unpublished paper, Brown University, April, 1982.

Matthaei, Julie. *An Economic History of Women in America: Women's Work, the Sexual Division of Labor, and the Development of Capitalism,* New York: Schocken Books, 1982.

Müller, Walter; Willms, Angelika; and Handl, Johann. *Strukturwandel der Frauenarbeit 1880–1980,* Frankfurt/Main: Campus Verlag, 1983.

Neuman, R. P. "The Sexual Question and Social Democracy in Imperial Germany," *Journal of Social History* (Spring, 1974).

Niethammer, Lutz; Hombach, Bodo; Fichter, Tilman; and Borsdorf, Ulrich. *Die Menschen machen ihre Geschichte nicht aus freien Stücken, aber sie machen sie selbst.* Einladung zu einer Geschichte des Volkes in NRW, Berlin/Bonn: Verlag J. H. W. Dietz Nachf., 1984.

Nolan, Molly. "Proletarischer Anti-Feminismus. Dargestellt am Beispiel der

SPD-Ortsgruppe Düsseldorf, 1890 bis 1914," *Frauen und Wissenschaft*. Beiträge zur Berliner Sommeruniversität für Frauen, Juli, 1976, Berlin: Courage Verlag, 1977.

Oakley, Ann. *Subject Women*, New York: Pantheon Books, 1981.

Oberschall, Anthony. *Empirical Social Research in Germany 1848–1914*, The Hague: Mouton and Co., 1965.

Ottmüller, Uta. *Die Dienstbotenfrage. Zur Sozialgeschichte der doppelten Ausnutzung von Dienstmädchen im deutschen Kaiserreich*, Münster: Verlag Frauenpolitik, 1978.

Pinchbeck, Ivy. *Women Workers and the Industrial Revolution 1750–1850*, New York: G. Routledge, 1930.

Plössl, Elisabeth. *Weibliche Arbeit in Familie und Betrieb. Bayerische Arbeiterfrauen 1870–1914*, Heft 119, München: Kommissionsverlag UNI-Druck, 1983.

Quataert, Jean H. "The German Socialist Women's Movement 1890–1918." Unpublished dissertation, University of California, 1974.

————. *Reluctant Feminists in German Social Democracy, 1885–1917*, Princeton, N.J.: Princeton University Press, 1979.

Recum, Hasso von. *Die Lebensformen der Industriearbeiterin im Zuge der Entfaltung der industriellen Gesellschaft in Deutschland*, Kiel: n.p., 1959.

Rowbotham, Sheila. *Hidden from History*, New York: Vintage Books, 1973.

Safa, Helen, and Leacock, Eleanor, eds. *Development and the Sexual Division of Labor*, *Signs*, Vol. 7, No. 2 (Winter, 1981).

Sagarra, Eda. *A Social History of Germany*, London: Methuen and Co., 1977.

Samuel, Raphael. "Workshop of the World, Steam Power and Hand Technology in mid-Victorian Britain," *History Workshop* (Spring, 1977).

Schlegel, Katharina. "Mistress and Servant in Nineteenth Century Hamburg: Employer/Employee Relationships in Domestic Service, 1880–1914," *History Workshop* (Spring, 1983).

Schneider, Lothar. *Der Arbeiterhaushalt im 18. und 19. Jahrhundert*, Berlin: Verlag von Duncker und Humblot, 1967.

Schorske, C. *German Social Democracy 1905–1917*, Cambridge, Mass.: Harvard University Press, 1955.

Schulte, Regina. "Dienstmädchen im Herrschaftlichen Haushalt," *Zeitschrift für Bayerische Landesgeschichte*, Band 41, Heft 2/3, München: C. H. Beck'sche Verlagsbuchhandlung (1978).

Schulz, Ursula. *Die Deutsche Arbeiterbewegung 1848–1914*, Düsseldorf: Karl Rauch Verlag, 1968.

Smith-Rosenberg, Carroll. "The New Woman and the New History," *Feminist Studies*, No. 1/2 (Fall, 1975).

Social Wellsprings, Fourteen Epochal Documents by Pope Leo XIII, Milwaukee: The Bruce Publishing Co., 1940.

Stearns, Peter. *Lives of Labor*, New York: Holmes and Meier Publishers, 1975.

Stolper, Gustav; Hauser, Karl; and Borchardt, Knut. *The German Economy 1890 to the Present*, New York: Harcourt, Brace and World, 1967.

Strasser, Susan. *Never Done: A History of American Housework*, New York: Pantheon Books, 1982.

Tentler, Leslie Woodcock. *Wage-Earning Women: Industrial Work and Family Life in the United States, 1900–1930*, New York: Oxford University Press, 1979.

Thönnessen, Werner. *The Emancipation of Women: The Rise and Decline of the Women's Movement in German Social Democracy 1863–1933*, London: Pluto Press, 1973.

Tilly, Louise A., and Scott, Joan W. *Women, Work and Family*, New York: Holt, Rinehart, and Winston, 1978.

Tipton, Frank. *Regional Variations in the Economic Development of Germany during the Nineteenth Century*, Middletown, Conn.: Wesleyan University Press, 1976.

Vicinus, Martha, ed. *Suffer and Be Still: Women in the Victorian Age*, Bloomington and London: Indiana University Press, 1974.

Weber-Kellermann, Ingeborg. *Frauenleben im 19. Jahrhundert*, München: Verlag C. H. Beck, 1983.

Willms, Angelika. *Die Entwicklung der Frauenerwerbstätigkeit im Deutschen Reich*, Nürnberg: Graphische Betriebe F. Willmy, 1980.

Winkler, Dörte. *Frauenarbeit im Dritten Reich*, Hamburg: Hoffmann und Campe, 1977.

Zetkin, Clara. "Der Kampf um das Frauenwahlrecht soll die Proletarierin zum klassenbewussten politischen Leben erwecken," *Arbeiterbewegung und Frauenemanzipation 1889 bis 1933*, Frankfurt/Main: Verlag Marxistische Blätter, 1973.

Index

About the Author

BARBARA FRANZOI is Associate Professor of History at the College of Saint Elizabeth in New Jersey. Her article, "Domestic Industry: Work Options and Women's Choices," appeared in *German Women in the Nineteenth Century, A Social History.*